SMITHSONIAN INSTITUTION
BUREAU OF AMERICAN ETHNOLOGY
BULLETIN 130

ARCHEOLOGICAL INVESTIGATIONS AT BUENA VISTA LAKE KERN COUNTY, CALIFORNIA

By

WALDO R. WEDEL

WITH APPENDIX

SKELETAL REMAINS FROM THE BUENA VISTA SITES, CALIFORNIA

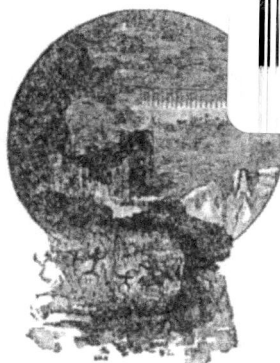

By T. D. STEWART

UNITED STATES
GOVERNMENT PRINTING OFFICE
WASHINGTON : 1941

LETTER OF TRANSMITTAL

SMITHSONIAN INSTITUTION,
BUREAU OF AMERICAN ETHNOLOGY,
Washington, D. C., June 20, 1940.

SIR: I have the honor to transmit herewith a manuscript entitled "Archeological Investigations at Buena Vista Lake, Kern County, California," by Waldo R. Wedel, with an appendix entitled "Skeletal Remains from the Buena Vista Sites, California," by T. D. Stewart, and to recommend that it be published as a bulletin of the Bureau of American Ethnology.

Very respectfully yours,

M. W. STIRLING, *Chief.*

DR. C. G. ABBOT,
Secretary of the Smithsonian Institution.

CONTENTS

ILLUSTRATIONS

PLATES

FIGURES

ARCHEOLOGICAL INVESTIGATIONS AT BUENA VISTA LAKE, KERN COUNTY, CALIFORNIA

BY WALDO R. WEDEL

FOREWORD

The excavations described in this paper comprised one of a number of archeological projects organized and financed by the Civil Works Administration in December 1933, as a means of reducing unemployment. To the Smithsonian Institution was given the task of selecting suitable sites, providing professional direction, and supervising the work so as to obtain a maximum of scientific information. As with the other similar projects, choice of a suitable location in California was contingent primarily on climatic and economic factors, i. e., upon mild winter conditions and proximity to abundant unemployed labor. Kern County, an important oil-producing region at the extreme south end of the San Joaquin Valley, met both these requirements. Moreover, it has long been known that aboriginal village and burial sites abound on the margins of the lakes and sloughs which formerly occupied a considerable portion of the valley floor in the southern part of the county. Some of the largest and most promising of these on the westerly and northwesterly shores of Buena Vista Lake were readily accessible by automobile to relief labor from several towns in the Sunset-Midway oilfield. Two large shell heaps on the southwest side of the lake, which seemed likely to yield a considerable depth of archeological deposits, were accordingly selected as the scene of operations.

Excavations began on December 20, 1933, and were continued as a Federal project until February 15, 1934. With considerable reduction in manpower, it was thereafter carried on as a county project, terminating on March 31. The Smithsonian Institution placed Dr. W. D. Strong and W. M. Walker, both of the Bureau of American Ethnology, in charge of the work as director and assistant director, respectively. On these two men rested the burden of administering the project in the field and of determining local policies. Actual excavation was supervised by two assistant archeologists: E. F. Walker, of the Southwest

1

Museum, Los Angeles, and the present writer, then a graduate student in anthropology at the University of California. Since the work was initiated at the beginning of the Christmas holiday period, it was possible to secure for a time the services of other graduate students as technicians. Their responsibilities included the recording of all field data, mapping of special features and profiles, clearing of burials, cataloging of specimens and labeling of containers, and other technical details. As these students left to return to school they were replaced through promotion of the more promising and capable local men. In general, this procedure worked out satisfactorily, although the frequent and unavoidable changes in personnel among the skilled workers and the lack of standardized forms for recording data entailed some confusion in the field records.

At the height of the work 160 men were employed as unskilled laborers, and the entire force numbered 187. With a few exceptions the men were oil-field workers from Taft, Maricopa, and nearby towns. Their number was reduced by about half with transfer of the project from Federal to county status. Thereafter, successive cuts further reduced the size of the crew until, at conclusion of the dig, less than two dozen remained.

All artifacts and skeletal materials discussed herein, unless otherwise stated, were shipped to the United States National Museum for study after completion of the field work. Specimens illustrated are on permanent deposit at the Museum. Duplicate collections have been returned to California for preservation in the Museum of Anthropology of the University of California and in the Southwest Museum at Los Angeles.

ACKNOWLEDGMENTS

It is a pleasure to acknowledge here our heavy debt of gratitude to the Honolulu Oil Co., its assistant superintendent, H. B. Stark, and other officials. Through their courtesy field offices, laboratory space, and photographic darkroom facilities were made available without cost at their main camp, as well as free quarters for the supervisory staff throughout the duration of the project. Thanks are likewise due a number of other individuals and organizations whose readiness to cooperate was an important factor in the successful prosecution of the investigations. These include the following:

Miller & Lux Land Co., owners of the property, and Manager Elmer Houchin, for permission to excavate.

John B. Stevens, geologist of the Associated Oil Co., for first reporting the sites and for other valuable assistance.

Robert Evans, purchasing agent for Kern County Fourth Division Road Headquarters, Taft.

Stanley Abel, chairman of the Board of County Supervisors, Taft.

George D. Nickel, district CWA head at Bakersfield.

Robert Patterson, United States Geological Survey office at Bakersfield, for loan of transit and other engineering equipment.

E. S. Stockman and the Standard Oil Co., Taft, for loan of two water tanks.

F. F. Latta, Shafter, for loan of unpublished ethnographic and archeological data on the southern Yokuts area.

John D. Henderson, Kern County Free Library, Bakersfield, for loan of books, notes, and other materials.

Kern County Historical Society, for loan of historical data.

Dr. H. I. Priestley, department of history, University of California, Berkeley, for loan of notes and manuscripts on early Spanish explorations in the southern San Joaquin Valley.

W. F. Barbat, Standard Oil Co. geologist.

Dr. G. D. Hanna, California Academy of Sciences, San Francisco.

R. G. Paine, aid in the Division of Archeology, United States National Museum, prepared figures 1, 2, 4, 5, 6, 7, 9, 10, 11, 12, 13, 14, 15, 16, 17, 18, and 19.

Analysis of the results of these investigations was begun by W. M. Walker, whose studies were well advanced when his appointment at the Bureau of American Ethnology was terminated in May 1935, owing to ill health. When the present writer subsequently undertook preparation of the report presented herewith, all of the material was reexamined and Mr. Walker's data, with some revisions, were incorporated.

INTRODUCTION

GEOGRAPHICAL BACKGROUND

The Central Valley of California is a great structural depression nearly 500 miles (804.6 km.) long, lying between the Sierra Nevada on the east and the Coast Ranges on the west. Its northern half is drained by the Sacramento River, the southern half by the San Joaquin. The two streams unite in a labyrinth of sloughs and marshes to discharge through Suisun Bay and Carquinez Strait into San Francisco Bay. The valley floor itself is a long narrow alluvial plain which rises gradually from virtual sea level in the Sacramento-San Joaquin Delta to an elevation of approximately 500 feet (152 m.) at either end.

Buena Vista Basin lies at the extreme upper or southern end of the San Joaquin Valley, with an elevation at its lowest point of under 300 feet (91.5 m.). Eastward, the ground rises gradually through a broad foothill zone to summits of 6,000 and 8,000 feet (1,820 and 2,427 m.) at the crest of the Sierras some 30 or 40 miles (48.3 or 64.4

km.) distant. To the west the valley is limited by the Temblor, easternmost of the Coast Ranges in Kern County. The Temblor rises much more steeply from the basin floor than does the Sierra but to a lesser altitude. It curves slightly eastward to join the San Emigdio mountains near the town of Maricopa. Between the San Emigdio and the Sierras are the Tehachapis. The Coast Ranges west and south of Kern County comprise a series of roughly parallel ridges enclosing valleys of variable width, all forming a rugged belt 40 to 50 miles (64.4 to 77.3 km.) wide between the Buena Vista Basin and the Santa Barbara coastal region. The Tehachapi mountains separate the San Joaquin Valley from the westernmost arm of the Mohave Desert.

Near the south end of the Temblor Range two low spurs project eastward onto the valley floor. These foothill ridges, the Elk Hills on the north and the Buena Vista Hills on the south, are separated from one another and from the main range by broad gently sloping valleys filled with gravel outwash from their flanks. Between the two spurs is Buena Vista Creek, an intermittent stream emptying into Buena Vista Lake. The Elk Hills touch the lake on its northwest margin near the outlet, while the Buena Vista Hills form a part of its southwest shore (fig. 1).

The San Joaquin Valley generally lies in the "rain shadow" of the Coast Ranges, and in consequence suffers from deficient rainfall. Moreover, since the Temblor is lower than its sister ranges to the west, moisture-laden air which clears the Coast Ranges passes on eastward across the valley to release its burden as rain or snow in the higher Sierras. Precipitation on the Temblor is thus so slight that only intermittent streams occur on its slopes, i. e., on the west side of the valley. Run-off is rapid and the water disappears in a few days. The eastern slope of the valley, on the other hand, has sizable streams of perennial nature, fed by innumerable smaller creeks which head in zones of heavy precipitation. Erosion is vigorous and there is a much more pronounced outwash of alluvial materials. This is deposited in great fans on the valley floor where the slackening waters drop their burden of sediment, and since there is no compensating deposition from the west side, the main axis of drainage in the valley proper has been steadily crowded toward that side. The Kern River, heading in the Sierras south of Mount Whitney and Sequoia Park, has in this wise pushed its fan of detritus entirely across the valley in northern Kern County at and just above the Elk Hills, forming a broad natural dam across which it meanders in a maze of channels to empty partly southward into Buena Vista Lake and partly northward into the Tulare Basin.

Lying south of this dam is Buena Vista Basin, measuring about 30 miles (48.3 km.) from east to west by 20 miles (32.2 km.). Its lowest point, which was occupied by Buena Vista Lake, is 268 feet

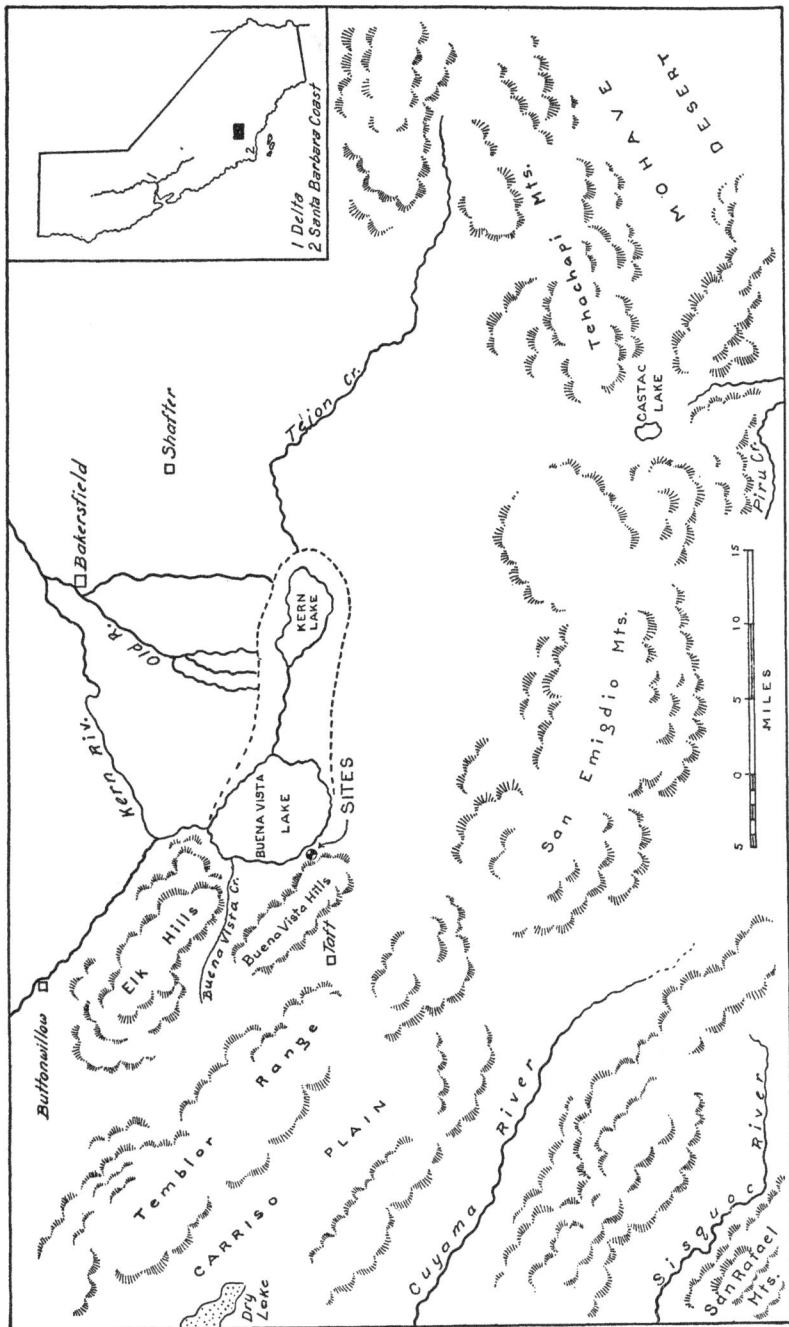

FIGURE 1.—Sketch map of Buena Vista Basin, showing site of excavations and surroundings. Inset, approximate location in relation to Sacramento-San Joaquin Delta and Santa Barbara coast regions.

(81.6 m.) above sea level, with the north rim just under 300 feet (91.5 m.). Within historic times considerable fluctuations have occurred in the height of water in the lake, wholly apart from the activities of the white man, and there is good evidence for similar phenomena in prehistoric days. The lowest stage on record was 282 feet (85.8 m.) in 1879.[1] At this time Buena Vista Lake was about 7½ by 4½ miles (12 by 7.2 km.) and was joined by a winding slough to the smaller Kern Lake some 7 or 8 miles (11.2 or 12.8 km.) to the southeast. In 1910 the shore line followed the 291-foot (88.7 m.) contour and Buena Vista Lake was roughly 8 by 5 miles (12.8 by 8 km.) with no outlet. At 295 feet (90 m.) or over, the two lakes formed a single broad sheet, overflowing northwestward around the Elk Hills through Buena Vista slough into Tulare Basin. It is represented at this approximate level by the broken line in figure 1.

In course of our excavations no less than six wave-cut terraces marking former beaches were uncovered. The highest was at the 300-foot (91.5 m.) level, the lowest at 291 feet (88.7 m.). Directly evidenced, therefore, is at least one 300-foot stage, at which time the combined lakes must have been about 8 miles (12.8 km.) wide by at least 23 miles (36.8 km.) long. The United States Geological Survey map (Buena Vista Lake quadrangle) shows a gap 1½ miles (2.4 km.) wide between the 300-foot (91.5 m.) contour lines on opposite sides of the slough draining this sizable body of water, though from the flatness of the ground on the east the marshes were probably much wider. It seems highly improbable from topographic considerations that the lake waters ever rose much over 300 feet (91.5 m.) above sea level, at any rate since the human occupancy revealed by the excavations began.

During the 295- to 300-foot (90–91.5 m.) stage, the waters washed directly against the northeast foot of Buena Vista Hills and the southwest base of Elk Hills. Elsewhere, only broad gently sloping plains bordered the lake. Lowering of the water to 285 feet (86.9 m.) would leave the now distinct Buena Vista Lake completely encircled by a strip of flat low-lying shore a half mile to several miles in width—slimy and almost impossible to cross on the west and south sides but somewhat firmer on the north and east. That some spots on the southwest side must have been habitable even at such times is shown by the occasional finding of artifacts, campsite traces, and even burials as much as half a mile from the foot (300-foot contour) of the Buena Vista Hills.

Since the perennial Kern River empties, or at any rate formerly did so, into the Buena Vista Basin, it is extremely unlikely that either of

---

[1] Data which follow on lake behavior, as well as subsequent comments on the environment, flora, and fauna of Buena Vista Basin are drawn from the excellent discussion by Gifford and Schenck (1926, pp. 14–20).

the lakes therein ever dried up completely in prewhite days. As Gifford and Schenck have aptly remarked:

The fluctuations of its [lake] margins were never great enough to cause the removal of a people situated on the 300-foot line. It was able to support a more constant and vigorous flora; and animal life as a source of human food would never be forced away. In short, it was the most suitable habitat for permanent residence in the southern San Joaquin valley. [Gifford and Schenck, 1926, p. 15.]

Diversion of Kern River by means of dams and irrigation systems has long since dried up Kern Lake. It and much of the bed of Buena Vista Lake have been placed under the plow, and today water normally stands even in the latter only where needed for reservoir purposes.

The mountain ranges enclosing the Buena Vista Basin on the east, south, and west could be crossed along any of several routes. These have been described by Gifford and Schenck (1926, pp. 15–17) but will bear repetition. Three gave access to the Santa Barbara coast and the Chumash region. With distances in miles from Buena Vista Lake, these were:

1. From the west side of the lake via Buena Vista Creek past the present McKittrick to Painted Rocks in the Carriso Plain; thence southward across another ridge to the Cuyama River, and down this stream to the Pacific Ocean south of the town of Pismo. Total distance, 105 miles. A shorter but more difficult alternative route would be southward from the Cuyama River across the San Rafael Mountains to the locality of present day Santa Barbara. Estimated distance 75 miles (120 km.).

2. From the south side of the lake by way of Maricopa and Sunset Valley to the Cuyama River near the mouth of Santa Barbara Creek; thence either down the Cuyama as before (90 miles, 144 km.) or else up Santa Barbara Creek over the divide onto Mono Creek, tributary to the Santa Ynez River just behind Santa Barbara. The airline distance from Buena Vista Lake to Santa Barbara is about 55 miles (88 km.); on foot by this, the shortest possible route, it would be between 65 and 75 miles (104 and 120 km.).

3. From Kern Lake south over Tejon Pass via Grapevine and Castac Creeks to the Santa Clara River near the present town of Castac, then down river to the coast near Ventura (115 miles, 184 km.). This could be shortened 15 miles (24 km.) by traveling from Grapevine to Piru Creek and down that to the Santa Clara River (100 miles, 160 km.). Where this route passed Castac Lake, it was within 15 or 20 miles (24 or 32 km.) of the western edge of the Mohave Desert.

4. From Kern Lake travel was possible in a general easterly direction up Tejon Creek, thence across the Tehachapi range onto the slopes overlooking the Mohave Desert. Keeping in the foothills, one

could then proceed southward to Elizabeth Lake and San Francisquito Creek to the Santa Clara River at Saugus and down river to the coast (145 miles, 232 km.). Alternatively, going east instead of south after crossing the Tehachapi, the traveler could reach the present town of Mohave, on the route to the Colorado River, some 70 or 80 miles (112 or 128 km.) from Kern and Buena Vista Lakes. Tehachapi Pass, still farther to the northeast, also provided a route, if a somewhat longer one, to the Shoshonean area of southern California and to the Colorado River tribes.

That some or all of these routes were extensively traveled is strongly indicated by archeological findings in the southern San Joaquin. Particularly noteworthy are cultural influences from the Santa Barbara coast peoples, to which we shall refer later in some detail. After a reconnaissance in the upper Cuyama and Sisquoc Valleys, Strong (1935, p. 72) concluded that, "Our own investigations do not indicate that the upper Sisquoc was ever an important trade route for shell and steatite from the coast." The Sisquoc heads just west of the Santa Barbara-Mono Creek route described above as the shortest between the Buena Vista Basin and the coast. From this it may be inferred either that the trade evidences on the upper Sisquoc remain undiscovered or else that the regular routes avoided this particular locality.

Climatically, much of the San Joaquin valley and especially its upper end, can be classed as little better than a desert. Precipitation in the Buena Vista Basin averages between 5 and 6 inches (12.5 and 15 cm.) annually, rarely totaling as much as 10 (25.4 cm.). Snow falls regularly on the Sierras to the east, less frequently on the ranges to the south and west, but only rarely on the valley floor. The moisture comes chiefly from November to April, and during these months heavy penetrating, often disagreeable fogs may blanket the entire plain. On a number of foggy mornings our workmen built fires to dispel the discomfort. Summers are excessively dry and hot, with temperatures from June through September frequently ranging well over 100° F. Subfreezing winter temperatures are uncommon.

Distribution of plant life reflects the semiarid conditions. Pine and juniper are found today only on the upper slopes of the San Emigdio, Tehachapi, and, of course, on the Sierras. Oak groves, the *roblars* of the early Spanish explorers, covered much of the lower valley slope east of the lakes. In favorable places these extended out onto the floor of the valley. Perennial watercourses, the sloughs, and the north shores especially of Buena Vista and Kern Lakes were fringed with stands of cottonwood, willow, and sycamore. On the sandy plain itself sage, greasewood, and some bunch grass was to be found. The west side of the valley, including the Buena Vista and Elk Hills and also the eastern slope of the Temblor bore only a sparse and low-growing vegetation. Even today the plain lying west of Buena Vista Lake is too arid for agriculture.

Wide zones of shallow water nearly or quite surrounding the lakes and also the connecting sloughs were the habitat of lush stands of marsh grass and tules. These marshes, or *tulares*, are a continuous feature of the San Joaquin throughout its length, having been noted again and again by the Spanish. Around the tule centered much of the economic activity of the marsh-dwelling Indians, who utilized it as raw material for house construction, balsas and rafts, textiles, and fuel.[2]

The avian, mammalian, and other faunal forms available to aboriginal man in the upper San Joaquin have been enumerated by Gifford and Schenck, and for details the interested reader is referred to their report. Here it is desired only to present lists of the species identified among the bone materials excavated from the village middens at the foot of Buena Vista Hills. These remains are most complete as regards mammals, and they indicate that almost every available species of any size was utilized. Possibly some of the bones of the smaller rodents were accidentally present, i. e., individuals which died in their burrows. By comparison the list of identified birds is surprisingly short. This is probably owing in part to the generally more fragile and fragmentary nature of their remains, secondarily to their frequent modification in manufacture of artifacts. It is certain the Indians must have drawn heavily on the numerous species of waterfowl which formerly swarmed about the marshy sloughs and lake margins. Fish bones were fairly common but none have been identified.

●

BIRDS [3]

White-faced glossy ibis (*Plegadis guarauna*)
White pelican (*Pelecanus erythrorhynchus*)
Little brown crane (*Grus canadensis canadensis*)
Goose (*Anserinae*)

REPTILES [4]

Terrapin (*Clemmys marmorata*)

---

[2] "This tule is the common bulrush of California, either *Scirpus californicus,* or *S. tatara.* Such tules were ten to twelve feet high and one to two inches in diameter. They had a bulbous branching root eight to ten inches long and six to eight inches in diameter. Their growth formed a belt as wide as two to three miles around the marsh. . . ." [Gifford and Schenck, 1926, p. 18.]

[3] Identified by Dr. A. Wetmore, Assistant Secretary, Smithsonian Institution.

[4] Identified by Dr. Doris M. Cochran, Division of Reptiles and Batrachians, U. S. National Museum.

MAMMALS [5]

Bison (*Bison bison*)	Raccoon (*Procyon lotor*)
Elk (*Cervus canadensis*)	Badger (*Taxidea taxus*)
Elk (*Cervus nannodes*)	Otter (*Lutra canadensis*)
Virginia deer (*Odocoileus virginianus*)	Mink (*Mustela vison*)
Deer (*Odocoileus* sp.)	Spotted skunk (*Spilogale gracilis*)
Pronghorn (*Antilocapra americana*)	Jackrabbit (*Lepus californicus*)
Dog (*Canis familiaris*)	Gopher (*Thomomys bottae*)
Coyote (*Canis latrans*)	Ground squirrel (*Citellus* sp.)
Desert fox (*Vulpes macrotis*)	Chipmunk (*Eutamias merriami*)
Red fox (*Vulpes* sp.)	Kangaroo rat
Wildcat (*Lynx rufus*)	Meadow mouse (*Microtus* sp.)

The molluscan remains, which comprised a very considerable proportion of the mound mass in each of the two shell heaps examined, were almost exclusively of the river mussel (*Anodonta nuttalliana* Lea), which must have been a very important dietary item for the natives. The only other identified freshwater mollusk was a univalve (*Planorbis* sp.), occurring both in old beach deposits and in occasional sand pockets throughout the middens. A number of marine species were present, but since these were clearly imported by man for other than food purposes and do not indicate the range of local resources, they will be listed and discussed in a future section.

The mammalian remains from sites 1 and 2 were tentatively identified in the field by Paul O. McGrew, then a graduate student in paleontology at the University of California, now Assistant in Paleontology at the Field Museum of Natural History. In his field report, McGrew calls particular attention to the large number of canid and jackrabbit bones. He points out further that among the numerous antelope remains, most were from very young individuals; that the skulls of most of the canids and mustelids were split open as though for removal of the brain. Noteworthy is his statement that "a horse upper premolar was supposedly found in mound 1 at a depth of 2 feet. The tooth was bleached white, in contrast to the bones which were originally deposited in the mound, and was quite obviously intrusive." The distribution of animal bones, based on this field study, is shown in the following chart; for site 2, presence or absence only, not actual numbers, are indicated:

---

[5] Identifications by Dr. Remington Kellogg, Division of Mammals, U. S. National Museum.

TABLE 1.—*Distribution of mammalian remains as identified in the field*

Animal bones	Site 1							Site 2					
	0-1'	1-2'	2-3'	3-4'	4-5'	5-6'	Total	0-1'	1-2'	2-3'	3-4'	4-5'	5-6'
Procyon, raccoon		1					1						
Mustela, mink	3	3	2				8						
Lutra, otter				1			1						
Spilogale, spotted skunk	1						1						
Taxidea, badger	3	3	3	2	1		12				+		
Vulpes, kit fox	7	7	4	4	2		24		+	+			
Canis latrans, coyote	6	5	4		1		16	+	+	+			
Canis familiaris, dog	5	4	4	3	4	1	21			+			
Canis sp	15	27	24	16	8		90	+	+	+	+	+	+
Lynx, wildcat		2	1				3						
Citellus, ground squirrel	1	1					2						
Thomomys, pocket gopher									+		+		
Dipodomys, kangaroo rat	3	3	3	1	1		11	+			+		
Microtus, meadow mouse	1	2					3	+	+				
Lepus, jackrabbit	42	58	59	21	10	3	193	+	+	+	+	+	
Sylvilagus, cottontail		2	5	1			8	+	+	+			
Cervus, elk	6	16	20	16	3		61	+	+				
Odocoileus, deer	+	+	+	+	+	+	+						
Antilocapra, antelope	13	17	9	3	2	1	45						
Birds, several species	74	234	56	31	13	3	411	+	+	+	+	+	
Turtle	29	45	42	17	7	2	142	+	+	+	+		

TABLE 2.—*Distribution of animal and bird remains represented by the much smaller collection of bones sent to the U. S. National Museum*

Animal bones	Site 1								Site 2						
	0-1'	1-2'	2-3'	3-4'	4-5'	5-6'	6+'	?	0-1'	1-2'	2-3'	3-4'	4-5'	5-6'	?
Unworked bone:															
Mustela vison			1						1						1
Taxidea taxus									2						
Lutra canadensis				1					1						
Spilogale gracilis	1								3						
Vulpes macrotis		2	1		2				2						
Canis familiaris	5	5	5	8	6	1			2	2	2	1			1
Cervus nannodes			1						3	2		1			
Odocoileus virginianus	1														
Antilocapra americana	2				2										
Lepus californicus	1	1	1		1	1	1								
Thomomys bottae											1		1		
Citellus sp											1				
Eutamias merriami											1				
Bison bison													1		
Worked bone:															
Odocoileus sp	1		3	1											
Odocoileus or Antilocapra sp		2	2						1						
Antilocapra americana										2					
Vulpes sp. (red fox)	1														
Canis familiaris															
Canis familiaris or Canis sp		1													
Lepus sp. (jackrabbit)									2			1			
Cervus canadensis		2													

Bird and reptile bones	Site 1								Site 2						
	0-1'	1-2'	2-3'	3-4'	4-5'	5-6'	6+'	?	0-1'	1-2'	2-3'	3-4'	4-5'	5-6'	?
Birds:															
Plegadis guarauna		1													
Pelecanus erythrorhyncus	1		2	1											
Grus canadensis canadensis															
Anserinae, goose		1													
Unidentified	4		4	4	2	1			1						
Reptiles:															
Clemmys marmorata			2												

HISTORICAL AND ETHNIC BACKGROUND

Since the time of its first discovery by white men the floor of Buena Vista Basin has been the habitat entirely of Yokuts-speaking tribes affiliated on a wider basis with the Penutian linguistic family. According to Kroeber,

The Tulamni . . . were the tribe in possession of Buena Vista Lake, at some point on whose western or northwestern shore where the hills come close to the water was their main settlement Tulamniu, "Tulamni-place." From there they ranged westward to Wogitiu in the vicinity of McKittrick. [Kroeber, 1925, p. 478; see also pl. 47.]

The domain of the Tulamni lay altogether west of the lower Kern River, extending north to about the latitude of Goose Lake, west to the watershed separating the San Joaquin from the Cuyama and upper Salinas drainages, and south to the vicinity of or just beyond Maricopa and Hazelton. The shores of Kern Lake were held by the related Hometwoli tribe. South of these two groups, the southernmost of the Yokuts, the slope of the San Emigdio mountains was occupied by the linguistically divergent Emigdiano branch of the Chumashan stock.

The first white man to leave a written description of the Buena Vista region is now believed to have been Don Pedro Fages (1775; Bolton, 1931), comandante of the presidio at Monterey. Early in 1772, in pursuit of deserters from the Spanish missions, Fages left San Diego by way of the Imperial and San Jacinto Valleys and Cajon Pass, skirted the west edge of the Mohave Desert, and entered the San Joaquin Valley by way of "the pass of Buena Vista." From here he made his way west across the Coast Ranges to San Luis Obispo, and up the coast to San Francisco Bay. Of much interest are his comments on the San Joaquin Valley, which he described as "a labyrinth of lakes and tulares" in the middle of "a great plain." This plain was "very thickly settled with many and large villages." Particularly germane are his statements concerning

a village called Buena Vista. This village, because it is on a fair sized elevation, overlooks a great plain along the course of the River San Francisco [San Joaquin]. . . . From the village of Buena Vista the plain continues toward the south for seven leagues more, over good lands with some water. And at the end of these seven leagues one goes toward the south through a pass, partly of valleys and arroyos, very thickly grown with groves of live oaks, as are also all the hills and sierras which form these valleys. Going now three leagues more in the same direction, one comes to a very large plain [Antelope Valley and the Mohave Desert], which keeps getting wider and wider, both toward the east and toward the south, leaving to the north and northwest many sierras.[6]

---

[6] Bolton, 1931, pp. 218–219. See p. 214 for reconstruction of Fages southward trip; pp. 215–216 and 219 for Bolton's identification of Buena Vista with Tulamniu and the latter with certain shell heaps at the foot of Buena Vista Hills.

Items of ethnographic interest with some possible bearing on archeology, include such observations as the following:

In their villages the natives live in the winter in very large squares, the families divided from each other, and outside they have very large houses in the form of hemispheres, where they keep their seeds and utensils. . . . They have some large stones like *metates* on which they grind their seeds.

. . . The natives, who live there in their spherical houses, in order to escape the discomfort which rain causes them when it is very abundant, are accustomed to move to a drier region during the rainy season and when it is over return to their houses. . . [Bolton, 1931, p. 219].

Elsewhere are reported stone jars and variously sized wood and reed trays decorated with grass roots in their natural permanent color (Fages, 1775, p. 73).

Unfortunately, no estimate of population or size of villages is given.

Four years after Fages, in 1776, a priest from San Gabriel, Francisco Garces, traversed the eastern slope of the upper San Joaquin while enroute to the Mohave area. There is no specific mention of the lakes or of the natives residing on their immediate shores. Most of his observations were on the eastern foothill tribes. Here he saw stone mortars and pestles, small baskets, flint knives, etc. In view of his personal acquaintance with the Santa Barbara channel area we note especially his mention of

vessels (bateas) with inlays (embutidos) of mother of pearl, like the shell-work (texidos de cuentas) on the handles of the knives, and all the other articles, (obras—manufactures) that it is said there are on the Canal [channel ?] with (the people of) which they carry on much commerce, and perhaps it is that very nation; according to the reports that I have they also agree closely in the dress and cleanliness of the women. [Coues, 1900, p. 278.]

The perennial search for fugitives from the missions on the coast led Zalvidea in the summer of 1806 from Santa Barbara northward through the Cuyama Valley and across the south end of the San Joaquin. Entering from the west or southwest he gives among others the following details for July 25:

This day after mass we marched northward; after eight leagues we came upon the rancheria of Buenavista, which consists of thirty-six men, one hundred and forty-four women, and thirty-eight children, according to the assertion of the Indians. The rancheria is on the margin of a lake eight leagues long and five wide. The Indians cross it on rafts (balsas) . . . [Zalvidea, n. d.]

Next day, after traveling eastward along the south side of the lake, Zalvidea turned north to reach a second village called Sisupistoi. Here he found 50 to 60 men and counted 28 huts, leaving us like his superior to "infer the number of souls approximately." At Sisupistoi trouble developed between its inhabitants and several Buenavista Indians in the party, and the former after shooting several darts at the "captain of Buenavista" finally took to the tules for cover.

The exact route followed is uncertain. Bancroft (1886, p. 48) held that the lake mentioned "seems too large for Buenavista or Kern Lakes or both, and too small for Tulare Lake, but was probably the latter." Gifford and Schenck (1926, p. 22) on the contrary believe the party skirted the shores of the combined Buena Vista and Kern Lakes, which at full stage would have formed a sheet about as long but only two-thirds as wide as the estimates of the Spanish. They further identify Sisupistoi with Pohalin Tinliu at the east end of Kern Lake, and Buena Vista with Tulamniu at the west end of Buena Vista Lake. For the two villages they estimate a total population of about 500.

A week later while making his way out of the San Joaquin through the Tehachapi, Zalvidea on the authority of the natives observed "that the Indians of the Rio Colorado of the rancheria called Majagua are continually coming to deal with them. The journey requires 10 days, and there are no watering places on the road." Departure from the San Joaquin was through a canyon "five leagues from the rancheria [Sisupistoi?] at the point of the lake, as many more from Buenavista. . . ."

The next account touching on the Buena Vista Basin seems to be that of Martinez.[7] He locates the village Buenavista "on the shore where the plain reaches the lake [and ?] there is a large grove of poplars growing over more or less sandy soil about one league in width." According to Priestley's interpretation of the narrative the village was on the north shore of Buena Vista Lake.

In 1819 [8] Estudillo, commandant at the presidio of Monterey, made a reconnaissance and inspection trip into the country of the *Tulareños*.[9] He appears not to have visited the Buena Vista Basin, and most of his observations concern the region about Tulare Lake and Kings River. There is frequent mention of the difficulties encountered in crossing the marshes, but relatively little definite information regarding the customs of the natives. Ethnographic items for the lake peoples include the balsa, snares for catching ducks, baskets, use of wild hemp for making fish nets, houses apparently made of arched-over poles covered with tules, and, in the foothills, stone mortars or mealing slabs. Though not seen, the village of Buenavista is several times mentioned since many of the Indians Estudillo hoped to contact had gone thence for a fiesta. He was further informed that Lieutenant Moraga had gone to Buenavista

---

[7] This appears to exist only in manuscript form. Since it is not available to me, I have incorporated in the above only the pertinent comments by Gifford and Schenck (1926, p. 24), and one from a manuscript on Franciscan Exploration of California, by Priestley.

[8] Bancroft (1886, p. 335) says that in this year "in the Tulares all ride," and that regular fairs for horse selling were held.

[9] Gayton, 1936; esp. pp. 71, 72, and 76 for references to Buenavista.

a few days previously, but the Indians had scattered to the lake upon his arrival.

On a punitive expedition against a fugitive band of rebellious neophytes from Santa Barbara, Portilla in 1824 marched into the San Joaquin via Tejon pass (Bancroft, 1886, p. 535). He stopped at San Emigdio, 9 leagues from the pass through which he had come and 5 or 6 leagues from Lake Misjamin. On or near the lake was the rancheria of Tulali (Tulamniu ?), but no further information is given.

After 1824 the history of the upper San Joaquin becomes only a local variant of the tragic story that was being written wherever the Indian and the white man came into direct contact. Americans and Europeans entered in increasing numbers, and so also did malcontents from the mission tribes along the coast.[10] It is only reasonable to infer that, as elsewhere, such readjustments of population were attended by cultural changes, and in particular by a weakening of attachment to the old native ways of life among the *Tulareños*. It is not altogether clear just how strong the cultural influence of the incoming coastal people was. The southern Yokuts themselves escaped the blight of mission life as such but because they inhabited the land best suited to ranching and farming they succumbed rapidly to the American penetration after 1850. Driven from the plains into the mountains, they were rescued from complete oblivion only through the reawakened interest of ethnologists in the early twentieth century (Kroeber, 1925, pp. 474–543).

The narratives from which the foregoing observations have been extracted are of interest for two primary reasons. In the first place, they afford suggestive if incomplete glimpses into the mode of life followed by the southern valley tribes prior to the decline of native culture before the impact of European civilization. As subsequent ethnographic researches have shown, in its material aspects it was a simple unspectacular culture in which the subsistence economy centered largely about the lacustrine and paludous features of the immediate environment. On the nonmaterial side we learn relatively little except that there was extensive intercourse and commerce with neighboring peoples to the east, south, and west, and that large intertribal festivals were held. To the Spanish soldiers and priests the details of social, political, and religious organization were utterly inconsequential, and whatever in native society and custom was not superficially obvious passed unnoticed. It is, therefore, to the ethnologist that we must turn for a succinct characterization of historic Yokuts civilization. To quote from Kroeber:

[10] Because of this ". . . a skeleton dug up on the shore of Buena Vista lake, if buried since 1800, is as likely to be that of an individual born on the coast." [Gifford and Schenck, 1926, p. 28.]

The affiliations of Yokuts civilization are nearly equal in all directions. To the north their system of totemic moieties connects them with the Miwok while certain detailed elements of their culture, such as the Y-frame cradle and the magpie headdress, link them definitely with the Maidu. To the east their twined basketry has close relations as far as the remoter edge of the Great Basin. Toward the Shoshonean and Yuman south there are innumerable threads: the Jimson weed ritual, the arrow straightener, the carrying net, to mention only a few. Toward the west the decay of Salinan and Chumash culture makes exact comparison difficult, but what little is known of the former people evidences a strong Yokuts impress, while with the nearer Chumash relations of trade were close and must have brought many approaches of custom in their train. It is difficult to say where the most numerous and most basic links stretch.

Equally impressive, however, are the features distinctive of the civilization of the Yokuts, or rather of the group composed of themselves and their smaller and less known Shoshonean neighbors on the immediate east and south. These specialities include the true tribal organization, the duality of chieftainship, the regulated function of transvestites, the coordinated animal pantheon, the eagle-down skirt, the constricted coiled basket, a distinctive pottery, and the communal house, to mention only a few points.

It thus seems that the Yokuts were a nation of considerable individuality. . . . [Kroeber, 1925, p. 542.]

From the viewpoint of archeology, it is of equal interest to note the persistent references by the Spaniards to a particular rancheria on the shores of Buena Vista Lake. Variously designated as Buenavista and Tulali, this appears to have been a settlement of some size and permanence. Unfortunately, the historical documents are indecisive as to its exact location. Fages, first to mention the village (1772), placed it "on a fair-sized elevation" overlooking the course of the San Joaquin River, 7 leagues north of a pass leading from the valley. From this Bolton (1931) infers that the location was at the east end of the Buena Vista Hills on the southwest edge of the lake; his sketch (opposite p. 216) and accompanying photograph identify it with our site 1 (cf. also p. 219). From Zalvidea's account (1806), Priestley (n. d.) also concludes that Buenavista was on or near the southwest corner of the lake. Gifford and Schenck (1926, p. 22) merely place it at the west end; elsewhere (p. 40), as site 33 in the Lake region, they equate it with our sites 1 and 2 at the southwest side. On the other hand, from what little is available regarding Martinez' journey (1816), the village appears to have stood on the north or northwest side (Priestley, n. d.). Certainly its environs, as given by Gifford and Schenck, conform much more closely to the situation near the outlet of Buena Vista Lake. This, as already indicated, is the location toward which Kroeber also inclines.

It is entirely conceivable, even quite probable, that the natives shifted their centers of abode from time to time, particularly in the period of unrest and turmoil initiated by the Spanish invaders. So far as the Yokuts of Buena Vista Lake were concerned, the southwest and northwest sides were equally suited to occupancy. Both were utilized, as proved by large shell heaps at the foot of Buena Vista Hills and also at the base of Elk Hills. Possibly between the time of Fages and that of Martinez, the main settlement was transferred from a point in the former locale to another in the latter. That this instability necessarily foredooms any attempt at precise identification of a given townsite is improbable, though it may well entail a critical re-examination of all relevant evidence. As elsewhere in the New World, so here in the San Joaquin the prehistoric past touches the historic present and makes possible the attack of archeological problems through history and ethnology. In the present instance, since the historical data are open to two interpretations, archeology may have the final word as to where the native villages stood at the dawn of the contact period. At any rate, one of the prime considerations in selection of the sites for present excavation was the distinct likelihood of establishing a connection between a defined archeological complex and a specific historic tribal group. We shall return to this point again after analysis of the archeological evidence.

ARCHEOLOGY

LOCATION AND GENERAL DESCRIPTION OF SITES

The area covered more or less intensively by the investigations herein described is shown in detail in figure 2. At its higher stages particularly (295–300 feet (90–91.5 m.)) the lake here washed the northeastern base of the Buena Vista Hills along a front of about 2 miles (3.2 km.). The shoreline trends from northwest to southeast, then curves sharply southward around the extreme easternmost spur of the hills. Between the shore and a parallel line some 750 yards (817.5 m.) inland to the south are three hillocks rising 75 to 125 feet (22.9 to 38.1 m.) above the former normal lake level and separated from one another by shallow gullies draining toward the north. Depressions likewise serve to isolate this area from the main and generally higher mass of the Buena Vista Hills on the south and southwest. At the mouth of each north-flowing draw is a small alluvium-filled embayment, normally dry and safely above even the higher stages of the lake. The hills consist of coarse, usually compact, gravels and sand, a Tertiary formation designated as the Tulare. As elsewhere, they are clothed here with a sparse growth of brush, but trees, and, for the most part, also grass are absent.

North and southeast from this immediate locale the hills recede from the old lake bed and give way to low flat-lying plains. Here the shores were generally wide, poorly defined, and swampy, much less suited to permanent habitation than along the flanks of the hills.

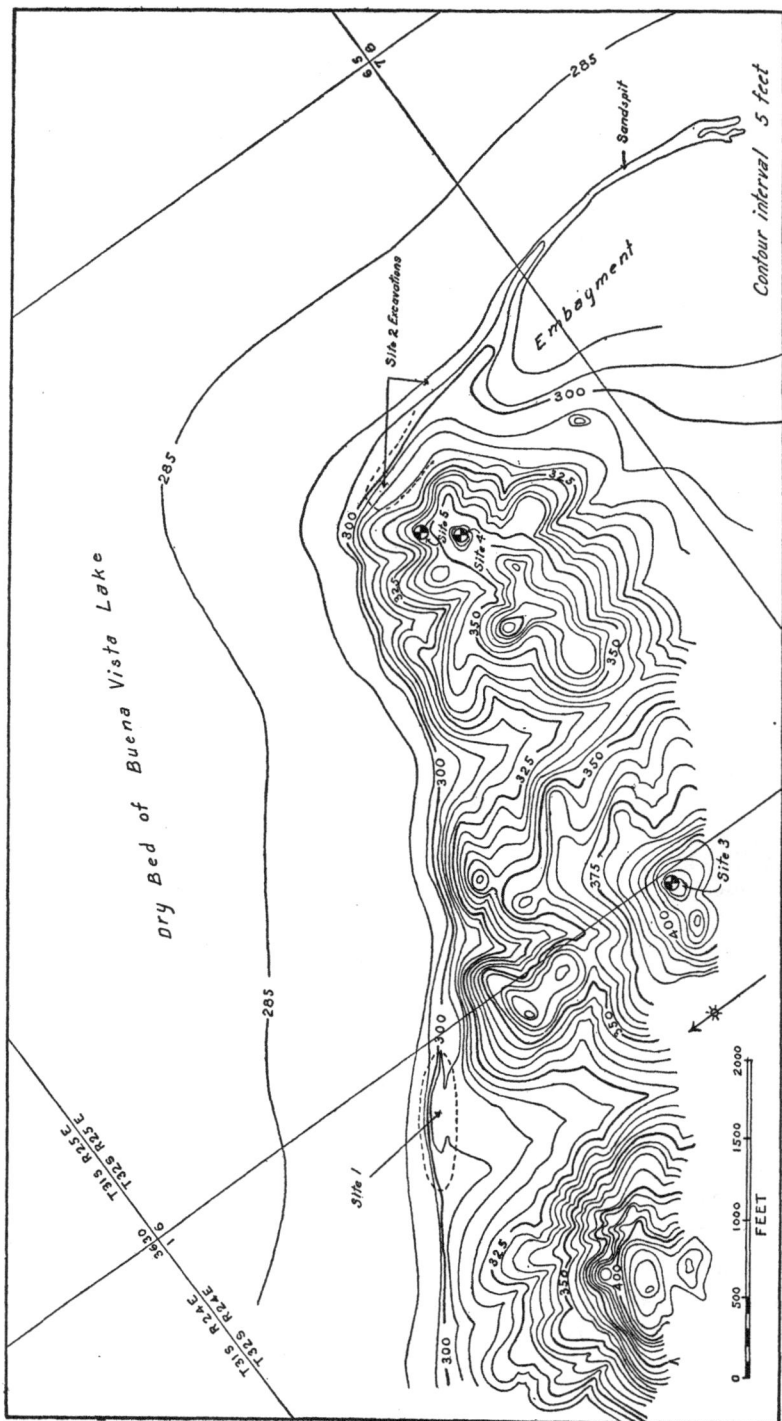

Figure 2.—Key map of village and burial sites excavated on southwest shore of Buena Vista Lake, 1933–34.

So far as the south and west margins of Buena Vista Lake are concerned, the most desirable and satisfactory localities for such occupancy were only two, viz, the base of the Buena Vista Hills and, 5 or 6 miles (8 or 9.6 km.) to the north, the borders of the Elk Hills. Traces of aboriginal activity occur everywhere along the northeast foot of the Buena Vista Hills, mostly at or just above the 300-foot contour. Owing to the action of currents and waves along this exposed stretch of shore, however, there were only a few spots where larger human groups could conveniently settle. The best, or at any rate the one most favored by the natives, was a small alluvial flat half a mile (0.8 km.) southeast of the Honolulu Oil Company water-pumping station (U. S. Geol. Survey, Mouth of Kern quadrangle, 1932), about midway along the northeast front of the Buena Vista Hills. Across the outer or lakeward end of this flat lies a large elliptical shell heap some 300 yards (273 m.) in length. Its location and outline but not its dimensions are indicated in a very general manner by the 305-foot contour on the topographic sheet just mentioned. In figure 2, as hereinafter, it is designated site 1.

Twelve hundred yards (1,092 m.) to the southeast and just around the shoulder of the easternmost hill, is site 2. This is a less clearly delineated occupational area centering at the eastern foot of the hill, and extending a long narrow arm several hundred yards southward along a sandspit onto the dry lake bed. Both sites are mainly on, or at most extend just below the 300-foot contour, but broken shell and camp debris are spread in a thinning mantle out onto the lake bed to and beyond the 295-foot line. Neither site can be seen from the other because of the curve in the shoreline. Shallow middens occur at the mouth of a small embayment between the two, at another near the water-pumping station, and, as already stated, to a much lesser extent all along the narrow shelf at the base of the hills. Sites 1 and 2 jointly comprise site 33 as reported by Gifford and Schenck (1926, pp. 40–41 and map 1).

On the highest of the three hills overlooking the lake, 700 yards (637 m.) due south of and about 125 feet (38.1 m.) higher than site 1, was found a prehistoric burial ground hereafter described as site 3. Two smaller native cemeteries were situated on lower summits 100 to 180 yards (91 to 164 m.) west of site 2 and about 50–70 feet (15.2–21.3 m.) above the latter. These will be discussed as sites 4 and 5. Sites 1 and 3 are in the east half of section 1, T32S, R24E; sites 2, 4, and 5 in the south half of section 6, T32S, R25E.[11]

Airline distances from the sites to modern towns and cities are approximately as follows: To Taft, 7½ miles (12 km.) west southwest; to Maricopa, 8½ miles (13.6 km.) south-southwest; to Bakersfield, 23 miles (36.8 km.) northeast.

---

[11] Designations refer to the Mount Diablo datum.

SITE 1

Site 1 (pl. 1) is in the N½ of SE¼ of NE¼ of section 1, township 32 south, range 24 east. The accumulated refuse, consisting of shells, ash, bones, sand, artifacts, and soil, extends along the shore continuously for 900 feet (274.5 m.) or slightly more, and back from the former water's edge some 100-200 feet (30.5-61 m.). At its highest point the summit of the shell heap is 310.4 feet (94.7 m.) above sea level; its base generally is just above the 300-foot (91.5 m.) contour. From this it is evident that the entire site was above even the highest possible stages of Buena Vista Lake and could have been continuously inhabited. As already stated, it lies across the lower end of a small alluvial plain through which drains the run-off from the nearby hillsides to the south. This eventually finds its way around either end of the shell heap into the lake bed. From its summit the midden slopes evenly in every direction to give a symmetric elongate elliptical outline. The 310-foot contour is not encountered again until the lower slope of the hill to the southeast is reached upward of 50 yards (45.5 m.) distant. On the side facing the lake a steadily thinning sheet of refuse continues down to the 292-foot contour. The exact limits of the shell heap are not easily determined due to modification of its outlines by wave action and other erosional factors. The probable width based on our cross sections may be given as circa 100-110 feet (30.5-33.5 m.), ending originally at the 302-foot contour on the lake shore (fig. 3). Lengthwise, it is delimited on the southeast by a small dry wash, with the shell deposits ending near the 303-foot contour. On the northwest the mound as such ends at the 302- or 303-foot line, with the last 100 feet (30.5 m.) showing only thin shell deposits. The area covered is estimated roughly at 80,000 to 90,000 square feet (7,500 to 8,300 sq. m.), more if the thin mantle of shell and refuse extending onto the lake bed is counted.

For excavation the site was laid out by a system of coordinates in 10-foot (3.05 m.) squares, with datum located well to the north off the mound (figs. 3, 4). Each square was designated by the number on a stake at its north corner. Test trenches soon indicated a lenticular rather than truly stratified internal structure; hence it was decided to remove the material in arbitrary 12-inch layers. Over most of the area dug, the dirt was sifted through ¼-inch screens, periodic checks being made with finer mesh to insure a minimum of loss of smaller objects such as beads. Specimens were placed in sacks and labeled according to the square and depth (within 12-inch vertical limits) from which they came. Artifacts in general can thus be located within a 12-inch (30 cm.) horizon in a 10-foot (3.05 m.) square. Special features, such as burials, pits, and fireplaces, were plotted with more exactitude, as were also artifacts of exceptional nature. Profiles were taken of the vertical face at 10-foot intervals, while post molds, graves, etc., were similarly plotted to scale on horizontal plans. Master profiles were prepared for each of the three principal cross-section trenches as well as for the lengthwise trench.

Three parallel cross trenches were made through the heap in a southwest-northeast direction so as to section its deepest portion on both sides of the highest point (fig. 4). Trench 1, the original test to determine possible stratification, was 220 feet (67.1 m.) long by 10 feet (3.05 m.) wide; the depth varied from 3 feet (0.91 m.) at either end to 11 feet (3.4 m.) at the point of maximum accumulation (pl. 1, c). Trench 2, 120 feet (36.6 m.) to the northwest along line 77 was 150 feet (65.7 m.) long by 5 feet (1.5 m.) wide. The third cut, along line 67, was 100 feet (91 m.) northwest of trench 2; it measured 190 by 5 feet (57.9 by 1.5 m.). At right angle to these, a 900-foot (274.5 m.) profile was secured by a longitudinal cut, continuous from the southerly end of the mound (row 118) to its junction with trench 3 (in square 67/37), whence 5- by 10-foot (1.5 by 3.05 m.) pits at 20-foot (7.1 m.) intervals ran on to square 30/37. All of these cuts were carried downward into undisturbed sterile soil formations and extended horizontally until the middens thinned to the vanishing point. None of the material in the trenches was screened.

From the cross sections just described it was clear that the greatest depth of refuse lay at or near the peak between trenches 1 and 2. Accordingly, it was decided to remove this entire block of the mound on the full 100-foot (30.5 m.) front starting on the westerly or landward side and screening all dirt layer by layer as previously explained. Hopes were entertained, and, indeed, steps actually taken, to extend this area of investigation 100 feet (30.5 m.) further toward the northwest, so as to include also the section between trenches 2 and 3. The work, though vigorously pushed from both sides of the shell heap by 75 or more laborers, progressed much less rapidly than anticipated. The width of the cut was reduced from over 200 (61 m.) to 100 (30.5 m.) and finally to 50 feet (15.2 m.) on which basis it was carried through the midden save for a 10-foot (3.05 m.) longitudinal control strip down the center.

The area thus excavated and screened covered approximately 16,000 square feet (1,500 sq. m.), which was worked to depths of 2 to 7 feet (0.7 to 2.1 m.) according to the thickness of deposit. The volume probably exceeded 50,000 cubic feet (1,407.5 cu. m.). The trenches and test pits, some 1,400 feet (427 m.) long in all, 5 to 10 feet (1.5–3.05 m.) wide, and up to 11 feet (3.4 m.) deep, represented in the neighborhood of 45,000 cubic feet (1,266.2 cu. m.). Including trenches and all screened and unscreened areas, the total amount of

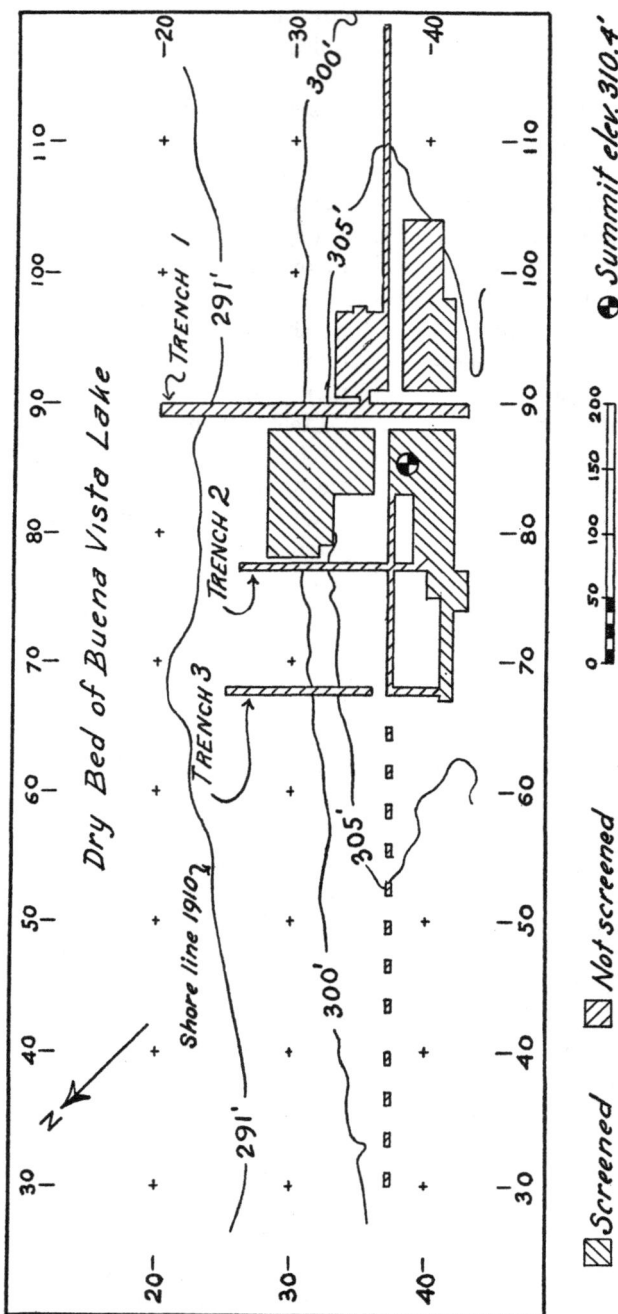

FIGURE 4.—Map of excavations at Buena Vista site 1, 1933–34.

midden worked over during excavation of site 1 can be estimated, probably conservatively, at nearly 100,000 cubic feet or approximately 3,700 cubic yards (2,812 cu. m.). The volume of the shell heap has not been accurately calculated, but the average depth over the 80,000–90,000 square feet may perhaps fairly be set at not over 3 feet (0.91 m.). This would give a total mound content of around 240,000 to 270,000 cubic feet (6,645–7,600 m.³), of which 35 to 40 percent was subjected to scrutiny during our excavations.

The oldest soil formation revealed by the trenches was a "hardpan" of very compact yellowish brown alluvium (fig. 5; pls. 2, a; 4, b). This appeared to be essentially the same clayey material as that which underlay the flat south of the mound, all of which was doubtless derived by geologically recent wash from the surrounding hills. The yellow brown soil graded upward into a darker gray zone, not much different in texture, hardness, and composition except for occasional bits of broken shell and charcoal. We attribute the color here to organic admixture, either from vegetation or else through human agency, perhaps both. In the field, this zone, from 1 to 2 feet (fig. 5, bed 1 A) thick, was called "gray hardpan" to distinguish it from the underlying yellow hardpan. The upper surface of the gray layer was quite irregular, with numerous trash-filled pits and basins alternating with humps and low ridges (pls. 2, b; 4, b). Its larger contours, as disclosed in the various diggings, are interesting. At the northerly end of the longitudinal mound profile, the hardpan surface was at or just above 301 feet (91.8 m.) above sea level. Thence it rose gradually and unevenly to about 304 feet (92.7 m.) under the summit of the mound only to shelve off again to 303 feet (92.4 m.) at the southerly end of the trench. Thus, at either end of the long axis it was mantled by only a few inches to a foot of refuse and topsoil. In the main transverse, trench 1, it maintained a level at or very near 303 feet for nearly 100 feet, about the estimated original width of the shell-heap base. Then it sloped rapidly downward to 290 feet (88.4 m.), a 12-foot (3.6 m.) drop, in about 80 feet (24.4 m.) under the beach. This slope began at its upper end some 10 or 15 feet (3.05 or 4.6 m.) inland from an old wave-cut terrace on the 301-foot (91.8 m.) level, the uppermost but probably not oldest, of six recognized terraces. More about these later.

It was suggested by visiting geologists that the yellow hardpan represented a natural ledge or reef of Quaternary to Recent alluvial material, which because of its height above the highest expectable lake levels tended to encourage human habitation. Though extended tests were not made in the flat to the south, i. e., inland from the shell heap, it is probable that the upper surface of the hardpan rises. Its decline at either end of the mound is presumably due to downward cutting of the intermittent washes draining the flat,

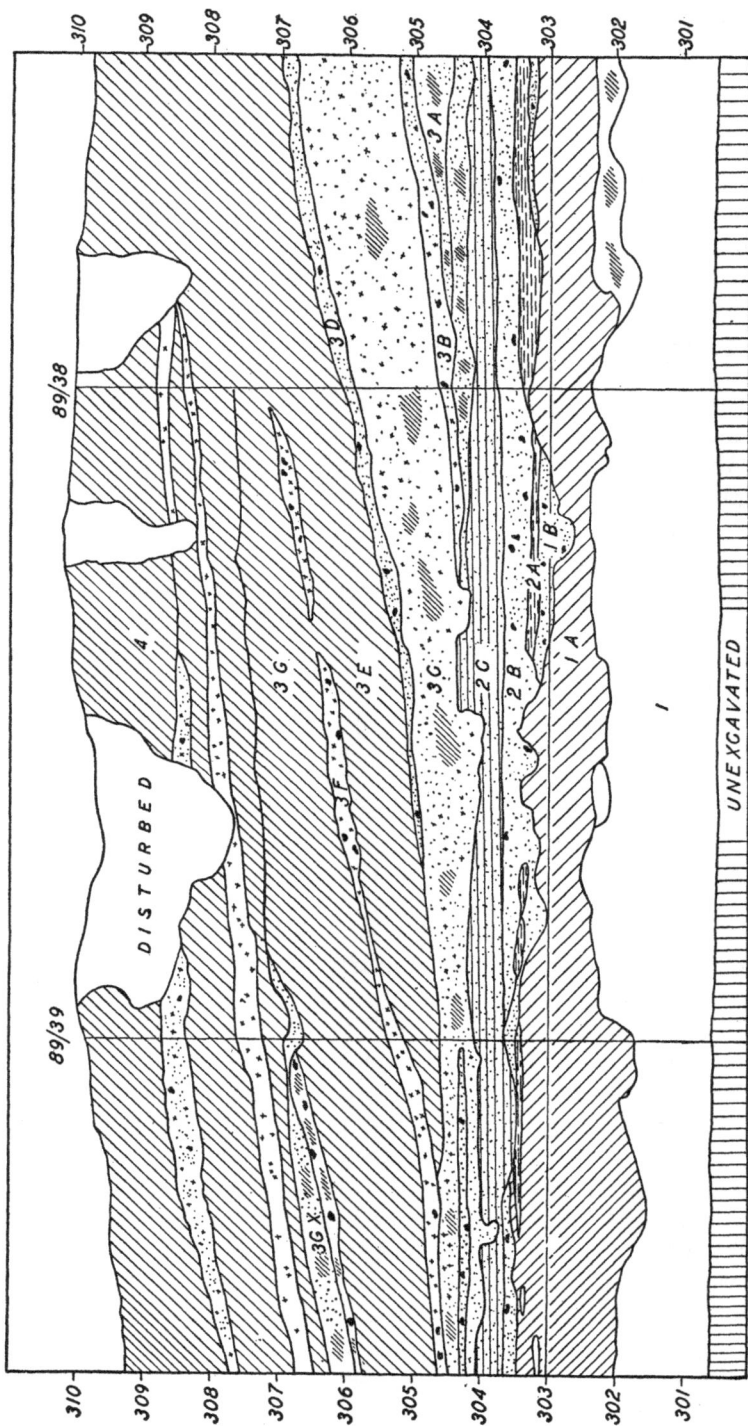

FIGURE 5.—Sample profile section from northwest wall of trench 1, Buena Vista site 1. Key to symbols: ///// shell; + ash; irregular black spots, charcoal; small dots, sand.

the rising shell heap itself forming an obstruction around which run-off would be forced to seek its way. The hardpan underlying the flat generally would not be very deeply invaded by the lake because of the hill to the northwest which deflected currents along the shore past the point occupied by the site.

That this "basement soil" was not entirely a prehuman deposit, at any rate not in its uppermost portions, was indicated by the discovery of artifacts unquestionably inclusive therein. These, significantly, included only mullers, at least 4 of which were found from 1 to nearly 3 feet (0.3 to 1 m.) below the contact between hardpan and the overlying less compacted layers of refuse. The top of the hardpan was from 5½ to 8 feet (1.7 to 2.4 m.) below the mound surface at every point where these objects occurred, whereas their specific depths were 6½ to about 9 feet (2 to 2.7 m.). There was also one small stone-filled pit, possibly a hearth or oven from which the ashes had been leached, in the upper few inches of this zone, as well as occasional pockets of fire-reddened earth. All this suggests that intermittent occupancy, perhaps by hunters or fishermen, may have occurred on the ledge even during final stages in deposition of the alluvium.

Along the front of the mound, i. e., on the side facing the lake, the gray hardpan was found to shade gradually into a thicker and somewhat softer mass to which the unorthodox but apt term "plum pudding" formation was applied. This was a dark gray rather formless mass apparently caused by churning and wave agitation of broken shell, sand, ash, and organic matter. It, too, contained evidences of human industry, though only in limited quantity, and undoubtedly represents an early period in man's occupancy of the site. We shall discuss its nature and probable significance later in connection with site 2, where a much clearer picture was defined.

The uncompacted portions of the shell heap, including all materials above the hardpan and "plum pudding" formations, attained a maximum thickness of about 7 feet (2.1 m.). They included beds of mixed shell, ash, charcoal, sand, dust, the bones of animals, birds, and fish, some stones, and cultural debris. True stratification, in the sense of definable widely spread strata markedly distinct from others, was not found, and the deposits are more accurately described as lenticular. Lest this characterization be thought unwarranted after a study of plates 2 and 4, it may be remarked further that the seemingly well-marked beds therein shown could not with rare exceptions be certainly identified 20 feet (6.1 m.) either way from the trench walls. Moreover, the profiles from each of the three transverse trenches show only very general but few specific similarities to one another. Certain of the thicker lenses were traceable for 20 or 30 feet (6.1 or 9.1 m.), seldom over a greater distance, and most of the seams pinched out much more rapidly. The internal structure thus is strikingly like that noted for the shell heaps of San Francisco Bay (Schenck, 1926, pp. 168–170).

Careful study of the walls of trench 1 suggests that the first permanent occupancy above the hardpan began on the immediate edge of the ledge north of the apex of the mound, between the lake and our longitudinal profile cut. The highest point of this nuclear mound lay some 15–30 feet (4.6–9.1 m.) to the right (northeast) of the section reproduced as figure 5. In figure 5, stratum 3B is indicated as rising gradually to overlap the flank of the older heap which appears to have reached a height of 2 feet (61 cm.) or more above the hardpan at the 303-foot level. It consisted of finely broken shell, ash, dirt, and sand, moderately compact. The extent of this original heap is uncertain but could not have been very great for there was no indication of it in trench 2. There may well be other still earlier such hummocks not noted or seen by us. From the standpoint of time and sequence, we may point out that an artifact, A, found near the top of this postulated and locally well-marked early zone, say at a depth of 3½ feet (1.06 m.) below stake 89/36 would be older than another, B, 6 feet (1.8 m.) deep under stake 89/39, because the bed in which A occurred sloped visibly downward to the southwest to pinch out under the horizon containing B. In other words, it cannot be assumed a priori that a higher level is younger than a lower regardless of its horizontal position. Schenck's observations (1926, p. 170) at Emeryville apply equally here when he says, "With lenticular construction only an area more or less directly under another area can be considered relatively older." In the present instance, however, it should be added that there appears to be no significant difference between objects recovered in this nuclear mound and those found generally throughout the later deposits in the main shell-heap mass.

The great bulk of the accumulations at site 1, then, comprised lenses and pockets of varying extent and thickness, distinguishable from one another only by the relative amounts of shell, ash, sand, and soil. The sample section reproduced in figure 5 is as representative as any, but could probably not be precisely duplicated anywhere else in the mound. The cross trenches generally show a definite upward slope of the shell beds toward the higher part. Between its crest, if this be considered as approximately indicated by our lengthwise profile line, and the lake, the bedding lines and lenses are traceable only with extreme difficulty or not at all. Perhaps this strip because it was highest was most intensively lived on by the natives. This, together with old filled-in pothunter's excavations, large burrows, and other pittings, has obscured structural details throughout virtually the entire lakeward slope. The general appearance of all this material is such as to suggest relatively rapid and recent deposition. Whereas picks and mattocks were well nigh indispensable in excavating the hardpan and were useful as well in the "plum pudding," the upper 6 or 7 feet (1.8 or 2.1 m.) were so loose and soft that they could be turned readily with the shovel. Some of the larger lenses and pockets consisted of little save whole shells and such dust as had filtered in among them. No long breaks in occupancy are indicated. The difference in age between this material and its contained human remains, on the one hand, and the underlying compact layers with little visible remaining shell and charcoal and but few artifacts must have been considerable. The dissimilarities may be readily visualized by reference to plates 2 and 4.

Particular mention should be made of one noncultural layer encountered beneath the inland slope of the shell heap. This consisted of fine yellow sand and dust bedded and sorted apparently by wind and/or water. It is shown as 2C in figure 5, and as a light-colored band in plate 2, *a*. As determined in trench 1, it lay on the 304-foot (92.7 m.) level, with a thickness of 4–6 inches (10–15 cm.). Appearing in the southerly inland end of the trench it continued in the walls for about 50 feet (15 m.), where its lower contact began to curve evenly upward. The upper surface maintained a perfect level throughout, so that as the bottom rose the stratum soon pinched out against the slope of the hypothetical nuclear mound. The edge of the layer on the side nearest the lake bed was found in squares 68/38, 79/37, and 90/36. Toward the northwest it was readily traceable for about 200 feet (61 m.) from trench 1, where it disappeared beyond the limits of our excavations in square 70/41. It was also strongly marked 100 feet (30.5 m.) south of trench 1 in square 99/41. Thus it covered an area at least 300 feet (91.5 m.) long by about 60 feet (18.3 m.) wide, running well under the highest part of the mound. Inland, its limits under the flat were not determined. Cultural remains were nowhere observed in this yellow sand, although there was a very thin seam of loose broken shells, ash, and occupational debris directly under it. This, we may note, thickened in the trench wall toward the northeast and proved to be continuous with the "nuclear" mound. A 1- to 2-inch (2.5–5 cm.) layer of extremely fine yellow dust underlay the occupational horizon, and where not broken through or missing served to separate it from the much harder gray subsoil.

Whenever seen in the excavations, the upper surface of sand layer 2C apparently lay at the same level, approximately 304 feet, and presented a uniform thickness save at its margins. It is believed this signifies deposition in standing water, and that the fine texture implies carrying in of small particles of sand and dust by winds. It seems not improbable that the stratum was laid down in a pond behind the mound, the pond itself being due to unusually heavy run-off filling a depression inadvertently formed by the slowly rising heap of camp refuse. The extent of this supposed body of water, as stated, was not ascertained, but circumstances suggest that stratum 2C was only the edge of a temporary lagoon which may have covered a sizable area beneath what is now a dry flat. There is no reason whatever for suspecting an inundation by the lake, since the yellow sand is well above the highest indicated or likely lake level. In light of certain features to be discussed presently from site 2, it would be tempting to regard the sand as the visible imprint of a period of excessive precipitation which occurred during occupation of the spot by the people whose refuse built up the shell heap proper. It should be stated in this connection that the few artifacts found in the softer refuse immediately below the yellow sand, like those in the "nuclear" mound, are essentially the same as those in the shell layers above 2C. The contact between gray hardpan and probably also the "plum pudding," on the one hand, and the softer shell heap proper on the other, *not* the 2C stratum just discussed, forms the line of separation for what archeology suggests were two vertically distinct occupational periods. The second and later period had already begun when 2C was laid down.

It is well nigh impossible to reconstruct satisfactorily the growth of the site except in a very general way. The only significant change which may be important over the entire mound area is between level 1A (top of gray hardpan, and possibly of "plum pudding") and the overlying unconsolidated materials. Anticipating ourselves slightly, it may be remarked that below this contact in the hardpan were found only a few hearths, mullers, and very rudely worked objects. Above, and immediately, begins a much richer deposit, so that the break between the two formations is apparently about as marked culturally as it is geologically. Neither the dust layer, 2A, nor the water-laid sand, 2C, appear to represent any prolonged period of time or a cultural break, nor is there any reason to believe they were attended by complete abandonment of the site.

Passing reference has been made to old beach lines now buried beneath the outer lakeward slope of the shell heap. Six of these were found during excavation of trench 1 (pl. 3). Each consisted of a well-defined bluff 6–18 inches (15–45 cm.) high cut into the hardpan by wave action and fronted by a gently sloping strip of sandy beach. Prior to excavation there was no hint of their presence, as broken shell and earth formed a fairly uniform slope from the mound down into the old lake bed. The highest terrace, No. 6, was 18 inches (45 cm.) deep; it stood at the 300-foot (91.5 m.) level, or 2–3 feet (60–90 cm.) below the top of the hardpan on which the middens rested. Since the outlet of Buena Vista Basin was such as to drain the lake whenever the water stood over 295 feet (90 m.) above sea level, it is extremely unlikely the waters ever exceeded the height represented by this terrace. Terrace 5, at 298 feet (90.9 m.) was 12 inches (30 cm.) deep (pl. 3, b), while terrace 1, at 291 feet (88.7 m.) was 18 inches (45 cm.). The latter was the level of the lake in 1910, though it is not certain whether the terrace was cut then or at some earlier equivalent stage. Between were terrace 4, 6 inches high at 297 feet (90.5 m.) elevation; terrace 3, 8 inches (20 cm.) high at 294.5 feet (89.8 m.) elevation; and terrace 2, 14 inches high at 292 feet (89 m.) With the possible exception of 4, the terraces are clear cut and were readily traced in either direction from trench 1 along the lake front. Several had layers of beach sand and gravel a few inches deep along their front slope, but all contained nonlacustrine, i. e., cultural, material as well.

The terraces bear ample witness to the wide fluctuations which characterized the height of water in Buena Vista Lake in the past. Unfortunately, the story they tell is almost impossible to read in some of its particulars. It is quite evident, though, that they do not signify a steadily rising or a shrinking lake, but that for periods of unknown length after each terrace was cut the waters receded to permit re-use of the newly formed beaches by man. There is no way of establishing the rate of terrace-cutting, which was undoubtedly affected by a number of geological and meteorological factors difficult or impossible to appreciate today. Still, it may be possible to infer with reasonable assurance the probable sequence of development for the upper three terraces at least.

As may be judged from plate 3, b, terrace 5 was filled with broken shell, dirt, and sand not very firmly consolidated, and attributable to the domestic activities of the natives living on the shell heap. The upper surface of this fill lay in the same plane as the beach of terrace 6. Two or three inches of beach sand covered the slope immediately in front of this higher terrace and, though not continuous, the same layer was noted resting on top of the shell bed in terrace 5. Terrace 5 must then have been cut and filled before terrace 6, since fill peculiar to and causally connected with the latter directly overlay that of the former. By analogous reasoning 4 probably preceded 5, though the evidence is not so clear. We may infer, therefore, that the lake once stood for a time at the 297-foot level where the waves carved out terrace 4. Then the waters fell and the widening middens spread down over the dry beach. A rise to 298 feet produced terrace 5, which was in turn covered with refuse as the lake again receded. Still later came a 300-foot stage, leveling off the older terrace fill and building a sandy beach over both the earlier ones. Subsequent high lake stages, if any comparable in height to these three again took place, are not demonstrable from our findings. They would have left scant traces in the loose materials now mantling the slopes toward the lake bed. As a matter of fact, since retreat of the water from terrace 6, the shell heap seems to have widened gradually toward the margins of the diminished lake, more or less uniformly overspreading the entire slope to a point about 5 feet (1.5 m.) beyond stake 89/30 (in trench 1), where the elevation of the hardpan is approximately 295–296 feet (90–90.3 m.). Here the lenses and strata fall more steeply, and give way to deposits in which sand and earth greatly predominate over shell and occupational debris. This suggests that the lake normally stood at and below 295 feet, and that occupation beyond this contour other than for cooking, camping, or similar transient activities was unsafe or impracticable.

It is impossible to reconstruct from the data at hand the sequence represented by terraces 1–3. That the highest of these (3 at 294.5 feet) may have been fairly recent is suggested by the finding of stone hearths and other materials similar to those from the upper midden layers at intervals along its front. Other materials included a steatite bowl found 14 inches below the surface in square 87/29 (pl. 6, a), and fragments of a stone vessel or mortar in a fireplace in square 81/29. Both these finds like the hearths generally were very close to or directly against the bluff of terrace 3. Beads occured in great profusion all along the lake slope, but obviously afford no such clear proof of domestic activities as do hearths and vessels.

The description of site 1 may be concluded with the observation that at 300 feet the lake would in no way imperil the occupants of the mound; at 291 feet the water would be within 50 yards (15 m.) of the settlement. Another 6-foot drop to 285 feet, would remove the lake margin some 300 yards (273 m.) from the site with an intervening zone of deep mud almost impossible to cross.

HOUSE REMAINS

Prior to excavation, the surface of the shell heap showed no pits or other indications of the former existence of definite habitations. In view of its elevation above the flat to the south as well as above the lake and its consequent general security from floods of any sort, it is only reasonable to believe that it was lived on throughout the period of its growth. Direct evidence of such occupancy was, indeed, found, in the form of post molds, fireplaces, and storage pits. Lodge sites and floors were never easy to find because of their similarity to overlying and underlying refuse layers, which also made difficult the task of distinguishing post molds satisfactorily. However, painstaking examination of large areas cleared horizontally resulted in delineation of slightly depressed areas of finely broken shell and sand containing ash-filled hearths and outlined by post molds. These are believed to represent habitation sites. Long thin horizontal lenses of sand, clean at the bottom and shading upward into darker organically discolored material at the top, were similarly identified. Whether through accident or by design, the house floors appeared to have been generally covered with thin layers of sandy earth. Location of the entrances is in most instances uncertain. Ethnographically, this locality was characterized by huts covered with tule and grass, and, as might be expected from such transient materials, nothing survived the ravages of time save occasional small masses of charred twigs, poles, and rushes.

Some evidence of wattle-and-daub construction was found in the form of lumps of burned clay impressed with twigs, tules, etc., strikingly reminiscent of earthlodge ruins in the Great Plains and Southeast. The structures revealed by our work would have been too light to support more than a very thin or partial covering of such material.

House 1, the first to be uncovered, was also most clearly defined. Most of the northwest quadrant was inadvertently destroyed before its nature was recognized (pl. 5, a). It lay near the southwest end of the midden, on the inland side, with its centrally located firepit about 3 feet from the north corner of square 99/41. The floor level was of clay covered by about a foot of loose shell mixed with soil. The firepit, 24 inches across, was shallow and ill-defined, but contained some ashes and bits of charcoal. The edge of the floor was marked by a circle of post molds, 19 in number. When dug out by hand, these averaged about 8 inches deep by 4–6 inches in diameter. All sloped inward at the top, indicating a conical or domed framework of poles converging at the top over the hearth. Four extra post holes occurred inside the circle, perhaps representing braces. The greatest diameter was 21 feet. There were no artifacts, nor was there any clue as to interior arrangement of furniture and household appurtenances. The direction in which the lodge opened is unknown.

Much time was given over to a search for additional house sites especially in the southerly third of the shell heap south of trench 1. For this the mound material was stripped off in layers 6–12 inches thick, the floor of the excavation being smoothed off at each successive level. The areas thus cleared included rows 91 to 102, sections 38 to 40, inclusive, and rows 91 to 97, sections 33 to 35, inclusive, a total of about 5,700 square feet. In depth these tests varied from 2 to 5 feet. They disclosed several groups of post molds outlining subcircular and irregularly oval areas each of which was designated a house site.

Numerous smaller groups were uncovered by the workmen but most or all of these are probably not to be regarded as habitation remains.

The areas cleared in a special search for house floors lay eastward from the highest point of the shell heap on the lakeward side of its longer axis. Nine so-called lodge sites were uncovered. The smallest of these, No. 10, was elliptic in form, and measured 9 by 15 feet. The others were more nearly circular, but in no case exceeded 16 or 17 feet in maximum diameter. They were outlined by post molds from 4–8 inches across and about the same in depth, somewhat unevenly spaced at 1- to 3-foot intervals. Floors in every instance were poorly marked and the doorways were generally doubtful. Fireplaces were indicated as ash-filled basins, either near the center or as often at one side near the ring of post molds. The latter placement seems a little curious if these were actually habitations, since the fire would have to be kept low or else closely watched to prevent its igniting the nearby wall. Moreover, as a source of warmth fires in such positions would be inefficient, since much of their heat would have been wasted on the unfeeling house walls. Since some of the rings of post molds overlap others, the structures which they represent must have been used at different times.

Just east of house 1 and apparently on a slightly lower horizon were four ash pits in a curving line enclosed by a roughly oval double series of post molds The double oval averaged about 22 by 25 feet across, with a 4-foot break at the south side. Wood ashes were scattered about the firepits and over the floor which was quite hard and discolored by charcoal and other rubbish. Considerable variation was noted in the size of the post molds. From the northernmost ash bed was taken a lump of asphaltum bearing the impression of small grass seeds, probably from some unidentified wild species used as food. It is not certain whether this was a dwelling used by several families or represented some specialized ceremonial or other structure.

In sections 38 and 39, rows 91 to 98, inclusive, were several charcoal beds whose meaning is conjectural. The largest measured about 18 by 7 feet but may have been much larger since it extended an unknown distance into the unexcavated part of the heap. It consisted of a mass of charred twigs, grass, and the like about 2 inches thick. Near its apparent center, and also extending into the undug mound, was an ash bed suggesting a hearth. There was no sign of post holes in or near the charred area. A few feet to the south was a similar but smaller mass, without an ash bed, but with the charcoal as much as 4 inches thick in places. A third charcoal area measuring 8 by 12 feet lay in square 96/39; it contained an ash bed. Scattered nearby were small pockets filled with fishbones and other refuse. There were no post holes or artifacts.

In square 91/39 was a shallow circular pit 6 feet across by 10 inches in greatest depth. At the center was a 12-inch firepit. Post molds, artifacts, and stones were not found in or around this basin but the fill was slightly discolored by ash and charcoal.

The significance of these charcoal areas is uncertain. That they represent the remains of regular habitations is unlikely because of the complete absence of post holes. At the same time the presence of ash beds in two of them would indicate considerable cooking or related activity on these particular spots. One interpretation suggested at time of their finding was that they mark the sites of temporary unwalled arbors consisting only of a brush roof suported by a few light poles. Such shelters were used by all the Yokuts in recent times and would have been much more comfortable during the hot summer months than the enclosed lodges. Whether burning down of such flimsy structures would result in a mass of rubbish as thick as some of those found is debatable. This suggestion, perhaps as good as any, is at best still a guess.

Although not wholly conclusive the archeological evidence suggests a house type unlike that reported in historic times for the lake Yokuts. According to Kroeber (1925, pp. 521–523), these were mainly of elongate gabled, wedge-shaped, or oblong form, in all cases with a ridge and vertical endwalls. Moreover, as is further stated in some of the historical accounts, they appear usually to have been communal affairs accommodating two or more families. The Yaudanchi, a hill tribe living east of Tulare Lake, built conical winter houses of tule, and similarly shaped structures are reported for several other groups residing farther north and off the valley floor. House 1 at Buena Vista Lake, site 1, was certainly of this general type, and inferentially the others were also despite the less definitive nature of the post molds and other remains.

FIREPLACES

These occurred in some numbers throughout the shell heap. They were of two kinds. Most abundant were shallow basins from 18 to 42 inches across and up to about 8 inches deep, filled with wood ashes and charcoal. One or more of these was found in each of the house sites, in addition to which a number were encountered in the general excavations. Exact locations for about 30 are on record, and these were all on the landward side of the mound. Sometimes they occurred in groups, at other times singly. All those noted were in the uncompacted shell-filled portion of the midden, in no case more than 6 feet below the surface.

Firepits of the second type usually contained much smaller quantities of ash and charcoal, their distinguishing feature being cracked and irregularly broken stones. These varied in number from a half dozen to several score. Broken and sometimes scorched animal bones and fragmentary artifacts were sometimes intermingled. Where they occurred in pits and basins these were seldom more than 18 inches across by about 6 or 8 inches deep (pl. 6, c). At other times the rocks formed small nests or piles on the contemporary surface (pl. 6, d). Hearths of this type showed an interesting distribution. Those certainly associated with the upper shell levels, 17 in number, all lay on the lake side, i. e., northeast of the long axis of the shell heap. Ten of these, moreover, were on one or another of the old lake terraces, off the mound proper, and in this area none of the stone-free hearths occurred. Several were directly against the wave-cut bluffs. The reason for this seemingly mutually exclusive occurrence of the two types is not clear. Possibly most of the cooking was carried out on the immediate lake shore, by stone-boiling or baking, while the other fires elsewhere on the site served primarily for heating or other non-culinary purposes.

CLAY-LINED BASINS

Immediately southeast of the center of square 92/33 was a shallow basin, 16 inches in diameter by 2 inches deep, lined with fine greenish clay 1 inch thick. This lining was very hard and could scarcely be penetrated with an ordinary plasterer's trowel, but showed no sign of having been baked or fired to this stage. In the basin was a quantity of soft greenish material superficially resembling the lining. This, however, was uncompacted and could be easily removed by light scraping with small hand tools. In plate 5, d, the soft fill appears white, while the clay lining is slightly darker. A somewhat smaller but otherwise very similar basin was found about 20 feet to the west near the east corner of square 91/35. This measured 15 inches across by 2½ inches deep with a hard 1-inch clay lining. It lay a few inches above the floor of house 8, with which it probably had no direct connection.

The purpose of these pits is not known, but they were certainly not hearths. No analysis was made of the contents of the larger, but the texture of the substance and its "feel" was about that of meal or coarsely ground flour. From this it was tentatively inferred that they might represent acorn leaching basins. However, as reported ethnographically, these appear to have been usually in sandy places where the water would readily percolate through the ground meal and so carry off the tannin. The clay lining the pits under discussion would seem to have been well nigh impervious to liquids, hence some other explanation is called for.

POCKET CACHES

In the extreme corner of square 91/38, 62 inches below the mound surface, a small carefully dug pit came to light (pl. 5, b). It was 14 inches in diameter by 15 inches deep, with the floor slightly depressed at the center. The sides and bottom were coated with a half-inch layer of greenish clay, visible in the illustration as a light-colored zone bordering the mouth of the pit. The opening had not been closed or covered in any way, and shell fragments, dirt, and ash from the overlying middens completely filled the cavity. There were no artifacts or other stored materials, but a similar pit 20 feet to the southwest yielded direct evidence of the use to which they were probably put. It lay near the east corner of square 90/40, and measured 8 inches in diameter by 19 inches. Besides ash, charcoal, and shell it contained also one large tapered pestle, fragments of two steatite bowls, and several stones. Some of the contents can be clearly seen in plate 5, *c*. Unlike the first this was unlined. Neither bore any marks of firing in the interior, and neither was in a lodge site. Presumably their sole purpose was the storage and concealment of small objects of daily use.

DOG "BURIALS"

Three more or less complete dog skeletons were found in the shell heap. One of the animals had apparently been placed in a shallow depression and purposefully covered over. It lay at 27 inches depth near the south corner of square 83/40 (cf. pl. 8, *b*). The other two were in square 87/29, at 36 inches, and in square 87/30 at 10 inches. There were no associated artifacts. They may or may not have represented burials of pets (cf. Heizer and Hewes, 1940).

BURIALS

Thirty-five burials and one dissociated human femur were uncovered during excavation of the shell heap. Twenty-four of these were infants and very young children whose age seems seldom to have exceeded 6 years. They were for the most part inconclusive as regards exact position, orientation, and other details. Six were classed as adults, five as subadults and older children. They were scattered at random in all parts of the diggings, and in depth they ran from 10 to 66 inches. With exception of burials 1 and 5 there were no signs of dug pits, the bodies evidently having been laid in shallow hollows and then heaped over with mound materials. Two burials came from each of the following squares: 82/37, 84/33, 91/36, 92/36.

Fifteen of the 35 offered fairly conclusive evidence as to position, these all being more or less tightly flexed (pl. 7). Not one could be classed as extended. Six lay on the back, three on the right side, five on the left side, and one appeared to be face down. Decay of the softer tissues and settling of the remains after burial may have altered somewhat the position of some of the skeletons since interment but the general practice governing placing of the corpse seems quite clear. As regards direction of the skull with reference to the trunk 20 burials were indeterminate. The orientation of the remaining

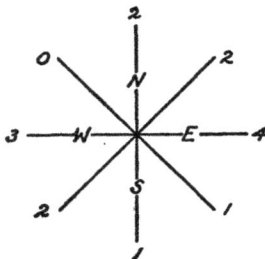

FIGURE 6.—Orientation of 15 burials at Buena Vista site 1.

15 is shown in the accompanying diagram (fig. 6) which indicates a possibly insignificant preference for a general northeasterly or south-westerly placement of the head.

Burial 1, an adult male, lay in a fairly well defined and apparently dug grave pit. Stones were found about No. 4, and there were also a few with No. 11. No. 5, skeleton of a child, lay partly in a subelliptical steatite bowl with a smaller hemispherical vessel of the same material near the knees (pl. 8, *a*). Beneath the larger vessel were traces of tule and asphaltum, possibly remains of a grave lining. The pit containing these remains was 27 inches in diameter, and its bottom lay 63 inches below the mound surface. There were two instances of multiple burial. Burials 25 and 26, an adult female and a child, respectively, were found at a depth of 36 inches in square 61/36, with the former partly overlying the latter (pl. 7, *b*). Nos. 29 and 30 were near the northerly end of the shell heap, 40 inches deep in square 42/37. Both were flexed and each lay on its left side; heads were at opposite ends of the grave so that the bodies faced each other. A few fragments of asphaltum were found in this grave.

Artifacts were generally absent. Aside from those incidentally noted above, there was a spear point under the left scapula of No. 3 (adult male ?); a shell bead with No. 15; traces of textile and two broken projectile points with No. 22; a projectile point with No. 25; traces of asphaltum on No. 27; a bone bead with No. 28.

In summary, the shell heap yielded surprisingly little information on burial practices, and it may be inferred that only a very small proportion of its inhabitants were buried therein. It is possible, of course, that cemeteries exist in the unexcavated portions, but our diggings sampled at least half—the more promising half, of the area. The evidence available indicates flexion of the corpse, little preference as to its orientation, general absence of dug graves, and rare association of mortuary furniture. The high proportion of infants and small children suggests that burial in the mound was largely limited to those who died young, most of the older children and adults being interred elsewhere and probably at a distance from the village. All of the burials at site 1, we may add, belonged to the occupation represented by the upper shell layers; none were of the individuals whose cultural remains were found sparingly in the gray hardpan.

OBJECTS OF MATERIAL CULTURE

California mounds and shell heaps, at least north of the Santa Barbara coast, have long been notorious for their low artifact yield per unit of earth turned. The sites on the southwest shore of Buena Vista Lake were no exception. In the present case, however, the large scale operations made possible through use of government relief labor netted a considerable number of specimens from a fairly representative proportion of each site investigated. There are in all about 5,000 entries in the field catalog. Many of these refer to single items; others may include strings of beads and similar groups of objects. Not all the material recovered and cataloged reached the National Museum, since some of the duplicate steatite sherds and other heavy articles were discarded to cut freight costs.

The several thousand artifacts retained from site 1, complete and otherwise, have been grouped first on the basis of material. They are further classified according to function; or, in the absence of evidence as to function, according to form and other superficial characters. The textual remarks are confined largely to brief definition and description of types; the number and occurrence by depth of each type of object or trait are indicated in table 8. Nearly all the types discussed herein are illustrated on one or another of the accompanying plates.

To integrate our findings with those of earlier investigators frequent reference has been made to the survey paper for the southern San Joaquin by Gifford and Schenck. The materials figured and described by them as coming from the Lake region were found in the Buena Vista Basin within 25 miles of our diggings. From time to time, similarities with the Santa Barbara coast and the San Joaquin-Sacramento Delta will be similarly noted.

WORK IN ASPHALTUM

This material, judging from its frequent occurrence and varied utilization, was well known to the occupants of site 1. Its source was, no doubt, the tar seeps or "breas" in the hills to the west and south of Buena Vista Lake. At present the nearest breas are in the vicinity of Maricopa and Hazelton, about 10 miles due south of site 1 and easily reached on foot by crossing Maricopa Flats. To the northwest near McKittrick, about the sources of Buena Vista Creek, were others. These would have involved a somewhat longer but otherwise not particularly arduous journey, which in any case need not have exceeded 20 miles.

Balls.—There are six of these more or less spherical objects, with the diameter in millimeters ranging as follows: 60, 57, 51, 38, 38, and 16. The second is slightly flattened on two sides. Best finished and smoothest of the lot is the smallest which has a fresh shiny look. All appear to consist of asphaltum mixed with some gravel, grass stems, and similar foreign substances. A small shell bead was found embedded in the surface of the 51-millimeter ball but this is probably accidental. None are perforated or ornamented (pl. 19, *a*, *c*, *f*).

The use to which these spheroids were put is uncertain. Harrington (1928, pp. 105–106, pl. 18) found numbers of apparently similar objects at the Burton Mound in Santa Barbara, and suggests that "they were apparently made and set aside so as to have always ready a supply of adhesive bitumen." If this be true we may also mention here the finding of other variously shaped but less carefully finished lumps of asphaltum at our site 1. They are generally roundish and somewhat flattened, and range in weight from less than an ounce to upward of 3 pounds. Pieces of broken shell, charcoal, and the like usually occur on the surface, and one lump has tule impressions on its side. All of these immediately suggested to us cakes and patties stored for future use, as Harrington also thought. A number of irregular fragments and shapeless masses may have resulted from breakage of such objects as the foregoing or are otherwise accidental.

Brush.—This interesting specimen (pl. 21, *a*) was uncovered on the final day of our work during filling of the excavations. It was made of a bundle of yucca (?) or other fibers held together by a coating of asphaltum over one end. The asphaltum which originally covered about 3½ inches (88 mm.) of its length still forms a smooth rounded butt. Total length is 5½ inches (140 mm.), and the maximum width at the brush end is about 2½ inches (63 mm.). The asphaltum is only a thin shell and seems not to have penetrated among the fibers. There is no ornamentation or inlay on the handle. The specimen, aside from its shorter length, is identical with several brushes recovered by the Wheeler Survey (1879, vol. 7, p. 249 and fig. 123) at Dos Pueblos and La Patera in Santa Barbara County and on Santa Cruz and San Clemente Islands.

Coated pebbles.—Three pebbles about the size of a small walnut are covered evenly with asphaltum. One is broken and shows the stone to be disintegrating as from repeated firing. It is presumed that such stones were heated and placed with asphaltum in a basket, being then "swirled round and round until every part of the interior was uniformly coated" (Rogers, 1929, p. 398), the stones serving to distribute the melted asphaltum properly. At two points in the mound, remains of coiled basketry so waterproofed came to light.

Inlays.—The use of asphaltum to accentuate decorative incisions in shell objects, reported from the Slough region north of the Buena Vista Basin (Gifford and Schenck, 1926, p. 53) was not noted at Buena Vista Hills. However, it was employed as a foundation for inlaying of shell and other materials. From square 67/34, at 30-inches depth, came a small hollow beehive-shaped object set with rodent teeth. This may have been molded around a grass core since the inside of the delicate asphaltum shell bears grasslike impressions. The teeth are closely set and run parallel to the hollow axis. About a third of the piece is missing and the upper (smaller) end is so broken that the manner in which it was originally finished off is uncertain.[12] The larger opening may once have been against a flat circular surface, though the evidence is inconclusive.

Other specimens of inlay in asphaltum from our diggings will be described in a future section.

Stopper.—This is a roughly circular piece measuring 3⅛ inches (80 mm.) across by 1⅛ inches (28 mm.) thick with one side flattened, the other convex. It is mixed with shell bits and gravel, particularly on its convex surface. The term "stopper" was given because the flat surface, 52 millimeters across, has a slightly raised border, suggesting use of the object for closing a small aperture. More plausible is the view that it represents merely a spheroidal mass of asphaltum which melted into a small depression and there solidified. The flattened shell-free face in this event would then have been the surface of the melted mass (pl. 19, *d*).

Miscellaneous.—In addition to the above, other important uses for asphaltum were as a cement in the mounting of chipped scrapers and cutting tools and for securing basket hoppers to the rims of stone mortars. No less than 60 instances of such uses were recorded; they will be discussed later. They add to the number of occurrences for

---

[12] This object recalls three excavated by the writer and G. R. Dunkel, in December 1932, at a small burial mound on the west side of Buena Vista slough, 12 miles due north of McKittrick and about 25 miles northwest of site 1. Now in the University of California Museum of Anthropology, they are described as follows in my unpublished notes:

"Each object consists of a thin casing or shell of asphaltum 1¼ inches (32 mm.) in height. This is funnel-shaped with a diameter at the smaller end of about 0.5 inch (13 mm.) and at the larger of 1¼ inches (32 mm.). A perforated subcircular piece of abalone shell is cemented to the larger end of the funnel. Immediately above the shell base is a row of rodent incisor teeth impressed into the asphaltum. Each of the (two) restored specimens is encircled by five such inlaid teeth. . . . The walls are seldom more than 2 millimeters thick. . . ."

See also Heye, 1921, pl. 122a.

the substance but do not materially increase the depth range. Most of the asphaltum was in the upper 4 feet, with a few occurrences to 6 feet.[12a] None occurred below the top of the gray hardpan.

WORK IN BONE AND HORN

Awls.—Most abundant of the artifacts of bone were awls. These have been classified for purposes of description according to the scheme used by Kidder at Pecos (1932, pp. 203–220). This divides them first into three groups on the basis of material, whether 1, mammal leg bone; 2, mammal rib; or 3, bird bone. Subtypes within the larger groupings are based on the treatment accorded the specimens in manufacture, as regards in particular the head or grasping end. Thus, we have:

1. Mammal leg bone:
    A. Head intact.
    B. Head unaltered except by original splitting.
    C. Head partly worked down.
    D. Head wholly worked down, or nearly so.
    E. Splinter awls, modified only by sharpening.
    F. Unclassifiable tips and fragments.
2. Mammal rib bone:
    A. Worked type (whole bone).
    B. Edge type.
    C. Splinter type.
3. Bird bone:
    A. Whole bone.
    B. Splinter.

Type 1. Of 63 awls from site 1, 59, or nearly 94 percent, were fashioned from the heavier leg bones of mammals. So far as the species can be identified, the awl-makers seem to have preferred those of the deer and, to a lesser extent, the ulnae of such carnivores as the dog and wolf. The latter required little modification, but the deer bones were in most cases split and then considerably worked down.

Subgroup A includes all specimens in which one articular end of the bone was left intact to form the head of the finished implement. Ten of these include 4 made from the cannon bone of the deer; in 3 the distal end was retained, in the fourth the proximal end. All are quite large, varying in length from 90 to 202 mm. Because of their sturdy nature they were doubtless intended for heavy work. All are highly polished from use (pl. 22, *a*, *c*, *e*). One specimen has shallow notches and a red stain on the inner concave surface. Five smaller specimens were made from the ulnae of some canid or similar sized animal (pl. 22, *f*), but only one shows evidence of much usage. This, the largest, is 113 mm. long, but was formerly a few millimeters

---

[12a] See footnote 29, p. 134.

longer; they range downward in length to about 85 mm. Also included in the subgroup is a well finished, highly polished awl fashioned from the os penis of the raccoon (pl. 22, *b*), 80 mm. long.

Subgroup B is not represented at site 1.

Subgroup C. In these the head of the original bone has been more or less ground down, but there still remains an appreciable swelling at the grasping end. Two specimens from site 1, though incomplete, are evidently from the proximal end of the deer cannon bone. Both are worn very smooth. Another is incomplete; it was also made from a split deer metapodial after which the joint end was smoothed down. It measures 180 mm. long (pl. 22, *i*). Five other smaller awls, 73 to 120 mm. long, all show much wear; three appear to be ulnae, the others are unidentified.

Subgroup D comprises 8 slender awls whose heads have been largely or wholly removed by grinding or by cutting off (pl. 22, *r–t*). One or two suggest ulnae, but because of the extensive modification, identification is uncertain. The complete specimens range in length from 69 to 158 mm.

Subgroup E is a miscellaneous assortment of 14 splinters and scraps modified only by sharpening of one end. Rare specimens have the shaft more or less smoothed and polished. The shape and size varies greatly, and they impress one as hastily improvised or makeshift productions (pl. 23, *b, c, f*). They are from 56 to 145 mm. long. The smallest has asphaltum stains on the head and over about half its length, and may have been set into a handle (pl. 22, *w*).

Subgroup F. Specimens here included differ from those immediately preceding in that they are evidently the broken remnants of formerly well finished artifacts. All show smoothed and polished surfaces throughout except where broken (pl. 23, *i–n*). Were they complete, they would doubtless be assignable to one or another of the well-marked subgroups already enumerated. The longest fragment measures 153 mm., the shortest 53 mm. Some are broad and heavy, others slender and evenly tapered. Because of their broken and indeterminate nature they are of relatively little significance in the determination of type distributions and in cross correlations between sites.

Type 2. There are but 2 specimens fashioned out of mammal rib, both falling under subgroup A. One is a long, slender, highly polished piece 201 mm. long, broken at the head (pl. 23, *p*). The other has been worked out of a heavier broader split rib, traces of whose inner cancellous tissue still show (pl. 23, *o*); the other surface is well polished over its entire length of 117 mm.

Type 3, characterized by use of bird bone, is also represented by 2 specimens. Both belong to subgroup A, i. e., are made from whole bones, pointed. One is a very slender bone (sp. unidentified) 219 mm. long, with one pointed end; the head is unmodified (pl. 23, *u*). The second example is from a larger bone; it now measures 111 mm. but the head is broken off and there is no way of determining its original length (pl. 23, *t*).

Bipointed objects.—Here is included a somewhat variable group of objects (pl. 24, *a*, *b*, *f*). Five range in length from 62 to 70 mm.; two with broken tips may have been slightly longer. In cross section they are slightly flattened. The maximum diameter, usually toward one end, is 7 or 8 mm. Three are well polished all over; the others are rougher but exhibit worn tips. The surface of one is generally striated and scratched except at the middle, where a thong or line may have been attached. Two others show similar evidence of unusual wear at the corresponding zone. This suggests their use as fish gorges. Somewhat similar objects from the San Joaquin-Sacramento Delta have been variously identified as parts of composite fishhooks, nose pins, hair pins, and needles (Schenck and Dawson, 1929, p. 350 and pl. 76, *n–w;* Lillard and Purves, 1936, pl. 10.)

There is one large double-pointed bone object which may have been a hair or nose ornament (pl. 24, *a*). This is 147 mm. long, thickest at the middle whence it tapers evenly and gradually toward either end. Faint striations from the grinding process are still visible despite the over-all polish of the surface (cf. Schenck and Dawson, op. cit., pl. 76, *x*).

Cut bone.—Twenty-four bone fragments, mostly the joint ends of leg and wing members, probably are rejectage from the manufacture of tubes, whistles, beads, and similar types. The cut ends are cleanly made in every case, but otherwise there was no effort at modification of the bone. From this it seems clear the craftsman was more concerned about the now missing portion than with the present end fragments. One sliver of mammal bone is somewhat rounded at the end, perhaps from use as a flaking tool. Two other scraps are cut and scored as though in the initial stages of production of some unidentifiable artifact. Excepting these last three, the pieces all look like bird bone, from which were made all the tubes and whistles presently to come under consideration. The vertical distribution of the cut ends is virtually identical with that of tubular artifacts.

Horn.—Objects of horn and antler were relatively scarce at site 1. Most abundant were the so-called flakers. Characteristically, these display a long slender body with oval, circular, or flattened cross section and rounded tapering ends (pl. 25, *f–h*). All show traces of the cancellous internal horn structure on one surface. The ends

WEDEL] ARCHEOLOGICAL INVESTIGATIONS IN CALIFORNIA **43**

are scratched and nicked, never polished or ground down. Both straight and curved specimens are present. Of four complete flakers the longest is 13.5 cm., the shortest 6.5 cm. The others are both 11 cm.; and to judge from their close similarity, the four additional fragments found are from implements of about this general size (Schenck and Dawson, 1929, pl. 81, *e*).

Three antler tips, otherwise unmodified, show evidence of some use in that the ends are worn away to an unnatural bevel. Two are badly nicked and scarred as though from action against sharp edges; they presumably were used for chipping flint. The third is very smooth, with a deeply worn notch or groove on one side. This suggests the action of a cord or some similar soft material rather than of stone. Just what function would produce such a feature is uncertain. A 7-mm. long tip of bison horn was at first thought to be a flaker since the tip shows a few scratches, but this is not certain.

The only other artifact of antler is the blade and part of the body of a wedge (pl. 25, *i*). This is 105 mm. long, with a well-smoothed bevelled working edge; its original length is unknown. It appears to be identical in type with those commonly found in the shell heaps of San Francisco Bay (Schenck, 1926, p. 229 and pl. 44, A–H).

Needles.—This term is applied with some doubt to 4 delicate objects made apparently from fish spines or very light bird bones. They are from 55 to 65 mm. long, hollow, and pointed at both ends. In size they only little exceed an ordinary toothpick. They were found together in a shell pocket at a depth of 12 inches. If intended as artifacts, they could have served only for very light use.

There were no true eyeletted needles.

Pins.—Uncertainty also accompanies this classification, though there is no doubt regarding the modification by man of the objects in question. Two are from the humeri of medium-sized birds; they are very delicate, and measure 101 and 135 mm. long (pl. 24, *l*). Another is shaped somewhat like the antler flakers previously described but is much lighter. Most of the others are merely well polished tips, not materially unlike some of the awl points except that they are somewhat more delicate. Three broken but well made objects with slender shafts and enlarged bulbous or spatulate ends could have been used as pins or fasteners.

Sweat scrapers.—Here are included tentatively 5 fragments of mammal ribs which are unusually well polished. They are incomplete and so not certainly identifiable but they suggest a definite type found more commonly at site 2 (pl. 25, *e*). It is possible the latter and the former as well were used to scrape the perspiring bodies of the natives after a session in the sweat-house.

Tubes.—Polished tubular objects of various sizes were found, though not in great profusion (pl. 26, *g–j*, *m–p*). All appear to be of bird bone, ranging from those of small forms up to the white pelican. The ends of the tubes are generally cleanly cut, save in a few instances where one extremity has been broken off. The largest is 97 mm. long by 14 mm. in diameter; another is 110 by 8 mm.; the rest range downward in size to grade into small beadlike forms not more than 8 by 4 mm. With three exceptions, they are undecorated, and the hollow interior shows no wear such as might be expected if they were meant to be strung as beads, the smaller specimens excepted. One tube, 77 by 10 mm., has been hacked at midway of its length but not cut through; it may have been intended as a whistle. Several other conform closely in size and proportions to some of the whistles from the site. Scoring or cuts, probably accidental, occur on two.

Three tubes bear simple incised decoration. Largest of these is 74 by 10 mm., tapering slightly toward the ends, each of which is encircled by a narrow groove. A second is 40 by 5 mm. Around each end are 2 grooves overlaid by a cross-hatched design of small diamonds about 1 mm. square. The decoration covers less than 4 mm. at either end (pl. 26, *k*). The third specimen is also encircled by a line at each end, with short parallel cuts running from the lip to this groove (pl. 26, *l*).

Whistles.—There are 15 complete, unfinished, and broken whistles, all exhibiting the same general characteristics. The largest of the series (pl. 26, *a*) is still intact and in fair working condition. It is 193 mm. long by about 9 mm. in diameter; both ends are squarely cut and smoothed off and one is closed with asphaltum. Forty-five mm. from the stoppered end is a 7 mm. aperture partially closed with a dab of asphaltum. By blowing into the open end one can produce a clear whistling sound. Three shorter specimens, respectively 62, 72, and 75 mm. long, lack only the asphaltum plugs to be similarly effective. Two smaller unfinished whistles each bear nicks marking out the position of the side vent, but the strip of bone between the two marks was never removed.

The eight fragments are from whistles broken at the vent. All have asphaltum stains or part of a smoothed hole or both at the fractured end, while the other is invariably carefully cut off. This definitely establishes their identity. They are quite uniform as regards diameter but the length can only be conjectured. Probably the shorter whole whistles described above are not far from the average size. The largest fragment is 11 mm. in diameter, and may represent an exceptionally large whistle.

No four-holed flutes, such as Kroeber reports for the historic Yokuts, were recovered.

Miscellaneous.—Aside from the foregoing more or less distinct types of bone objects there are several complete and fragmentary specimens which might be lumped under this heading. They include a small flat arrow-shaped object, with blunt edges but otherwise well made (pl. 24, *p*). It is 24 by 12 mm., with concave base; the point is thinned somewhat. There is no sign of hafting, and its use is wholly problematic. A perforated bird claw (pl. 24, *n*), unidentified as to species, is the only one of its kind recovered. There are two pieces of turtle shell each with a single neatly bored hole. The larger has been identified as from the carapace of the small land terrapin (*Clemmys marmorata*) (pl. 24, *o*). Possibly they are all that remains of larger articles of ceremonial paraphernalia.

WORK IN CLAY

Fired clay objects are of several kinds but from the standpoint of actual numbers they formed a relatively small fraction of the total artifact yield.

Beads.—Three fusiform objects in which the diameter exceeds the length are classed as beads (pl. 20, *g*, *i*). All are centrally pierced, the hole apparently having been left by a small stick or stout grass stem about which the objects were molded. The largest is 37 mm. across by 22 mm. thick; the smallest measures 20 by 15 mm. They are carelessly modelled and irregular, and decoration is lacking.

Decorated pellets.—Only two pieces show evidence of an attempt at decoration. One is a modelled fragment 32 mm. long by 20 mm. wide, with a deep narrow encircling groove around its middle. One half of its flattened upper surface is divided by a horizontal and two vertical incisions into 6 unequal areas, each wholly or partly filled with minute punctures produced by a grass stem or similar small point (pl. 20, *h*). As illustrated the lower end seems to be broken. Another small scrap less than an inch across bears 21 similar but larger and deeper pits arranged in four incomplete rows.

Fillets.—This term has been used to designate 5 small cylindrical pieces under 15 mm. in diameter and less than 55 mm. long. Most of them appear to have been pinched off at one or both ends. The smallest, less than 8 mm. thick, is hollow as though shaped around a twig or grass stem; possibly it is a crude bead. Any or all of these could have been produced by children at play in the mud.

Molded circular objects.—Here are included 11 complete and fragmentary specimens closely akin to the so-called baked-clay "balls" commonly found in the Sacramento Delta. (Schenck and Dawson, 1929, pp. 360–364; Lillard and Purves, 1936, p. 17; Heizer, 1937.) Only 2 are actually spheroidal. The characteristic form is a short cylinder with flattened or concave ends (pl. 19, *i*, *j*). They were molded out of rather coarse clay mixed with gravel and occasional bits of tule. The interior of the fragments is sometimes fissured and porous. In color they range from buff to dark gray. All bear the impression of tule wrappings passed around and around the green clay, crossing each other over the two ends. Most of the specimens also show the imprint of a single element running around their circumference. Sometimes this was applied before the end-wise wrappings; as often, after most of the latter were in place, so that the two sets of elements interrupted each other. The depressed ends are evidently the result of pressure applied where the crisscross tule wrappings were thickest. None of the objects is truly spool-shaped as the single element encircling the middle produced at most a nearly imperceptible constriction.

The wrapping appears to have been done with some care, but just why is not clear. Heizer (1937, p. 41) has suggested its possible objective as the retarding of the rate of evaporation which otherwise might have proceeded so rapidly as to crack the unfired clay. Whether this is based on actual experiment or not I am unable to say, but a priori the suggestion seems as good as any yet advanced.

These tule-wrapped objects vary considerably in size, diameter always exceeding thickness. The largest, weighing 38 ounces, is 4¾ inches (120 mm.) by 2½ inches (64 mm.), with end cavities ½ and ¾ inches (13 and 19 mm.) deep. At the opposite extreme is a spherical pellet ⅞ inch (22 mm.) in diameter. The remaining specimens are mostly from 2 to 3 inches (50 to 75 mm.) across by about 1½ inches (37 mm.) thick, and weigh but a few ounces.

Related but less elaborate forms are also present, some consisting of fragments only. One type comprises 3 circular flattened objects lacking any impressions or ornamentation. The largest and best made (pl. 19, *g*) is 2⅛ inches (54 mm.) across by 1 inch (25 mm.) thick, the smallest 1¼ by ½ inch (32 by 13 mm.). Two other fragments are from specimens apparently similar in shape and diameter to the larger of the above but somewhat thicker. A different type is indicated by five broken pieces from larger undecorated spheroidal or ovate objects, whose exact conformations and dimensions can not be ascertained. Still another scrap bears a few faint impressions of twisted cordage.

All of the above artifacts show strong resemblances to the baked clay "dough-haddies" of Sacramento, San Joaquin, and immediately adjoining counties several hundred miles north of Buena Vista Lake, where, however, they are both more abundant and more varied in form and finish. That the Buena Vista specimens were locally made there is no reason to doubt, but their similarity to certain tule-wrapped often tamalelike forms farther down river must imply a direct connection. If so, the borrowers were in all probability the Buena Vistans whose accomplishments in the plastic arts generally seem to have been, if anything, even more perfunctory than those of the Delta dwellers.

As to the function of the objects there is no satisfactory evidence. Farther north, in the stoneless alluvial Sacramento Delta, the analogous forms are said to occur commonly in ash beds or hearths and it has been suggested that some may have been substituted for stones in cooking or roasting (Kroeber, 1909, p. 17; Heizer, 1937). No similar association was noted at Buena Vista, nor is it likely that objects intended for such use would have been so carefully prepared as were those with tule impressions. Equally dubious is their identification as sinkers, weights, or sling stones. Ethnography apparently offers no clues and the writer has no suggestions of his own that would seem to carry conviction.

Molded cylindrical objects.—These differ from the preceding in that the length consistently exceeds the diameter. Their use, which is unknown, may have varied as much as does their probable shape and size. With one exception, the present series includes only fragments broken from longer specimens. The exception (pl. 20, *e*) is of gray clay containing particles of sand. It is 2⅝ inches (67 mm.) long with a maximum width of ¾ inch (19 mm.); the cross section is slightly flattened. One end is tapered and rounded off; the other has been squeezed out to a blunt flat edge. The fragments range from one 37 mm. long by 23 mm. in diameter down to one 17 by 11 mm. The largest piece is also pinched off to a sort of wedgelike tail. Included in the group is a large fragment nearly 50 mm. thick by 90 mm. long bearing traces of a coat of red paint on its sides and at one roughly finished end. Possibly this should properly be included in the preceding series.

Potsherds.—Eight pieces of pottery of probable local manufacture came to light at site 1 (pl. 20, *a–d*). They are crude and of uneven thickness with cracks and cavities of varying size and depth. Color ranges from light buff to dark gray, differing considerably in the same sherd; paste is coarse and uneven, with gravel and rarely shell added as tempering; surfaces are rough and undecorated. Thickness is from 5 to 15 mm. Vessel forms can not be inferred due to the small size of the sherds. So far as finish and general ineptness of workmanship are concerned all of the fragments could have come from such creations as Gayton (1929) and Kroeber (1925, pl. 51) report for the Yokuts and western Mono, where medium-sized thick-walled pots and bowls seem to have been characteristic. One sherd has a ground-down edge, seemingly from efforts to give it a circular shape. Another vaguely suggests the bowl of a tubular pipe.

So far as the present evidence goes no great antiquity need be postulated for the potter's art here. The sherds and all but one of the other intentionally shaped clay objects were found in the upper 3 to 4 feet of the shell heap, and on the youngest (inland) side of the mound. As will be shown elsewhere, the age, though uncertain, may fall as late as the eighteenth century.

Miscellaneous pieces.—Far outnumbering the artifacts thus far described are sundry odds and ends of fired clay which are mostly too fragmentary to merit more than passing mention. Many are concave on one side as though pressed over a round stick or large reed, but there is nothing to indicate that these were anything other than accidental. Others may have resulted from the disintegration of "dough-haddies," but cannot be positively so identified. Impressions of tules, withes, twigs, and grass in some cases possibly indicate daub from house coverings, but none of these were found in association with identified post-mold configurations. If any of these pieces were artifacts, their original character is today utterly impossible of determination. Because of their highly doubtful nature they have not been included in the summary table, but it may be noted that all such traces were found above the gray hardpan.

ARTICLES OF EUROPEAN MAKE

In view of the tentative identification by various workers of site 1 as the Tulamniu of the nineteenth century Yokuts, it was expected that contact materials would be rather plentiful, at any rate in the upper portions of the shell heap. Such was not the case. A few glass beads were found on the surface, it is true, as others have been from time to time in years past. But with all our excavating in what was very probably the most recent part of the shell heap, only 4 specimens in any way suggestive of contact with white men came to light. These included a small bit of rusted iron, possibly a (modern ?) key fragment, from square 87/35, between 2 and 3 feet deep; a facetted red clear glass bead 5 mm. in diameter from the 1- to 2-foot level in square 83/38; and two larger spheric opaque beads from a depth of 18 inches in square 96/34. Of the latter, the smaller is of paste, with a diameter of 10 mm.; the other, 15 by 12 mm., is glassy with a narrow inconspicuous raised band about its middle.

All of these specimens were submitted to Arthur Woodward of the Los Angeles Museum, who reported as follows:

. . . The large glassy white bead 1–2009 does not seem to correspond in age with the duller white bead on the same thread. Apparently at one time the larger bead was covered with a silvery metallic lustre which had since worn away. Beads of this type appeared during the middle 19th century. The duller white paste bead seems to be either early in the 19th century, say around 1810–1820, or possibly in the late 18th century. The small red faceted bead 1–2458 belongs in the 1850–1860 category. . . . [Letter of February 15, 1939.]

In evaluating this particular evidence it must be borne in mind that much of the mound surface had been dug over by pothunters and collectors in previous years. Only the larger and more obvious of these old diggings are indicated on the map of site 1 (fig. 3). Smaller disturbances frequently were not visible until partially exposed in our trenches. Most of these diggings were not over 2 or 3 feet deep, about the depth to which our contact materials were found. Contact sites are said to exist at the base of the Elk Hills and elsewhere about the lake. The beads in question could have been excavated at some other location and carelessly dropped where we subsequently recovered them. There is nothing in our field records to indicate that they were or were not in areas of former disturbance. The nineteenth century dates in particular seem too recent since by that time the volume of trade between Indians and whites should have been great enough to leave far more quantitative evidence than we found. This would apply especially in the case of villages of several hundred individuals, such as Zalvidea reported for the Yokuts in 1806. In my opinion, the glass beads and iron found at site 1 may be intrusions within comparatively recent years, and do not necessarily establish a date for aboriginal habitation of the levels in which they were found.

PIGMENTS

Paint materials at site 1 included a number of lumps of red and yellow ochre. In several instances these were soft and friable, and seemed to have been mixed with clay. It is quite possible that these represent remains of prepared cakes of paint materials. Similar molded specimens from Santa Barbara are in the Wheeler and other collections in the National Museum.

There is one piece of white chalky substance that may have been used as a source of white paint.

WORK IN SHELL

At site 1 shell was utilized exclusively for manufacture of beads and other small ornaments, never apparently for strictly utilitarian objects. So far as they are identifiable, the species are all marine, occurring along the California coast west of the San Joaquin, whence they were brought inland by trade.

Species actually used in the manufacture of artifacts include the following,[18] listed in order of their frequency:

Olivella biplicata Sby.
Marine clamshell (sp. ?).
Haliotis cracherodii.
Haliotis rufescens.
Diadora aspera.

Shells and shell fragments of the following have also been identified but are not represented in the artifact series:

Cardium quadragenarium Con.
Spondylus princeps Sby.
Trivia sp.
Erata vitellina Hinds
Cerithidea sacrata Gld. (brackish water).

Clamshell.—Beads and ornaments were generally made from the heavy shell of an unidentified marine clam. Specific identification of our materials has not been practicable but it is possible they are of the species *Tivela crassatelloides*, which Gifford and Schenck (1926, p. 58) report as represented in the shell objects studied by them from the upper San Joaquin. The species is stated to be found in the vicinity of Pismo Beach and the Santa Barbara Channel, neither more than 100 miles from Buena Vista Lake via one or another of the natural routes described elsewhere.

Clamshell beads at site 1 are nearly all thick disks, 4 to 15 mm. in diameter and up to 6 or 8 mm. thick (pl. 27, *m–q*). Diameter is usually about three times the thickness, but variants include specimens in which thickness exceeds diameter so as to give a tubular form. Tubes are extremely rare at this site, however. Except in a few of the very thinnest, the drilling is biconical. All are flat with square-dressed edges; there are no globular, oval, or other forms, nor are there any blanks or unfinished specimens. A few are almost chalky in texture but most are firm and a few have an ivorylike appearance.

Decorated disk beads, frequently found by collectors in the Lake and Slough regions, are represented by a single example. This is 12 mm. across by 3 mm. thick. The squared edge bears three groups of closely set vertical scorings (pl. 27, *n*). It was found within a foot of the surface.

A short tubular or barrel-shaped bead, 8 mm. long by 7 mm. in diameter, is more elaborately ornamented. Two areas of vertical and horizontal crisscross lines alternate with two hourglass figures filled in with lines parallel to the ends of the bead (pl. 27, *k*).

There is one fragment from a large clamshell disk originally about 45 mm. in diameter. Owing to scaling and the irregularities of the shell used, thickness varies but probably never exceeded 5 mm. There

---

[18] Identifications by Dr. H. A. Rehder, Division of Mollusks, U. S. National Museum.

is a 4 mm. perforation at the center.   It is well smoothed but entirely undecorated (cf. Gifford and Schenck, 1926, p. 62).

Haliotis shell.—Beads believed to have been made from abalone shell include numerous small disks 5–11 mm. across by 2–5 mm. thick, thus averaging somewhat smaller than those of clamshell (pl. 27, *i*).   All are characterized by a pinkish color, besides which the flat surfaces occasionally show a faint iridescence.   One surface is generally rough, and on the whole the beads are not as well finished as those of clamshell. Some are nearly or quite flat, others concave.   All are biconically drilled through the center.   They are probably identical in type with those described by Gifford and Schenck (1926, p. 60) as having been made of the "salmon-pink epidermis of the *Haliotis californiensis.*"

So far as can be determined, most or all of the pendants found at site 1 were made of abalone shell.   Though not numerous, these are quite varied in form and other details, and resist easy segregation into distinct categories.   Four thin flat rings, under 15 mm. in diameter, have been termed spangle disks, on the supposition that they were sewn or otherwise affixed to garments, baskets, or other articles for purely ornamental purposes.   One at least was inlaid in asphaltum, but to what this in turn was attached is not clear; others may have been similarly used.   All are thin and tend to scale into thin flakes which may be handled only with extreme difficulty.   There are a few larger, heavier, but otherwise very similar, flattened rings up to about 25 mm. across, with a central hole whose diameter is roughly a third the total of the piece.   A half dozen fragments of variable length in all likelihood are from long curving pointed pendants cut from the lip of the abalone (pl. 28, *a*).   These seem to have been identical with several hundred specimens now in the national collections from the Santa Barbara coast and island region.   They have been identified as *Haliotis cracherodii.*   Two other scraps with rounded edges and broken perforations are probably from a large circular or oval disk.

The remaining ornaments of *Haliotis* are small, and their varied nature may be inferred from plate 27, *r–u, x, y*.   In outline they run from circular through oval and oblong to rectangular and square.   All are under 26 mm. in greatest dimension, and not over 2 mm. thick. Two circular pieces each have a large central perforation and one or two smaller holes near the edge (pl. 27, *r, s*).   Two elliptical pendants are pierced at either end (pl. 27, *t*), a third at one end only.   A half dozen small rectangular and oblong specimens also have holes at each end.   A single broken piece, pierced at one end, has milled edges on one face (pl. 27, *y*).   Another squarish object has a central and two corner perforations (pl. 28, *c*), while several other oblongs bear two or more holes near one or more margins (pl. 28, *d*).   The specimens have been arbitrarily and not altogether satisfactorily classified in the summary table where the vertical distribution and total numbers are given.

Keyhole limpet.—Only two artifacts of limpet shell came to light at site 1. They are small ovals made by grinding down the shells until only a narrow ring remained. They measure 21 and 23 mm. in maximum length, with the shell less than 4 mm. wide. In form they somewhat suggest the inlay pieces described and figured by Heye (1921, pl. 121). There is also one small limpet shell with enlarged aperture but this may not have been a completed artifact.

Olivella.—Despite considerable variation in their size the *Olivella* beads have all been identified as a single species (*Olivella biplicata*). The shells were manufactured into beads by any of three procedures. Simplest to produce but least numerous were those in which the spire was ground off to permit passage of a cord through the whole otherwise unmodified shell. These have been listed and are hereafter described merely as spire-lopped beads. The few specimens found differ considerably in size (pl. 27, *g*, *h*).

More common were half-shell, or split, beads consisting of about half the original shell with a slight liplike inward projection near one end (cf. pl. 27, *e*). These are mainly in the neighborhood of 20 mm. long, with a medium to relatively large (2–5 mm.) hole crudely cut or punched through the center. Included in the series are specimens lacking the lip but otherwise of the same general appearance. These are usually the crudest and most irregular of the *Olivella* beads. Presumably for this reason Gifford and Schenck (1926, p. 59) suggest that "it is possible that the *Olivella biplicata* half-shell beads are not a finished product, but represent a stage in the manufacture of the disc beads. . . ." This view is doubtful insofar as the present examples are concerned because the punched holes are almost invariably two to five times the diameter of those drilled in the disks. Dressed down, they would have been even more unlike the latter product. Moreover, occasional half shells do have well-finished edges and are evidently completed beads. Two bear incised lines, either single or paired, which intersect at the perforation (pl. 27, *f*).

Greatly outnumbering the above types are well-made, concave, rarely flat, disks about 1 mm. or a trifle more in thickness, with an average diameter of 8–11 mm. and an extreme range of 4–13 mm. The hole for suspension rarely exceeds 2 mm. Edges are usually well finished, seldom or never lipped (pl. 27, *d*). None are decorated in any way. Besides occurring in considerable numbers throughout the middens, *Olivella* disks were far and away the most frequent articles accompanying the dead. For this they seem to have been strung and worn as necklaces. Another use, to which smaller disks especially were sometimes put, is for inlay work with asphaltum base. One specimen has two disks and traces of abalone shell on a lump of asphaltum, the reverse side of which is concave as though the entire mass once covered the end of a round square-cut stick or bone object.

WORK IN STEATITE

Artifacts and variously worked fragments of steatite were exceedingly common, occurring in every portion of the shell heap above the hardpan. The summary table shows the distribution by depth of the specimens on which the present discussion is based. Actually, a large number of additional vessel sherds and other heavy pieces were discarded after brief examination in the field due to the impracticability and expense of transporting such materials across the continent. Smaller artifacts were generally retained. The discarded potsherds far exceeded in number those which were kept and were probably about as numerous as the total of steatite specimens entered in the field catalog.

Two kinds of steatite are represented. Thick potsherds and the larger heavier specimens generally were carved from a coarsely crystalline stone usually greenish in color. We were informed that this variety was obtainable in Santiago Canyon near Mount Pinos in the San Emigdio Range about 25 miles south of Buena Vista Lake. Efforts to locate the reported quarries and to secure unworked samples of stone for comparison were fruitless. Smaller objects, including thin-walled vessels and objects cut from their sherds, were of a finer-grained compact material of grayer tone. This is said to resemble the stone still quarried commercially as talc near Lindsay, in Tulare County, about 100 miles north of Buena Vista Lake. Sources nearer at hand, if such were available to the aborigines, are apparently not known today. It may be significant that in all the hundreds of steatite specimens uncovered there was not a single blank or unworked piece. Except where the outline and original conformations had been too much altered by reworking into small objects, all seem to have been fashioned from pieces of broken vessels. This might imply that only finished or nearly finished vessels were brought to the village site, the rougher preliminary work all being done at the quarry.

Also included in this section are small beads and ornaments made of serpentine, a near relative of steatite. These specimens are generally highly polished and black in color. Provenience of the serpentine is unknown, but it may have been procurable in some of the mountain ranges bordering the Buena Vista Basin or in the Santa Barbara region.

Arrow straighteners.—Two broken shaft straighteners, apparently of southern California type, were found (pl. 43, b). One was broadly elliptic in outline and also in cross section. The upper slightly convex surface is crossed transversely by a highly polished groove 13 mm. wide by 6 mm. deep. It is of fine steatite. The second specimen is of much coarser stone, broken at both ends so that the original dimensions of its narrowly elliptic form are largely conjectural. The bottom is flat, and the convex upper surface is crossed by a single deeply worn transverse groove. Neither has any other marks, decorative or otherwise.

According to Kroeber (1925, p. 530), "this implement is undoubtedly associated with the employment of cane for arrows; the Yokuts are known to have used this plant, though not exclusively. The joints were warmed in the groove and bent by hand or on the [lengthwise] ridge after the stone had been heated; the groove was also used for smoothing. . . ."

Another type was apparently an improvisation. It is represented by several sherds, otherwise unaltered, bearing worn grooves transversely across the convex outer surface at what would have been a right angle to the rim. They vary considerably in size, shape, and thickness. The largest is 96 by 70 mm., the smallest 65 by 40 mm. Five out of ten such smoothers are certainly rims, and all have one, rarely two, grooves (pl. 33, *v*). Two are perforated near the edge, one twice, but these holes probably had nothing whatever to do with use of the specimens as shaft smoothers. Both coarse and fine steatite were utilized.

Bars.—This designation covers a rather poorly assorted lot of elongate specimens of problematical and perhaps varied use. One finished piece, circular in cross section, measures 69 by 12 mm. The ends are cut off squarely and the entire piece is well smoothed down (pl. 33, *r*). One, or possibly two, broken fragments of comparable size and shape occur. Otherwise, the group includes variously cut, occasionally bored or scored bits whose ultimate form can only be guessed at. Mostly they are smaller than the whole specimen described above.

Two pieces in shape vaguely suggest old fashioned clothes pins. One end is knobbed, i. e., bears an encircling groove as though for suspension. The complete one is pointed at the other end, and has a groove along one curving edge (pl. 33, *p*). It is 67 mm. long. The other is fragmentary but appears to have been of about the same size and shape.

There are three short wedge-shaped pieces with more or less expanded heads and flat points. One is 20, the others 33 mm. long.

Beads.—Steatite, or serpentine, beads were relatively scarce, less than two dozen being recovered during the general digging at site 1. All are black in color and very highly polished.

Seven beads are tubular in form (pl. 31, *a–g*). The smallest is 12 mm. long by 5 mm. in diameter; the largest is 16 by 11 mm.

The larger specimens tend to be somewhat barrel-shaped, i. e., taper slightly to either end, whereas the smaller ones are straight tubes. None bears any decoration. The holes for stringing appear to have been bored from both ends with a slender tapered drill, presumably of flint, and are remarkably uniform throughout.

There are 11 disk-shaped beads, ranging from a tiny one 3 mm. across up to one 13 mm. in diameter by 8 mm. thick. The larger specimens, of which there are five, have rounded or bulging sides, and tend to be of uneven thickness (pl. 31, *k*). The smaller ones are flat and straight-sided. All are biconically drilled.

One large, thick, ringlike object is evidently unfinished (pl. 31, *l*). It measures 19 mm. across by 14 mm. thick with a large biconical perforation. The outside is irregular and covered with scratches. It is well polished, however, and despite the shoddy craftsmanship may have served as a bead.

Biperforate objects.—These have in common a more or less rectangular, quadrilateral, or otherwise elongate form with a drilled hole near each end. The holes are either on the long axis or else are set near one of the longer sides. Generally, the objects are quite well shaped with definitely cut edges (pl. 33, *a–c*). Only one is decorated; it has 15 notches on one edge. Bowl rims were occasionally so treated and, since this particular piece appears to have been a rimsherd, the notches may have been retained from the earlier object.

The largest complete specimen is 79 by 48 mm., but two broken and unfinished ones were probably from larger pieces. The smallest is 43 by 24 mm., with one scrap possibly from a still smaller example.

Groove-edged objects.—Occurring commonly at site 1 were variously shaped steatite articles with more or less well-finished edges into which grooves have been cut. Some look like little more than slightly altered sherds, while at the other end of the gamut are carefully made labrets. The grooved edge sometimes encircles the piece completely; in others it includes only a short section of the periphery. The groove itself varies from a heavy incised line to a broad deep V-shaped trough. There is nothing to indicate their use, although Gifford and Schenck (1926, p. 70) suggest several possibilities: for creasing tule sewing elements, as guides for string or thread, and as a substitute for beeswax in the finishing of twine and cords. Latta (unpublished notes) states that Yokuts women lashed such pieces to the baby cradles and from them secured a talcum powder as needed by grinding material off the flat sides. Few or none of the objects here considered show traces of such grinding. Some were pretty certainly used as labrets. Doubtless their uses, like their shape and size, were varied.

Four general types of groove-edged objects may be recognized in our series, though the line separating the several types is sometimes arbitrarily drawn. Plates 31 and 32 will convey a clearer notion of the range and variety which exists than can any number of words.

Type 1 includes oval, subcircular, or otherwise elongate objects completely encircled, or nearly so, by a smooth edge groove (pl. 32, a–h). In shape some vaguely suggest the baking plates or comals of the Santa Barbara region but they are generally smaller. Two or three each have a perforation near the smaller end but these cannot be conclusively linked with their present form and most recent utilization; they may have been in the sherds from which the objects were fashioned. About half the objects seem to have been made with some care; the rest are either fragmentary or else very clumsily worked. Some of the smaller specimens are suggestive of unfinished labrets or grooved plugs. In size they run from 167 by 110 mm. down to 23 by 9 mm.; in thickness from 12 to 25 mm. Except for the smallest pieces, nearly all show the concave-convex profile of the vessel sherd from which they were originally manufactured.

Type 2 differs from the preceding in the flangelike appearance of the edges when viewed in profile (pl. 32, i–n). This is owing to the smaller size of one surface (usually the convex), which in some specimens has been reduced to little more than a ridge or crest. The specimens are usually thinner and a great deal more variable than those of type 1. The largest is 106 by 65 mm. with a hole at the small end and a worn notch (for tule creasing?) at the other. Some of the larger examples differ but little from type 1, while the smaller ones grade into the next group.

Type 3 includes three smoothed disks from 21 to 40 mm. across, 7 to 15 mm. thick, with deep rounded grooves (pl. 31, m, n, q). Two others, more carefully made, are reminiscent of type 2, i. e., are spool-shaped with one large and one small surface. The best is 41 mm. across the larger face, 22 mm. across the smaller, and has a 17 mm. neck connecting the two (pl. 31, r). The other is 39 mm. in maximum and 31 mm. in minimum diameter, with a slightly constricted neck (pl. 31, p). These two are respectively 19 and 16 mm. thick, and were probably intended as labrets.

A sixth somewhat pyramidal object is placed in this group (pl. 31, o) but cannot be certainly identified as a labret.

Type 4. To this group have been relegated the miscellaneous groove-edged pieces either too fragmentary or too little worked to be ascribed to one of the other groups. They are irregular scraps and misshapen pieces with one or two edges slightly grooved. They may represent broken artifacts, unfinished specimens, or merely the results of purposeless cutting.

Plugs.—Five thick circular objects vary in thickness from 8–23 mm., in diameter from 16–41 mm. (pl. 33, d–h). Three are 31 mm. across. One is slightly concave on the under side. Two have small pockmarks in the center of one face. They have been shaped and finished with some care, but there is no ornamentation or anything to suggest their manner of use. A deep narrow groove encircles the smallest. Possibly they should be classed as lip or ear plugs.

· Under this designation are included two hemispherical forms each 39 mm. across, one 20, the other 26 mm. thick. Each has one flat surface. The periphery of the smaller is irregularly marked by 55 tiny nicks (pl. 33, *d*) and its surface is bumpy and uneven though superficially somewhat smoothed from use. The larger is not so well finished and bears no marks of any sort.

Reellike objects.—These curious objects are very nearly as numerous in our series as are those with grooved edges, and, barring vessel sherds, constitute otherwise the most abundant artifact type of steatite at site 1. Characteristically, they are flat and usually elongate with a deep groove or notch at each end, which gives the general shape of the capital letter H (pl. 34). Actually, there is considerable variation. The notches may be deep or shallow. In some, one upright of the H has been nearly or quite worn away so that little except a knob remains on the cross bar. Comparatively few show any marked degree of finish or of care in shaping and workmanship, and the majority are rather rough and carelessly made. The largest is 123 by 60 mm., irregularly elliptical in outline with a rounded notch at either end. At the other extreme is one 25 by 20 mm. The average size is indicated by the examples illustrated. Length generally exceeds width, but there are a number of exceptions. In thickness they run from 6 to 20 mm., but few are over 10 or 12 mm.

A satisfactory explanation for the use of these distinctive and abundant objects is wanting. The bottom of the groove as a rule shows the most wear, as though a thong or cord or some similar soft material had been repeatedly drawn through it. From this circumstance they were termed "tule creasers" by members of the field party. According to Latta's unpublished notes, they were fastened to cradles like the groove-edged pieces, and scraped with sharp stones to provide talcum powder. Since this observation is said to come from surviving Yokuts it can not be lightly dismissed. In this case, however, it seems improbable that the residual pieces would exhibit such a consistent uniformity of shape, or that the notches would have a worn rather than cut appearance. Perhaps Latta's informant was rationalizing. Otherwise, ethnography has as yet offered no convincing explanation.

Tube fragment.—The only specimen from site 1 which could possibly be construed as evidence of the tubular pipe is an inconclusive piece 79 mm. long with both ends rounded off (pl 33, *s*). One end seems to have been slightly bulbous and was conically bored. It is possible that there has been some whittling subsequent to breakage; if not, the inside was most clumsily and unevenly bored out. The walls are of very unequal thickness, one broken edge being as much as 6 mm., another less than 2 mm. The maximum diameter of the tube prior to breaking is conjectural but probably did not much exceed 25 mm. There is no tobacco "cake" or other indication of use for smoking.

Kroeber states that the historic Yokuts of the area ate rather than smoked tobacco; further, that such pipes as occur were small in size and made of wood or cane (Kroeber, 1925, p. 538). Probably for this reason our evidence was so overwhelmingly negative.

V-shaped objects.—There are two of these (pl. 33, *i, j*). The larger has a perforation near the point of the V. In both, bottom of the notch is much worn, after the fashion of the grooves in the reels above described. They are smoothed as though from much handling. They may have been used as ornaments or, with equal plausibility, for the same unknown purpose that was served by the reellike objects.

Vessels and sherds.—Broken vessel fragments were by all odds the most abundant objects of steatite. Those retained, although too small to permit accurate reconstruction of the original vessel shapes, seem all to be from open round to subrectangular bowls and platters of varying size and depth. One or two fragments suggest small handled vessels, possibly ladles. There is no evidence of large globular small-mouthed ollas such as occur commonly in the coastal Chumash area. The larger vessels at Buena Vista Lake were made of coarse-grained Santiago Canyon (?) stone, the smaller ones of finer-textured material. Most of the sherds are faily well smoothed on the exterior as well as interior surfaces, though the former is in some cases rougher and of poorer finish. Vessel lips are usually bevelled or tapered to a rounded edge thinner than the wall below. Square or flat lips sometimes occur in the thinner vessels and more rarely in the heavy ones.

An analysis of 81 rimsherds from site 1 indicates that nearly half (47 percent) are 16 mm. thick or over, while 38 percent are 10 mm. or less. The majority of these, and particularly the thinner ones, are seen to be drilled, the holes occurring typically at more or less regular intervals just below the rim. In the specimens available, these are spaced from 20–25 mm. apart, and suggest that the vessel from which they were broken was completely encircled by holes. In a few instances, perforations occur further down the vessel beside a break. These undoubtedly indicate primitive attempts at mending fractured vessels by lashing the fragments together. Only four sherds are decorated, if we may so term the notches cut at intervals across the lip.

In addition to the many sherds, site 1 yielded two nearly intact and three broken but restorable vessels. Two came from burial 5 (pl. 8, *a*), that of a young child, on the lake side of the shell heap in square 70/32. The larger is a shallow irregularly shaped bowl or platter, curving evenly from rim to rim in cross section (pl. 35, *a*). Maximum diameter is 382 mm.; minimum diameter is uncertain because part of the rim is broken out but seems to have been about 300 mm. or slightly over. The depth is 89 mm. Thickness varies from a maximum of about 18 mm. at the bottom to 7 mm. at the rim, which is rounded, undulating, and has various nicks and other small irregularities. Both surfaces are uneven, and the interior is covered in spots with masses of charred organic matter.

The second vessel is a subhemispherical bowl roughly circular in outline. Its diameter varies between 153 and 160 mm., and the depth is 69 mm. The outer surface is bumpy and uneven, but the interior has been fairly well smoothed; it, too, has a thin spotty "cake" of carbonized substance. At one point the lip has 19 notches covering a 55-mm. sector. Like the larger specimen, this is made of a moderately fine-grained steatite (pl. 35, *b*).

Near the south corner of square 87/29, lying directly in front of the hard clay ledge marking terrace 3, were the partly nested fragments of a large oblong bowl (pls. 6, *a*; 36, *a*). It lay 14 inches underground, a few feet from a poorly marked stone fireplace. The maximum dimensions were: length 312 mm., width 286 mm., depth 130 mm. Tool marks show on the exterior, which is very rough. The walls are irregular in thickness, and the bottom appears to have been worn through, or else to have broken out because it was ground too thin in manufacture. There is no lip decoration. The specimen is of unusual interest because it was broken and mended by the aborigines. A fracture runs lengthwise through the vessel. At either end just below the rim are two pairs of drilled holes, one hole of each pair lying on either side of the break. Grooves connect the holes of each pair across the crack, so that the lashing would lie flush with or below the surface of the bowl. Traces of the lashing, which was of some unidentified plant fiber, were noted in some of the holes. Near the bottom on either side of a missing bit of the bowl were three pairs of smaller holes also bordering the main breaks. Probably the vessel broke into two pieces lengthwise, was mended, and then broke a second time into so many pieces that effective repairs were not considered practicable, with the result that the fragments were discarded.

Two other broken vessels, each with several sherds missing, were found in square 111/36, near the southwest end of the shell heap. They were at a depth of 30 inches, on the hardpan at the very bottom of the refuse. One was an oval bowl 383 by 310 mm., with a depth of 190 mm. (pl. 35, *c*). Walls averaged about 20 mm., with a maximum of 30 mm. The lip is thin, sharpish, undulating, and undecorated but has four small notches at 4-mm. intervals beside one of the breaks. Tool marks show on the outside, and the interior is uneven. Perforations indicate that a diagonal break across the bowl was mended at one time. Two pieces of the rim, totaling about 300 mm., are missing.

The second of these vessels was subcircular, with the sides and ends tending to be very slightly flattened (pl. 36, *b*). Dimensions are 333 by 337 mm. with a depth of 136 mm. The outside is better finished than in the preceding, but the inner surface is again somewhat uneven. The lip is thinned and undecorated. Here again a lengthwise fracture has been repaired. At one end are three pairs of holes, one pair being joined across the break with a groove so as to countersink the lashing. At the opposite end are three similar holes, the second of each pair missing with the broken out sherd. One of these pairs also was connected with a cross groove.

Miscellaneous objects.—This category is a catch-all to which are assigned the numerous worked pieces of steatite not readily placed in one or another of the type groupings described above. It includes materials summarized under three separate headings in the summary table. The miscellaneous unidentified group alone suggests partly completed, finished, or, in some cases, broken artifacts, though in no case is there even a hint as to their function. Some are triangular in outline, others squarish or rectangular, while still others are irregular. All have been cut, scored, scratched, scraped, worn, bored one or more times, or worked in some other way. Plate 33, *k–o*, *q*, *t–w*, *x*, shows a few of the forms; we shall not attempt further comment here.

Even more numerous than the foregoing odds and ends are other scraps, mainly sherds, which have been bored or cut but otherwise exhibit no efforts at purposeful alteration. Thirty-seven have been variously cut and scored; mostly they are very small pieces. Forty-six others have been drilled from one to four or more times each. They would make satisfactory weights for fish nets or lines or similar light materials, though why more than one hole was needed is not clear.

As a matter of fact, many of these miscellaneous specimens suggest nothing so much as the heterogeneous leavings of an erstwhile village whittler plying his art in soft stone instead of in wood. It seems futile to describe each piece in detail since this would involve us in a welter of trivialities out of all proportion to their probable cultural significance.

WORK IN CHIPPED STONE

Chipped-stone artifacts were found in abundance at all of the sites examined on Buena Vista Lake. They include projectile points, knives, gravers, drills, scrapers, sawlike forms, and miscellaneous objects. Materials used were mainly cherts of various colors—gray, greenish, and brownish, in addition to which there was some jasper, chalcedony, quartz, and obsidian. The exact source for the different raw materials is not known, though the stream boulders on the lower slopes of the nearby mountain ranges would probably yield most of them. Obsidian is uncommon as compared to the crypto-crystalline silicas so that a more remote source of supply may be inferred. This may have been somewhere in the eastern Sierra Nevadas.

To simplify description, projectile points, blades, and knives have been herein classified on the basis of form or outline. Basically the scheme followed is that of Wilson (1899), which has been utilized and modified by numerous other workers in various regions. The form chart and accompanying outline of diagnostics is taken directly from Strong (1935, pp. 88–89). The number and vertical occurrence of each of the recognized types at all Buena Vista sites treated in this paper is indicated in the summary table.

CLASSIFICATION CHART FOR CHIPPED POINTS

N, Not stemmed

A, Leaf-shaped.
  a, Pointed at both ends.
  b, Pointed at one end.
    1, Convex base.
    2, Straight base.
    3. Concave base.
B, Triangular.
  a, Straight base.
    1, Two side notches.
  b, Concave base.
    1, Two side notches.
C, Diamond-shaped.

S, Stemmed

A, Contracting stem.
  a, Shouldered only.

A, Contracting stem—Continued.
  b, Shouldered and barbed.
  c, Neither shouldered nor barbed (lozenge).
B, Parallel-sided stem.
  a, Shouldered only.
  b, Shouldered and barbed.
  c, Neither shouldered nor barbed.
C, Expanding stem.
  a, Shouldered only.
    1, Convex base.
    2, Straight base.
    3, Concave base.
  b, Shouldered and barbed.
    1, Convex base.
    2, Straight base.
    3, Concave base.

Arrowpoints.—The great majority of specimens at site 1 classed as arrowpoints fall under type NBb. They are made chiefly of gray to almost black chert, but red jasper is also quite common. Only 11 are of obsidian. There is much variation in size and proportions, but in general they tend to be rather long and narrow with straight finely retouched edges and concave base (pl. 38, *a–i*). They range

PROJECTILE POINTS AND BLADES

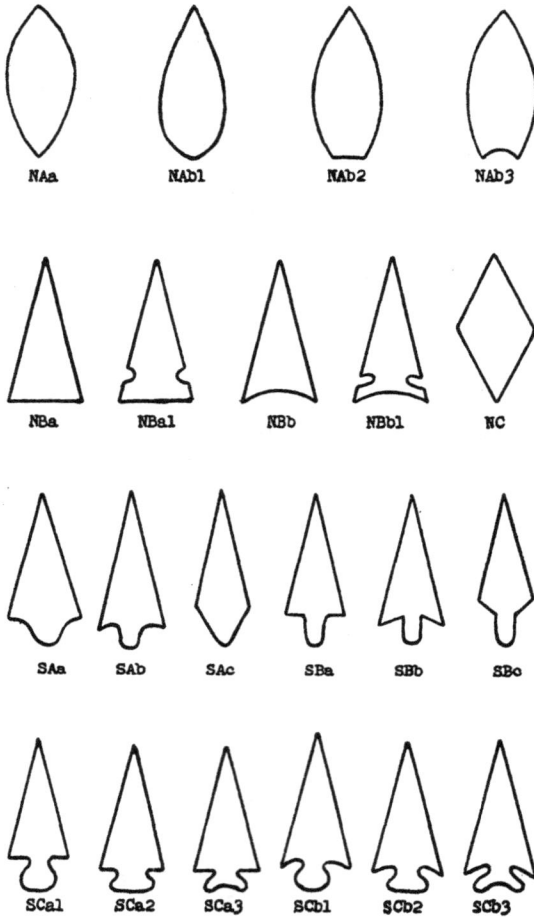

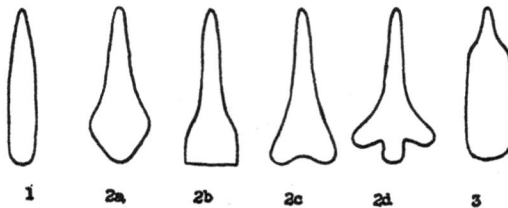

FIGURE 7.—Classification chart of chipped-flint forms.

from 19 to 70 mm. or a little more in length, but average between 25 and 38 mm. Points over 40 or 45 mm. are rare. The ratio of width to length, judging from a random sample, varies from 1 : 1.4 to 1 : 3.2, with most specimens approximating 1 : 2.5. Greatest variability is found in depth of the basal concavity. In some points this is all but absent; in others it equals as much as $\frac{1}{5}$ the total length of the point so that pronounced basal barbs are present. Usually the concavity is between $\frac{1}{7}$ and $\frac{1}{12}$ the length. Many of these specimens are well made and symmetrical, those with deep "swallow-tail" bases often being especially graceful and nicely chipped. A number exhibit finely serrate edges. In view of the abundance of this type, it is quite probable that many or most of the unclassifiable tips and other fragments are actually from similar specimens. Vertically, the type was found to a maximum depth of about 6 feet, with a marked increase in the upper layers of the shell heap. Nearly half (100 specimens) of the total yield came from the uppermost 12 inches. Throughout it consistently outnumbered all other types combined, and in the topmost foot it overshadowed them two to one.

Second in order of abundance were slender leaf-shaped points of NAb1 type, with rounded base, gently curving or nearly straight sides, and sometimes with fine serrations (pl. 38, *o*, *p*). These are all of cherty materials, obsidian being wholly absent. Complete specimens are from 34 to 76 mm. long and from 11 to 18 mm. wide. The longer ones tend to be proportionately narrower than the medium and short. The longest example (pl. 38, *o*) is 76 by 12.5 mm., a ratio of about 1 : 6, and there are several others which approach these proportions. Probably the majority average longer and more slender than the preceding type. A few are rather crudely chipped and heavy but for the most part they are about as graceful and well finished as the others. They were found to a slightly greater depth than the NBb form, but otherwise parallel the occurrence of the latter.

Differing from the first type in a few minor details are 25 incomplete fragments with straight bases, which have been classed as NBa. One is of obsidian, the others of gray chert. The majority are about the same size as the NBb examples, but a few are larger and heavier. Workmanship is essentially the same and their stratigraphic dispersal accords with both NBb and NAb1. Another variant, NBb1, finds the concave base triangles provided with a single pair of lateral notches. Of 18 such, 8 are obsidian, the rest chert. Only one or two appear to have been as much as 30 or 35 mm. long; most were under 25 mm., down to about 18 mm. For the most part, these were apparently cut first on the same pattern as the much more common NBb points, since they have the same general form and workmanship and about the same variability in details. They differ chiefly in the presence of the side notches.

Of 345 unstemmed projectile points (NA– and NB–) susceptible of classification only 20, or about 6 percent, are of obsidian. These, together with 12 unclassified fragments of obsidian points, are from the upper 3 feet with two exceptions; none were over 4 feet deep.

Stemmed points were numerically insignificant at site 1. In nearly every case they are heavier and less carefully fashioned than the unstemmed. To some extent this is attributable to the intractable nature of the material occasionally used. Seven specimens are crudely made from quartz porphyry; they are thick, coarse, and represent probably the poorest examples of flaking from the site. With chert and jasper somewhat better results were gotten. Most common is type SAc with 14 specimens. These are from 45 mm. up in length, the largest being a quartz porphyry nearly 80 by 26 mm. Width usually is about ⅓ the length. Type SAa is second with 3 specimens. Two complete ones are of quartz porphyry, respectively 29 and 40 mm. in length, while the third is the basal part of a large red jasper point. The larger of the quartz porphyry points has a notch in the base (pl. 38, z). Like basal notches occur in two other points made of similar stone, both of SBc type, 40 and 53 mm. long. There is one well made SAb point of greenish stone 50 mm. long, with broken tip, and the base of a heavy SCa2 point of quartz porphyry.

Before leaving the matter of projectile points it may be worthy of note that the triangular and "swallow-tail" points, and probably the leaf-shaped ones as well, bear a striking resemblance to some of the common Santa Barbara types. Rogers (1929, p. 404 and pl. 75) comments on the high quality of Canaliño points and observes that ". . . The greater part of them conform to two distinct patterns. One of these is elongate-triangular with a forked base. The other is the elongate, leaf-shaped variety with rounded base. There is no trace of notches or stem in either variety. . . ." (See also Wheeler Survey, 1879, pl. 3, and Heye, 1921, pls. 39 and 40.)

Beyond this, adequate statistical, illustrative, and descriptive data are not at hand for that region. However, judging from materials available at the National Museum many of the Buena Vista specimens, if mixed with their corresponding forms in the Wheeler Survey and other collections from the Channel, would be inseparable so far as size, shape, and technology are concerned. Significantly enough, sites farther north show a steady decrease in proportion of these particular forms. In the Tulare basin, NA– types predominate (Gifford and Schenck, 1926, pp. 82–83). The Stockton-Lodi district appears to yield mainly stemmed points, with few leaf-shaped forms; triangulars are almost absent and are quite unlike those at Buena Vista (Schenck and Dawson, 1929, p. 371). At

Emeryville large leaf-shaped and stemmed forms exclusively were present (Schenck, 1926, p. 240). For the Cosumnes-Deer Creek locale small obsidian NA– but no triangulars or NBb points are reported (Lillard and Purves, 1936, pls. 23, 24). In Colusa County, stemmed forms likewise are overwhelmingly predominant (Krieger, n. d.). It thus appears that Buena Vista is much more closely linked in this respect with coastal areas to the south than with anything yet recorded in or near the San Joaquin and Sacramento Valleys, a significant fact in view of other near identities to which attention will be called from time to time.

Disk.—There is a single thin subcircular object of gray banded chert (pl. 39, *v*). Its diameter averages just under 25 mm. with a maximum thickness of 4 mm. The edges have been carefully retouched, as have both surfaces.

Gravers.—This group includes three retouched pointed objects with heavy unfinished butts and thick cross sections. They suggest use in the incising and marking of bone, shell, and other softer substances.

Knives.—In addition to the great number of small projectile points already classified and described, several larger chipped blades of similar outline were brought to light. Judging from the complete or near complete specimens, 8 in number, a characteristic form was the leaf-shaped (NAb1) type. The whole pieces and most of the similar fragments are of brown to nearly black jasper, never of the light gray chert so popular for small points. The largest found is 173 by 35 mm., with very slightly enlarged butt, convex base, and finely retouched edges (pl. 40, *a*). Its average thickness is under 7 mm. On one face, about 10 mm. up from the base, are very faint traces of asphaltum. Another measures 105 by 33 by 8 mm. (pl. 40, *b*). It, too, has asphaltum stains on the base, and on this there is the indistinct imprint of a flat wooden surface. The others are smaller, ranging downward to a broad specimen 50 mm. long. There is one double pointed example (NAa) of dark gray banded chert 73 by 23 mm. Eight broken pieces, thin and chipped in the manner of the foregoing, are in all likelihood bases of as many knives, and there are six other sections with two retouched and two broken edges which may have come from still other similar objects. These fragments were found to a maximum depth of 5–6 feet, but 22 of the 23 were in the upper 3 feet. Asphaltum stains were noted on one or two of the scraps. From this it seems likely that these long leaf-shaped blades were intended for hafting, probably having been set with asphaltum into a wooden handle.

Omitted from the statistical summary because of their indeterminable identity are a few small triangular bits of obsidian and light gray chert that may have come from either knives or projectile points. They show two retouched and one broken margin. Small whole triangular specimens, which could likewise be assigned to either class, form a relatively insignificant group.

Perforators.—Twenty-three specimens have been included here. All are of flint or jasper. Most of them are broken, but insofar as classification is possible they may be divided into several types on the basis of form.

Commonest is type 1, a simple straight form with oval, diamond, or triangular cross section (pl. 39, *s*). Two seem to be little more than slivers broken from the edges of knives or points, but seemingly readapted for use as drills. The longest complete specimen is 53 mm. Type 2 includes all drills with the basal portion more or less expanded, in which the stem comprises half or less of the object. Three have the butt expanded and the base convex, and range from 32 to 44 mm. in length (subtype *a*). Subtype *b*, represented by a single specimen, has a broken butt, with very slender stem and sharp point. Subtype *c*, in which the bas is bifurcate, includes one 55-mm. drill, and probably a second incomplete one. A single straight example with two wings curving backward from a point just above the base, has been classed as subtype *d* (pl. 39, *r*). Type 3, also represented by one piece, is a thin well-made artifact 49 by 16 mm., of whose length the drill proper comprises only 10 mm. (pl. 39, *t*). The remaining specimens are too incomplete to permit identification, although seven certainly have expanded basal portions.

Saws.—More than 50 fragments of cutting implements which seem to be of rather distinctive type have been placed in this category. Almost without exception they are of gray green often brecciated chert evidently quarried from seams not exceeding 8 to 10 mm. thick. The flat surfaces of every specimen bear a calcareous deposit representing the matrix which enclosed the original vein of chert. The thickness of the implements was thus limited by nature to a proportion suited to convenient grasping. Not one is complete, and the original shape like their size is wholly conjectural (pl. 41, *a–c*). One or two pieces suggest oval knives perhaps 85 or 90 mm. long by about a third as wide. Another, slightly over 50 mm. wide, has two nearly parallel edges 85 and 100 mm. long; both ends are broken (pl. 41, *c*). Several others have straight or nearly straight edges upward of 100 mm. long, but are broken on all remaining sides. The edges are generally more abruptly thinned than in the knives above described, and the faces show scant evidence of dressing over a half inch from the extreme edge. For the most part they look like thin slabs roughly shaped to a size suitable for handling and then given a cutting edge. Edges are frequently blunted from long or hard use.

These implements must have been intended for heavier work than the more carefully chipped knives from the site, or for service against tougher and more resistant materials. Using one of the objects in question, and a blunt one, the writer was able in a little over a minute to saw a steatite sherd 8 mm. thick to the point where it finally broke along the line of the cut. Aside from its newness, the resulting fracture was indistinguishable from those on dozens of native-cut sherds recovered during our excavations. This suggests one possible purpose of the "saws." At least 90 percent of the steatite at site 1 occurred in the upper 3 feet, from which zone came 92 percent of the "saws."

Scraper knives.—This term covers a series of 181 chipped objects which could have functioned about equally well for cutting and scraping, or both. In general, they are oval, subcircular, and oblong in form, with the margin partly to almost wholly retouched to give an efficient cutting or scraping edge. About one-third, comprising the better made specimens, are 10 mm. or less in thickness, with maximum diameters not exceeding 55 mm. The smallest is 32 by 29 mm. Edges are usually thinned down all around, even at the back where the flint was mounted. Some are best described as thin disks or ovals.

Another group, including specimens both larger and smaller than the preceding, consists of less carefully shaped spalls or small cores in which the retouching is limited to one edge, i. e., to about a third of the periphery. In these the maximum thickness is commonly at the back, opposite the sharpened edge. In a few, the width along the cutting edge is two or even three times the length. That these variations have any far reaching significance is doubtful, since the evident manner of use made it well nigh impossible to utilize more than a short section of the edge irrespective of the extent to which the artifact borders were retouched. Perhaps the better nature of some was due primarily to the owner's preference for a better tool than the shoddy ones possessed by his or her neighbors.

Nearly a third of the scraper knives, 56 to be exact, have various amounts of asphaltum on part of the edge and on one or both faces. On the single-edged specimens this is always over the unsharpened portion of the margin; on the better made ones with all around retouching it covers a considerable part of the edge. The significance of this asphaltum is clearly indicated by some 10 or 12 examples whereon it occurs in unusual quantity. One, single-edge, has been set into the notched end of a small stick and fastened in place with a wad of asphaltum (pl. 42, *c*). Several others show the impression of larger split or notched sticks up to 20 or 25 mm. in diameter (pl. 42, *a*, *b*, *d*). It seems safe to assume that the majority of these implements were mounted in this fashion (cf. Wheeler Survey, 1879, pp. 59–61 and pl. 4), in which case they would have served very effectively as cutting and skinning tools, for hide scraping, etc. Their comparative abundance indicates that they must have been of some importance in the everyday domestic activities of the ancients,

and in a primarily hunting and fishing economy their utility is
evident. Their deepest occurrence at site 1 was in the 5–6 foot level,
and from the beginning asphalt was evidently used in direct
connection with them as above described.

WORK IN GROUND STONE

Balls.—Ten spheroidal stone objects, all more or less symmetrical
and well finished, were found in the upper 4 feet of the shell-heap.
All are of granite or very hard sandstone (pl. 43, *c, d, e*). The largest specimens, represented respectively by a ½ and a ¼ sphere, were
at least 110 and 80 mm. in diameter. The average is around 45 to
50 mm., and the smallest is just under 30 mm. in diameter. None is
perfectly true but nearly all the complete ones can be rolled in a
reasonably straight line. It is difficult to determine whether they are
natural river boulders picked up because of their unusual roundness
or have been subjected to artificial shaping by man. One of softer
limestone looks very much as though it had been shaped on one side
but even this is uncertain.

A clue to the possible manner of use of these objects is offered by
Latta (1929) who says that the hill Yokuts east of Tulare Lake
"used to roll round stones at a hole in the ground . . ." as one
form of recreation.

Charmstones.—Of this widespread and varied Californian type
only two examples were recovered at site 1, both in the upper 2 feet.
They are of very hard fine-grained stone. The one illustrated in plate
44, *e*, has a maximum diameter of 22 mm., a present length of 55 mm.,
and is generally well finished. One end remains intact; it is square
cut and smooth. With some uncertainty, this may be assigned to type
WBb1 (unperforated, with pile, i. e., secondary end curves, and with
plain ends) of Gifford and Schenck's (1926, p. 94) classification. The
second is yet more incomplete, consisting of a 57-mm. tapered and
split midportion with one squared end. Perhaps it, too, is from one
of the long narrow spindle-shaped type.

Decorated block.—This is a tapered piece of chalk or marl, with
both ends broken off. Its present length is 50 mm., its maximum width
32 mm., and its thickness 14 mm.; the cross section is flattened elliptic.
On one flat side is a rude incised design separated into three zones
by short transverse lines. The end zones are cross-hatched; between
is an hourglass-shaped figure, one half of which is filled in with short
incisions. The entire area is much like the edge decoration elsewhere
described for one of the thick clamshell disk beads. This surface
also has traces of red ochreous material, but it is not certain that
this was intentionally applied.

Knives.—In plate 40, *h, i,* are illustrated two ground stone knives
wholly unlike any other specimens recovered at Buena Vista. The

larger and rougher is made from a spall of fine-grained slaty-gray sandstone, with one end pointed, the other rounded. On one edge and side may be seen the bulb of percussion; the other edge is straight and has been thinned by grinding to a smooth even cutting or scraping blade (pl. 40, h). It measures 97 by 47 mm. The second is incomplete but was distinctly better made. The curving edges, if projected beyond the broken ends, converge to give an elliptical or bipointed outline about 150 by 40 mm. The thickness nowhere exceeds 8 mm. Both surfaces are smoothed but show some irregularities due to the original contours of the flake used. The edges are even and smooth. The surfaces are very dark from discoloration, but the freshly broken ends show the material to be fine greenish quartz or quartzite.

Both these knives are out of place at Buena Vista. They are strangely like certain knife fragments figured by Jochelson from the Aleutian islands.[14] Both were found within 12 inches of the surface of site 1. Whatever their actual age they thus fall within the closing period of occupancy—a period possibly, though not certainly, extending into the years just subsequent to arrival of white men in the general region. One wonders whether these particular specimens are in some indirect fashion to be connected with the presence of Aleut sea-otter hunters in the service of the early nineteenth century Russian fur companies on the southern California coast and in the Channel Islands (Bancroft, 1886, pp. 84, 94).

Mortars.—According to Kroeber, the Yokuts mortar was usually "a pit in an outcrop of granite, used until the depth of the hole became inconvenient. . . . On the alluvial plains portable mortars were necessary," these being usually of wood. He states further that:

Loose mortars of stone were found and used on occasion by all the tribes, but the univeral testimony is that they were not made. . . . It is reported that the Yokuts sometimes fastened a hopper of basketry to the edge of a stone mortar; but this practice is established only for the southern California tribes, and needs confirmation. There is no Yokuts mortar basket, and the few available specimens of the combination suggest that an American may have cut the bottom out of a cooking basket and asphalted it to the stone. [Kroeber, 1925, pp. 527–528.]

The present excavations yielded broken fragments of a few mortars, but their apparent scarcity where pestles were rather common is in line with Kroeber's observation that a wooden form was more typical. We are also able to confirm the presence of the hopper mortar for the Buena Vista Basin.

This conclusion is based on four specimens found at site 1 at various depths down to 52 inches. All are of sandstone, naturally or artificially shaped, whose upper surface in each case bears in-

---

[14] Cf. our pl. 40, h, i, with Jochelson, 1925, pl. 16, figs. 1, 4, 7, 8, 12.

disputable evidence not only of use as a mortar but also of asphaltum used to fasten in place a basket hopper. One specimen from the upper 12 inches is a round boulder with an outside diameter of 100 mm. and a height of 73 mm. The top has been hollowed slightly to a depth of 3 or 4 mm., and around this depression is a thick smear of asphaltum which extends down the outside for about 25 mm. (pl. 45, *b*). The bottom has been flattened somewhat by pecking so that the utensil stands upright with slight tendency to rock. A slightly larger spherical mortar 128 mm. in diameter has a similarly flattened base, while the top has been worked out into a basin 85 mm. across by about 8 mm. deep. Only a trace of asphaltum remains about the outside just below the rim. Still another specimen is nearly identical with the last except for smaller size—diameter 102 mm., height 83 mm., with flattened bottom. The cavity is 62 mm. across by 25 mm. deep, and is completely surrounded by asphaltum running 25 mm. or more down the exterior (pl. 45, *c*). The fourth example, 52 inches below the mound surface, is flat and roughly elliptical, measuring 188 by 162 by 63 mm. The flat much-worn upper surface has a ring of asphaltum about 25 mm. wide and 135 mm. in diameter. All of the wear from grinding activities is confined to the area within the ring, and is most pronounced at the center (pl. 45, *a*). Bits of asphaltum adhere to the under side also, which shows no evidences of subjection to grinding. While none of these four mortars shows basket impressions, the spherical ones are essentially identical with much larger and deeper specimens seen by us in the upper Cuyama valley, whereon the asphaltum bore distinct marks of coiled basketry. There seems no reason to doubt, therefore, the meaning of the Buena Vista mortars.[15] As to their origin—whether truly aboriginal or due to American inspiration—it can be stated that they were found at site 1 in levels well below any suggestion of white contact. That they are not necessarily of great antiquity, however, will become apparent presently when the time factor is attacked.

One battered but otherwise mostly intact mortar found at 65 inches depth may also belong with the above. It is of white calcareous sandstone 80 mm. in diameter, 50 mm. thick, with a pit 62 mm. across by 25 mm. deep. A dark band 18 mm. wide, which may or may not be of asphaltum derivation, encircles the rim exterior just below the grinding basin. Because of its small size it was dubbed a paint mortar in the field but there is no proof that it was actually so used.

Three other fragments of similarly shaped, i. e., spherical, mortars larger in size, were also found. They are devoid of asphalt stains.

---

[15] ". . . Some of these southern [California] tribes cement a basket to the rim of the stone; the Chumash asphalt it also to slabs. . . ." [Kroeber, 1925, p. 632.]

Of very different type are other mortars represented by six rim fragments from five specimens. All show carefully dressed interior and exterior surfaces, the latter sometimes being dimpled but never rough. The interiors are smooth from use. All have thick flat rims, which in two instances are slightly wider than the wall immediately below. They are of tough crystalline rock. Only one sherd is large enough to permit even a rough calculation of former size; here the interior diameter, lip to lip, appears to have been about 260 mm. It is inferred that the greatest diameter was at or just below the rim, with sides sloping or curving slightly to a base smaller than the mouth. This type may have resembled the better specimens or show mortars from Emeryville (Schenck, 1926, pls. 49, A, and 50, A, B). They were found from 12 to 60 inches deep at Buena Vista.

Mullers.—Only 10 specimens definitely identifiable as handstones for grinding are represented in our collections from site 1. They were distributed vertically from the surface to a depth of nearly 9 feet—a markedly greater range than is shown by any other artifact type from this midden. Two or three are of sandstone, the rest of granite. They are elliptical, oblong, or subcircular in outline, and generally show two smoothed grinding faces. Largest of the series is a thick block 130 by 109 by 76 mm., weighing 4 pounds; one end is pitted and the other appears to have been battered. The smallest, of sandstone, is 80 by 38 mm., weighs 14 ounces, and has one flat and a convex surface, i. e., bun-shaped. The general type can be inferred readily from plate 43, *i.* Curiously enough, no metates or mealing slabs were found.

One small circular flat sandstone object 63 by 24 mm. may have been a rubbing stone, but has been included with the mullers in the summary table.

Pestles.—Twenty-six pestles were recovered, including two whose exact provenience is uncertain. The maximum depth was 5–6 feet, but of the 24 whose location is exactly recorded, 21 were in the upper 3 feet and 9 in turn came from the topmost 12 inches. Thus, they appear later than the mullers, and unlike them show a marked numerical increase in the later periods of occupancy.

As to type there are only minor variations which show no apparent correlation with depth or other factors (pl. 47, *b–d*, *g*). All are of hard sandstone or granite. Four are heavy and barrel-shaped or subcylindrical with slightly tapered ends both of which could have been used for pulverizing. The largest is 195 by 100 mm., the smallest 150 by 60 mm. Most of the remainder may be characterized as subconical, with the maximum diameter at or just above the grinding end, and an even or slightly curving taper to a rounded handle. Here the largest is 290 mm. long, with a maximum diameter of 85 mm. The handle end is about 30 mm. thick. From this size they range downward to small "paint" pestles. A fair average would be about 165 by 65 mm. Five or six "paint" pestles vary in length from 100 to 54 mm., in diameter from 48 to 33 mm. The smallest is encircled by a low raised ring 1 cm. wide just below the upper end (pl. 43, *g*). Another slightly larger one, possibly broken from a long slender pestle, also has such a ring. Otherwise, in general form and in every respect save size these are virtually identical with the common larger type. One larger specimen has the handle elaborated into a knob below which is a raised ring (pl. 43, f). As to vertical distribution, two ringed pestles are from the upper 12 inches of midden; the third (ringed and knobbed) is from the 5–6 foot level.

Three other less carefully finished elongate pebbles, whose ends show evidence of battering, have not been included in the above series.

Miscellaneous.—At a depth of 1 foot (30 cm.) in square 97/39 was found an irregularly shaped subcylindrical object of soft friable brown sandstone. It is about 80 by 50 mm., with the ends not quite evenly squared off. Encircling the midportion is an erratic finely incised line. At right angles to this and paralleling the long axis are other carelessly executed and unevenly spaced scorings which do not extend onto the ends. A calcareous incrustation containing bits of shell covers part of one side.

Somewhat similar in shape but smaller and more slender is the fine-grained sandstone object shown in plate 20, *f*. It is 68 mm. long, 27 mm. in maximum diameter, and the ends are slightly bruised. It has been rather carefully shaped, but it is not polished or ornamented.

Two or three unshaped sandstone objects were evidently used as abradants. One is 345 by 65 by 40 mm.; one surface is flat as if used for grinding, while into the other face have been worn irregular depressions perhaps from sharpening or shaping objects of bone, etc. The other pieces, much smaller but equally irregular, show similar sharpening or grinding grooves.

SITE 2

Twelve hundred yards southeasterly from site 1 the shore line of Buena Vista Lake curves around the easternmost spur of the hills, swinging westward a short distance and finally southward again. Inside the hook thus formed is the lowest of the three hillocks mentioned in the geographical description given elsewhere. It is connected with its neighbors to the west by a saddle about 50 feet lower than the summit. When the lake stood at the 300-foot level, its waters washed the spur on the north, east, and south sides. At 290 feet or below there was no water to the south. (See fig. 2.)

At the extreme eastern foot of the spur, between the hill and the lake shore is a small roughly triangular bit of ground built up in part by erosion from the slope above and in part by other agencies (pl. 9, *a*). The northeast and south sides of this area today conform to the 300-foot contour; on the west it is bounded by the 310-foot contour beyond which rises the hill (pl. 9, *b*). From the southeast corner of the triangle a long narrow sandspit extends south by east onto the lake bed for about 500 yards, at which point it turns due south to splay out after another 400 yards. From the northeast shoulder of the hill to the end of the spit, including also the alluvial flat, is a distance of about 1,200 yards, all of which would have been above water when the lake level was at 290 feet. At 295 feet the southern half of the spit, and at 300 feet nearly its entire length, must have been submerged. Between spit and mainland there was a wide shallow embayment or lagoon whenever the lake level was 290 feet or higher.

All this area, including both alluvial flat and sandspit, shows evidence of frequent and extended human occupation; it comprises our site 2.

The manner in which the sandspit was probably formed and its history are of some interest. The former is inferred from certain topographic considerations based on the 1927 survey map of Buena Vista Lake and its relations to the immediately adjacent Buena Vista and Elk Hills. As already pointed out when the lake held water up to the 290-foot level or above, it impinged directly on the steep northeasterly front of the Buena Vista Hills. Currents moving in counter clockwise direction southward along the west shore would have been deflected toward the southeast at this point, and in so doing would tend to wear away the base of the hills. The force of the currents would then sweep past the shoulder of the spur into the open lake or into the bay to the south. In the protected lee of the spur there would be little or no current, and in consequence the waters would tend to deposit there such sand and silt as had been carried or rolled from points to the northwest. Deposition being most rapid and pronounced at the edge of the slackening currents, in course of time a narrow ridge would gradually rise on the floor of the lake. Such activity would probably be most pronounced during periods of high water. The marked fluctuations to which the water level of the lake was clearly subject would during lower stages leave a dry strip whose emergence invited parties of native fishermen and hunters to camp there. The resultant camp debris, as is directly demonstrable, was an additional factor in the growth of the spit. Where the latter touched the mainland, run-off from the hill during times of excessive precipitation added its burden of alluvium thus widening the ground available there for human occupancy. That the latter area was thus augmented there is clear proof in the profile trenches in form of alluvial strata which are absent on the spit, protected as it was from run-off sedimentation by the intervening embayment.

Within the memory of present day residents of Taft the entire spit is said to have been under water. How many times previously it had been subjected to alternate submergence and emergence it is manifestly impossible to say, because there is no way of reconstructing accurately the movements of the lake surface. The six buried terraces at site 1, together with others still, or recently, observed farther from the late shore line indicate that the lake had repeatedly dwindled to small proportions and then risen again. All of the terraces, even those noted well out toward the middle of the lake, are littered with camp refuse, showing that the natives had camped and buried on the immediate shores of the receding sheet, where their traces were covered by water as the lake refilled. The high water marks at site 2 are far less clearly marked than at site 1. Nevertheless, it seems reasonable to infer that the spit was probably submerged not only for short periods in the spring when melting mountain snows temporarily raised the lake, but also for longer intervals when unusually heavy rainfall or a wet cycle in plain and sierra might keep the lake full for years at a time.

It is clear that the spit has undergone considerable erosion and disintegration as well as aggradation. At time of our dig a wave-cut bluff was apparent along most of its length on the side facing the open lake (pl. 9, c). This steep front contrasted sharply with the even, gradual slope toward the embayment. At times of heavy storm, the partially submerged spit must have been exposed to heavy pounding by waves driven before winds sweeping across 5 to 8 miles or more of open water. In places, these had eaten nearly through the formation. Whether this has happened before, with the spit being rebuilt one or more times after partial demolition, is uncertain. From its position it seems reasonable to believe the same factors which originally built it would have operated similarly—given identical conditions—to restore its shape.

The latter phenomenon, i. e., the partial destruction of the spit, has noteworthy archeological implications, at any rate in theory. It is estimated that the strip was at one time at least 100 feet wider than in 1933–34. If this or a comparable portion has been repeatedly cut away and then rebuilt, it is extremely difficult or impossible to establish the relative age of materials in that portion now covered by beach sands. Actually, excavation showed that the two or three feet of occupational levels left under the present beach were continuous with the lower part of the surviving spit. This deduction rests partly on the evidence of the strata themselves, partly on the essential similarity of artifacts from the two areas. It thus appears likely that however much the upper part of the spit has been mutilated by the elements, the deeper and older layers have remained substantially untouched since arrival of primitive man on the scene.

The maximum area and depth of occupation at site 2, and the portion best adapted to human habitation was, then, at the base of the hills where the spit joins the mainland. The subtriangular flat, as defined, measures roughly 300 feet or more on its southern by 350 feet on its western edge—or something under 2 acres of ground. Its surface is flat and slopes evenly downward from the base of the hill toward the crest of the wave-cut terrace. At one time the terrace front may have been farther out, but if so, its former extent is wholly conjectural. In front of the bluff is a wide strip of beach sand, below which our excavations revealed surviving traces of what is believed to have been the earliest occupation of the site. Our main excavations at site 2 lay approximately 1,400 yards southeast of site 1, and, as in the latter, were intersected by the 300-foot contour. A test trench was cut through the spit, and somewhat more extended work was done where the spit joins the flat (fig. 9).

A contour map showing one-foot intervals was prepared for site 2, covering the flat and a portion of the spit (fig. 8). This area was then staked off in 10-foot squares following a system of coordinates similar to that at site 1. The coordinate numbers indicating squares began at a hypothetical point well off the site to the northwest. Each square was designated by the number on the stake at its northeast corner. All specimens and similar features were located first by square, then by depth. Depth was usually recorded to the 12-inch level only, i. e., as 0–1 or 3–4 feet, such levels being arbitrarily established to expedite the work and the recording. These levels did not necessarily conform to such natural strata as occasionally occurred. Objects of unusual nature, burials, etc., were recorded, plotted, and cataloged more explicitly.

Sample profiles designed to give a check on all stratigraphic observations were obtained by means of two parallel trenches running east and west through the site. Trench 1 was in the north part of the flat near the shoulder of the hill (pl. 10, a). Beginning at the east side of square 135/32, just above the 285-foot contour and well out on the lake shore, it ran due west between lines 32 and 33 until soil devoid of cultural admixture was encountered at line 100. It measured 350 feet in length, 10 feet in width, and varied in depth from 2 feet at the east end to a maximum of 12 feet under stake 111/33, whence it gradually diminished toward the west uphill end. Throughout the entire length it was carried down into unmixed soil

formations, thus giving a complete and probably representative cross
section of the area of main occupancy. Trench 2 was 530 feet to the
south, and due to the southwesterly trend of the terrace front its
west end lay nearly due south of the east end of trench 1. Like the
latter, this cut was 10 feet wide and reached undisturbed soil throughout the 190 feet of its length. Its east end began at the 290-foot contour in square 153/85, whence it ran west to and through square
135/85.

With stratigraphy thus established, subsequent attention was de-
voted to the excavation of certain selected areas in that part of the
site which promised the best results, namely, on either side of trench
1. Eleven 10-foot squares on a staggered front were opened about
150–200 feet due north of the west end of trench 2. Otherwise, south
of trench 1, along the bluff and on the flat between it and the hills,
82 similar squares were excavated to varying depths, while on the
north side 59 others were dug. In all, the area excavated totaled
some 20,600 square feet (fig. 9).

Since trench 1 gave the longest and most complete cross section
through that portion of site 2 which was also most intensively occupied by man, it will be well to review briefly the picture revealed in
its walls. Owing to its great length as compared to the depth, it is
impracticable to reproduce a satisfactory diagram here. A sample
section where the trench cuts the heart of the habitation site and half-
tones to which reference will be made may suffice.

The trench may be divided for purposes of description into three
unequal sections. The first begins at the east end and is limited on
the west by the 294-foot contour, which crosses the trench at stake
119/33. There is a steady rise of 5 feet in 160 feet of the trench surface in this strip. Section 2 extends from 119/33 to 114/33, a 50-foot
stretch with a surface elevation rising from 294 to 303 feet. This
relatively abrupt rise represents the bluff cut by the lake from the
alluvial and other materials extending east from the foot of the hills.
Section 3 comprises the remaining 140 feet of trench, wherein the
surface rises evenly from 303 to 311.5 feet. This we may term the
terrace.

Most of section 1 bore a thin superficial covering of beach sands,
nowhere more than a few inches deep, and quite obviously owing to
the recent presence of the lake waters (pl. 9, c). While the last shore
line of any permanence seems to have been about at the 291-foot contour, it is also true that higher levels have obtained within the past
century, and this undoubtedly explains the presence of the wide sandy
beach. Directly beneath the sand was an exceedingly hard fine compact material difficult to work even with picks. This may owe its
origin to an underwater cementing process involving alluvial matter
and masses of fine loesslike soil carried into the lake by high winds

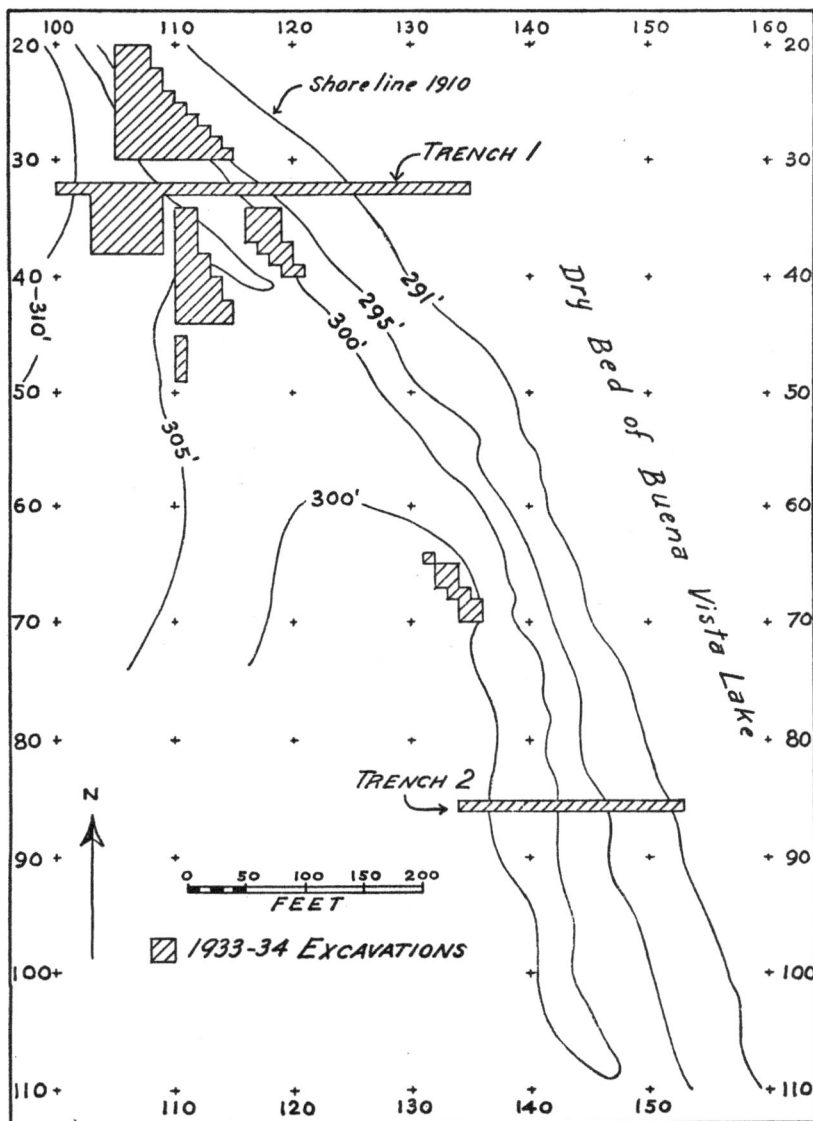

FIGURE 9.—Map of excavations at Buena Vista site 2, 1933–34.

from the barren dusty hills. Some ash and shell were also present, but definite strata and even clearly marked lenses were absent. In general, this material correlates with the so-called "plum pudding" formation at site 1. The exact manner in which it was formed has not been satisfactorily explained. Geologists to whom it was shown were able to offer little beyond the suggestion that its confused character may have been due to the churning and working over by

water of mixed cultural and noncultural deposits at depths too great
to permit sorting of materials by the waves. Whatever its origin, the
formation has been developed since human industry was carried on
at the site, since mullers and hammerstones were inclusively present.
Below this was a lighter colored but equally hard deposit of sand and
gravel containing no cultural traces whatever. From square 130 to
122 this was underlain by a bed of softer yellow sand. Underlying
all of these horizons was a bed of clear greenish clay, where work
ceased owing to presence of ground water.

The middle section under the bluff presented a profile dominated
by the "plum pudding" formation, with an average thickness of
about 3 feet. Below this the trench penetrated a very hard sterile
greenish sand which gave way to the equally resistant Tulare formation in square 116/33. Above the "plum pudding" were irregular
masses of material which contained dirt, shell, ash, etc., in varying
proportions, all giving an impression of having been churned into
a hopelessly unstratified and chaotic state. Except for the upper 2
feet or so, all of this was very hard and compact.

Beginning in square 114/33, there was some semblance of stratification, although the lines separating the layers were irregular and
often broken. The lowermost soil zone was the Tulare formation,
which from square 114/33 to at least 106/33 was from 8 to 10 feet
below the present ground surface. At 106/33 it sank below the floor
of the trench to reappear at a higher level in square 103/33. Thence
it rose rapidly but unevenly until at the end of the trench it was
covered by only a few inches of loose topsoil. Overlying this was
the "plum pudding," here consisting of compact yellow sand, gravel,
and some shell, mixed with alluvium washed down from the hill.
Through its upper portion ran dark streaks of what may have been
very old camp debris. From this level, also, came two of the deeper
burials, Nos. 17 and 18 (fig. 10 and pl. 15, a), while mullers and
hammerstones were not infrequent. Fireplaces and other evidence
of prolonged occupation were conspicuously absent, however. The
"plum pudding" faded out or at least lost its distinctive character
not far from the west end of the trench.

A typical section 20 feet long, taken where the various layers are
most clearly marked, is shown in figure 10. Above the basic Tulare
formation and the "plum pudding" (stratum 1) were 7 or 8 other
strata traceable almost throughout the length of the terrace profile.
Stratum 2, reading from the bottom up, was of gravel, sand, and
scattered shell, not differing greatly in appearance from stratum 1
but less compacted. In stratum 3, broken shells, ash, and charcoal were much more evident, indicating a period of fairly continuous activity by man. All of these layers contained a large propor-

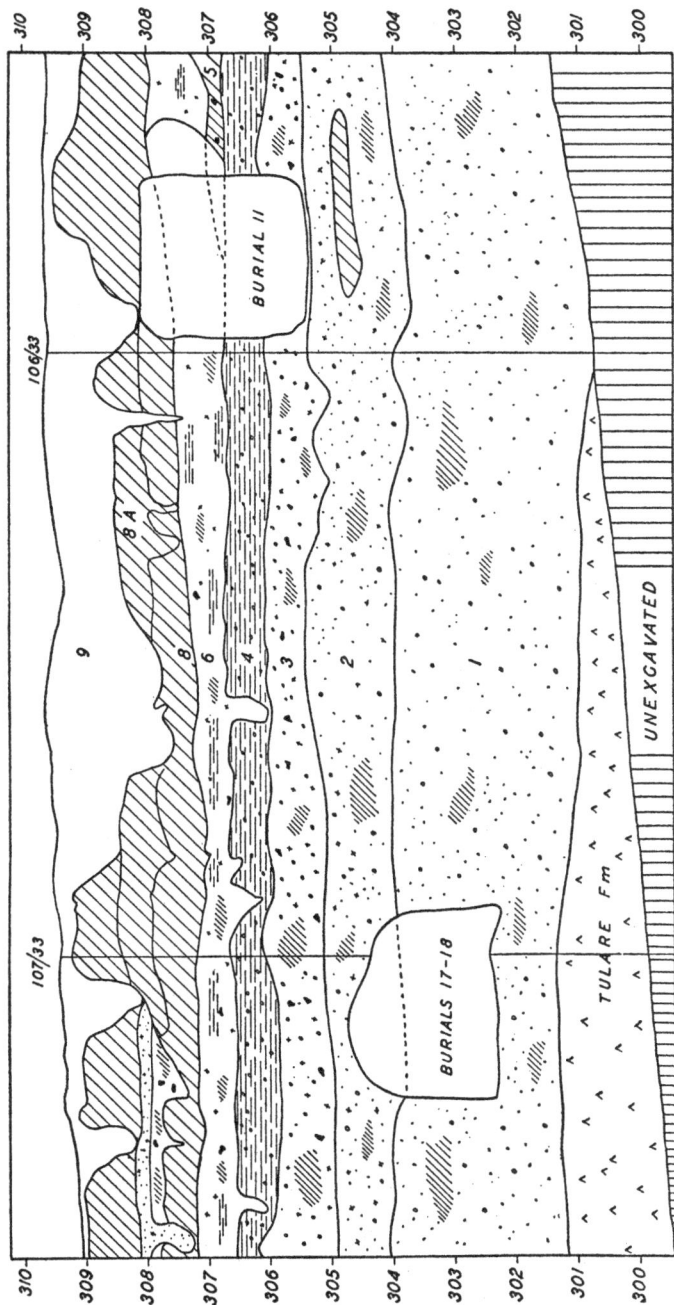

FIGURE 10.—Sample profile section from south wall of trench 1, Buena Vista site 2. Key to symbols: ///// shell; + ash; ° gravel; irregular black spots, charcoal; small dots, sand.

tion of gravel and sand, in all probability owing to wash from the higher ground on the west.

The bed marked as stratum 4 in figure 10 and in plate 11, *b*, is of exceptional interest and significance because in a general way it seems to separate two more or less distinct cultural manifestations. It consisted of yellow sand, gravel, and occasional shell fragments, but was notably devoid of charcoal, artifacts, and other cultural debris. Lighter in color than most of the horizons above and below, it was a conspicuous feature easily traced from beginning to end. To the east, toward the lake, it disappeared in square 112/33 at the 300.5-foot level. Its upper surface generally was much pitted and quite irregular, and in a few places the bed had been wholly penetrated by rodent (?) burrows and other holes filled with quantities of overlying materials. However, it was traceable westward to the middle of square 104/33, a total distance of about 90 feet. At its upper (west) end it merged into the fading "plum pudding" at an elevation between 305–306 feet, a rise of about 5 feet. Its upper plane of contact thus maintained a depth below the surface of 30–36 inches. The thickness varies between 6 and 10 inches. From its general appearance, make-up, and mode of occurrence, it can best be interpreted as a sheet of alluvium carried from the hillside during a period of heavy rainfall and spread over a pre-existing but temporarily uninhabited flat which in turn had been built up partly from occupational debris and partly through natural processes. Its outwash character is further proved by its presence under the terrace wherever tests were conducted, and its absence in the sandspit which was protected from slope wash by the embayment. It will be spoken of hereafter as stratum 4 or as the "alluvial stratum."

The soils overlying stratum 4 were generally softer and looser than those below, and contained a much larger proportion of shell, ash, charcoal, and artifacts. Stratum 5, immediately above, consisted of well-bedded shells, charcoal, and occupational detritus. Firepits and post molds were found here, too. Its eastern limit in the trench is indicated at the extreme right of the sample section (fig. 10) at burial 11, whence it was traced westward some 30 feet before it too merged into the "plum pudding." Stratum 6, from 6–10 inches thick, was of camp debris, charcoal, ash, shell, and some alluvial materials—undoubtedly a living level. West of our section was stratum 7, a very local feature not more than 20 feet in extent, and in composition quite similar to 5. Stratum 8, shown in plate 11, *b*, as a lighter colored horizon, consisted of shell, ash, bones, etc. Stratum 9 was made up of whole and broken shells, ash, and refuse, colored very dark by organic materials and humus. Topsoil proper was not over 3–6 inches thick, very loose and dusty, and evidently derived for the most part from stratum 9.

Probably the most significant feature of the vertical section, as noted, was the sterile alluvial horizon, stratum 4. No positive correlation could be established between this and any of those at site 1, but on general grounds we suggest the possibility that stratum 4 may equate with 2C, the sterile sand underlying most but not all of the looser portions at site 1. Both hint at a very wet interval partly or wholly interrupting human habitation at about the same apparent stage of cultural development. Such a phenomenon would have left much more marked evidences at site 2 for topographic reasons, and would thus have been in accord with our actual findings.

Generalizing for site 2, we may note that at the west end of the trench most of the horizons grade almost imperceptibly into the hillside (pl. 11, a), probably due to the recurrent deposition of run-off materials there as the terrace further out was being built up by accumulating camp and village refuse. At the east end they also give out in and near square 112/33, beyond which is a 20- to 30-foot zone whose upper half is mostly unconsolidated shell, sand, ash, gravel, and refuse. This again suggests that the eastern edges of the strata, comparatively well marked throughout much of the trench, have been mutilated and disturbed by high water where exposed to the direct action of waves. If these strata once extended farther out into the lake bed there is at present no way of determining their erstwhile limits.

Trench 2, crossing the sandspit, varied in depth from 6 feet at the east end to 10 feet at the center (square 140/85) to 4 feet at the west end. The entire surface to a depth of about 6 inches was loose aeolian material. Beneath this came a stratum up to 18 inches thick of harder wind-laid (?) earth, sand, and shell, whose lower contact lay wholly above the 298-foot level. Next came a 3–4 foot layer of hard clay, sand, some shell, and ash, with occasional dark stains possibly representing transitory occupational surfaces. In general, this horizon was quite sterile and unprepossessing from the standpoint of archeology. Beneath the crest of the spit, from square 139/85 to the middle of 143/85, a horizontal distance of 35 feet, was a series of thin shell and ash strata pretty certainly owing to human activity. Lying at elevations between 295.5 and 297 feet, these would have been habitable for considerable periods prior to deposition of the superincumbent 3 to 5½ feet of other materials. Sealed over by these slowly accumulated deposits, burial 28, one of the 4 extended interments (pl. 15, b), was exhumed from the occupational zone 80 inches below the surface of the spit. Below, and attaining a maximum thickness of 18 inches, was loam, sand, and shell forming a compact culturally sterile mass. None of these horizons could be directly correlated with those in trench 1, but it is probably safe to assume that the 295.5- to 297-foot habitation lenses and burial 28 are older than stratum 4 in the terrace. The hard clay-sand-ash overburden may, therefore, correspond to the "plum pudding" in trench 1. Since the general elevation of the spit is materially less than that of the terrace, it is possible that such transient occupancy as it experienced has been either washed away entirely or else was obliterated in loco by the reworking of the deposits under water into an unstratified and characterless mass. The trench did show a probably very old occupancy at least, and viewed in conjunction with the evidence from trench 1 may indicate that the earliest residence here took place during a comparatively dry period when the lake level was below 295 feet. Very few artifacts were recovered from trench 2.

Subsequent excavations involved the removal and screening of material along the terrace front over a total area of about 5,500 square feet. In addition, it was decided to strip off by layers a few inches thick a large area immediately south of the west end of trench 1. This excavation, adjoining the south wall of the cut, covered an area 50 by 60 feet. By combining the evidence thus gotten with that revealed by the trenches, it was possible to establish the true nature of the terrace and its history. Part of the excavation north of the trench was similarly stripped off, so that in all some 4,000 square feet or more were subjected to scrutiny in this fashion. As a result of findings so made, this area became known as "the camp site," under which heading it will be considered presently. The approximate limits of the camp site were determined by a large number of test pits scattered systematically over the entire terrace. Since the rectangular area south of trench 1 was most painstakingly examined, it alone will be discussed in detail. The other nearby cuts served primarily as a source of information concerning artifact types, burial practices, roasting pits, and local stratigraphy.

THE CAMP SITE

The area so designated was excavated to a total depth of 36 inches (91.4 cm), i. e., until the upper surface of the sterile alluvial layer (stratum 4) was reached. Termination of the project most unfortunately precluded similar study of the older horizons. Stripping was accomplished in 3- to 4-inch levels, with a detailed ground plan of the entire 50- by 60-foot area prepared for each level as cleared. Each successive surface was carefully smoothed with square-pointed shovels and then swept off with brooms. The freshly exposed surface then presented a uniform appearance—a dark ash-stained plane with flecks of white shell. A few minutes exposure to sun and air quickly dried most of the area to a light-gray color, leaving post molds, pits, and graves showing as slightly darker spots (pl. 13, *a*).

Over the surfaces generally it was noted that the shells lay horizontally or nearly so, but in the pits they lay on edge.

The general appearance and principal features of two of the levels may be inferred from figure 11 and plate 10, *b*, where the former

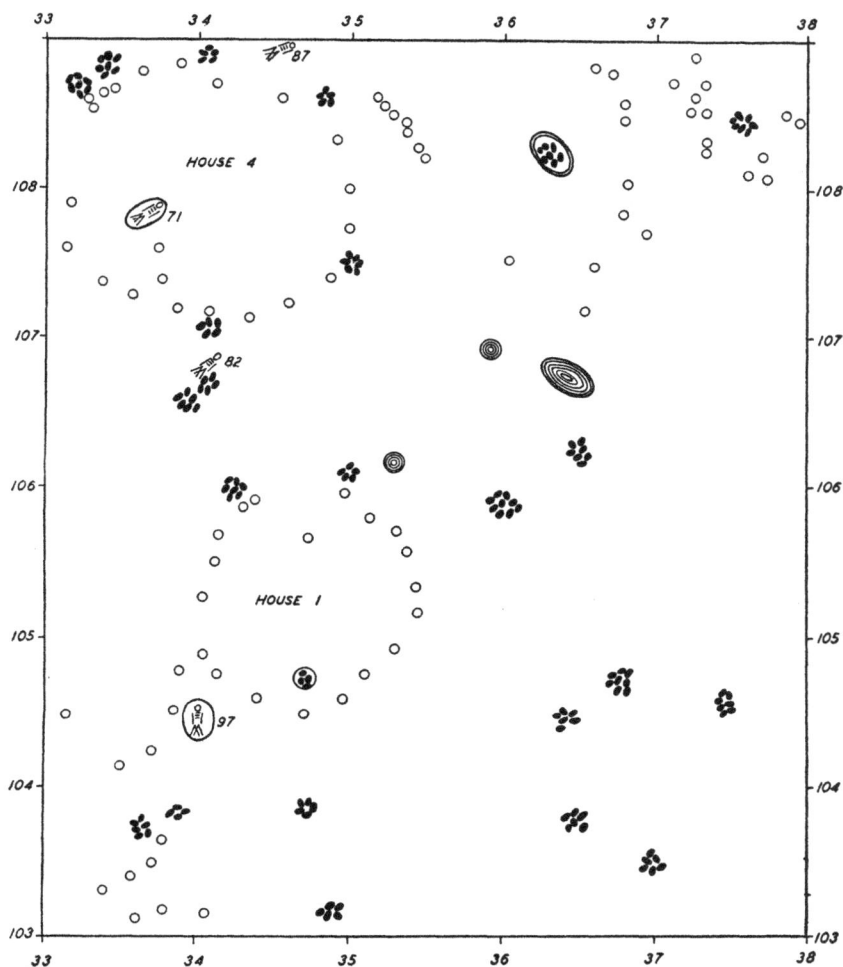

FIGURE 11.—Plan of portion of camp site at 9- to 12-inch level showing post holes (small circles), basins (concentric circles and ellipse), burials, stone hearths (clustered black dots), and other features; Buena Vista site 2.

depicts the 9- to 12-inch, the latter the 20-inch surface. Scattered about over these as over the others were numerous post molds from 2 to 5 inches across by 2 to 9 inches deep, and characterized in general by a looser fill than the surrounding matrix. In several instances these holes assumed definite patterns. In the 9- to 12-inch level, for instance, there were two circular groupings, the circles measuring approximately 14 and 18 feet in diameter (pl. 12). The post molds were arranged at 1- to 3-foot intervals, with longer gaps on the east and northeast sides. Both had hard-packed floors, and were identified as house sites. As at site 1, house 1 here had a firepit near the back wall. There was no hearth in the second, house 4, but surrounding both were several stone-filled firepits. These it may be said occurred in close association with each of the seven houses reported for site 2.

Significant data concerning the so-called house circles uncovered are summarized in table 3, prepared from the report of the assistant archeologist in charge at site 2. No details are available for house 2.

TABLE 3.—*Data on house circles uncovered at site 2*

Measurements and observations	House No.					
	1	3	4	5	6	7
At depth of	12 in	15 in	9 in	16 in	16 in	22 in.
Diameter	14 ft	15 × 13 ft	18 ft	15 × 13 ft	20 × 17 ft	21 ft.
Floor	Hard, dark	Hard, dark	Very hard, black.	Hard yellow soil and sand.	Hard, black	Hard clay.
Number of post molds.	18	13(+8?)=21	19	27	42	None; floor outlined by heavy shell ring.
Depth of post molds.	2½–5 in	2–3½ in	2–5½ in	2½–4½ in	2–6 in	
Diameter of post molds.	2–7 in	3½–9 in	2–8½ in	2–6½ in	2–9 in	
Center posts	Off-center, near doorway.	1 near center.	2 between hearth and west wall.	2 near center.	2 near center.	2 clusters of 4 each near center.
Direction of door.	East	Northwest	North	North	North	South.
Fireplace	Clay basin with stones; at rear.	Stone hearth outside near door.	Clay basin near center.	Of clay and stones, near center.		
Square No	106/35	106/36	109/35	106/35	105/33 and 105/36.	108/33 and 107/33.

If the circular configurations are correctly identified as lodge sites, they would indicate that the characteristic dwelling was a round surface structure 14 to 21 feet across, built of light materials. The holes are so small and shallow that relatively small timbers only could have been set in them. There was no evidence of clay daub, which would indicate that the covering was probably of tules and grass. The absence of firepits from several and the tendency toward a north-facing door look a little strange unless these were intended primarily as summer habitations. In winter, winds blowing off the lake would have made them, if unheated, quite cheerless and uncomfortable. Other than these, however, there was no evidence of possible house sites of other types. This, too, seems curious since the rectangular form recorded for the plains Yokuts in historic times might be expected to show up archeologically.

The post molds scattered indiscriminately and in considerable numbers about each cleared level should probably be regarded as indications of posts for granaries, or for scaffolds and platforms erected to keep provisions and equipment out of harm's way.

Fireplaces marked by small clusters of stones, sometimes mixed with ashes, were a highly characteristic feature of the upper levels at site 2. These were most numerous at depths between 9 and 16 inches, but were found down to 36 inches. The type is illustrated in plate 14, *a*, which shows one of the better examples from the 24-inch level. They were mostly shallow, seldom over 4–6 inches in depth, and ranged in diameter from 1 to 4 feet. As shown in figure 11, they occurred frequently in proximity to and sometimes within the house circles. None came to light in the trenches or elsewhere below the alluvial stratum. This contrasts significantly with site 1 where they ran downward to depths of 6 feet or slightly more. Shallow ash-filled hearths without stones, from 12 to 36 inches across by 2 or 3 inches deep were present everywhere.

Equally characteristic of the upper levels at site 2 were the variously sized clay-lined basins and pits encountered above the alluvial stratum. These were generally readily distinguished from the stoneless hearths mentioned above, but their exact function is uncertain. Some were small (pl. 13, *b*), but there were others from 2 to 3½ feet across by 1 to 3 feet deep, usually with vertical sides and flat bottoms which were believed to represent roasting pits. Some contained fire-cracked and blackened stones (fig. 11), others only trash which had been thrown in to level off the spot. Many had served secondarily as grave pits (pl. 16, *b*), and in at least one instance the partially scorched bones suggested that interment had been made while the pit was still hot.

BURIALS (UPPER LEVEL)

Of the total of 108 burials found at site 2, all but 4 may be ascribed to the cultural manifestation represented by the upper 36 inches of material on the terrace. A few are listel at depths from the surface which would place them well below the alluvial stratum, to a maximum of 78 inches. These were found to be in pits whose walls were traceable up to the 34-inch or a higher level. In other words, it is believed that all interments considered in this section represent individuals buried by occupants of the terrace after deposition of stratum 4.

Burials for which sex and age could be approximately ascertained in the field fall into the following groups: adults, 61 (24 males, 18 females, 19 indeterminate); adolescents, 9; children and infants, 28. Here, as at site 1, there was a disproportionately large number of children and babies, though the actual percentage was considerably lower (28.5 percent as against 67 percent) and there were many more adults. At site 2, moreover, there were nearly 2½ times as many children in proportion to the total as at the nearby hilltop cemetery, site 4, again suggesting that it was customary to bury very young persons at the village site whereas adults were about as often carried elsewhere for sepulture.

As to posture of the body in the grave we have the following for 84 determinable burials:[16]

	No.	Percent		No.	Percent
Flexed	(73)	(86. 8)	Semiflexed	(11)	(13. +)
On back	35	41. 6	On back	4	4. 7
On right side	14	16. 6	On right side	2	2. 4
On left side	21	25.	On left side	4	4. 7
On stomach	3	3. 6	On stomach	1	1. 2

Since the majority of burials were from pits and cists whose diameter rarely exceeded 36 inches, there was a practical basis for the custom of flexing the corpse. Some of the bodies had been compressed into such small compass that one suspects they were bound into tight bundles with rope or cords soon after death. It is not known whether the burials were habitually wrapped in shrouds of tule or other native fiber, but five or six graves yielded some few traces which tend to support such a view. Drainage and soil conditions in the terrace and spit were hardly favorable to preservation of materials of perishable nature.

Burials seem to have been oriented with heads toward every point of the compass. In 92 identifiable cases the directions were as shown in the accompanying diagram (fig. 12). Here 57.6 percent were to-

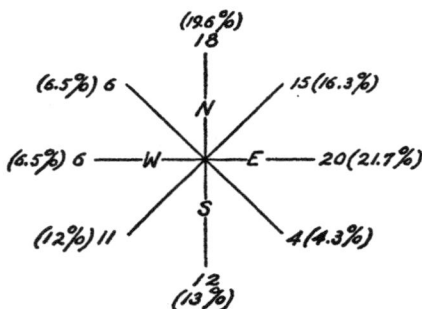

FIGURE 12.—Orientation of 92 burials at Buena Vista site 2.

ward the northeast quadrant (north, northeast, or east), the general direction least favored at the two hilltop cemeteries described in a future section. The southeast was used least commonly, west and northwest only a little more frequently. South and southwest were next in order of popularity after the northeasterly directions. Eighty-two percent of the individuals, in short, lay with the head

---

[16] Flexed burials have the knees drawn against the chest, the feet against the innominates ; semiflexed differ only in having the knees at a right or obtuse angle to the trunk.

either northeasterly or south-southwesterly, which hardly seems like a chance distribution. This does not conform to the distribution at any of the nearby sites currently described. However, it is not clear whether this reflects merely local preferences or has wider significance.[17]

Artifacts were found with 6 children, 2 adolescents, and 12 adults, but very young persons (7 infants) were unaccompanied by cultural material. Worked shell was found in 13 graves, bone in 7, chipped stones in 4, steatite and turtle shell in one each. Asphaltum-covered pebbles found in numbers with a female skeleton were probably used for asphalting baskets. Four other graves contained bits of asphaltum on basketry or native cloth, but the latter were too minute to be identified as to type. Other materials from the graves include red and white pigment, and bird wing bones found near the faces or necks of five adults and one adolescent. A summary of the burials accompanied by artifacts follows in table 4:

TABLE 4.—*Burials accompanied by artifacts found in site 2*

No.	Age	Sex	From level	Associated objects
			Inches	
8	Child		27	11 pierced fish vertebrae.
16	Adult	M	25	Flint scraper.
29	----do	M	12	Marine clamshell.
34	Adolescent		16	34 *Olivella* beads.
36	Child		29	1 abalone receptacle, 81 *Olivella* beads.
56	Adult	M	16	1 *Olivella* bead; pencillike steatite ornament.
62	----do	M	32	Stone knife; bone dagger.
65	----do	M	34	950 *Olivella* beads; 8 limpet ornaments; stone knife, drill.
66	----do	M	30	Stone knife.
72	Child		33	47 *Olivella* beads.
76	Adolescent		23	*Olivella* beads.
78	Adult	F	29	137 asphaltum-coated pebbles.
80	----do	M	28	90 *Olivella* beads.
84	Child		32	19 limpet ornaments.
85	Adult	F	16	Bone awl.
88	----do		26	1 abalone bead; 477 *Olivella* beads.
91	----do	F	19	Turtle shell.
94	----do	M	34	2 abalone beads.
104	Child		19	5 *Olivella* beads, 1 elk bone.
106	Adult	M	31	1,500 *Olivella* beads; 9 limpet ornaments; 2 abalone disks.

The typical upper-level burial at site 2 may be characterized as a more or less tightly folded bundle laid on its back or on one side, in an abandoned roasting pit or intentionally dug cist, head to east or north, possibly wrapped, and usually without grave furniture (pl. 16). So far as the associated cultural material shows, these burials all equate with the artifact types found in the general horizons from which the graves are believed to have been originally dug.

---

[17] "At Howells Point mound, Colusa County, a University of California expedition under the writer's direction in 1935 uncovered 58 graves in which 76% of the skeletons lay with the head to northeast or east." [Krieger, n. d.]

BURIALS (DEEP LEVEL)

Distinct as a type from the foregoing burials at site 2, and also from all others found at sites 1, 3, 4, and 5, were 4 interments definitely made from a living surface or surfaces beneath the alluvial stratum. These included Nos. 17 and 18, in square 108/32, at 76 inches; No. 28, in square 142/85, at 80 inches; and No. 40 at 101 inches. All were fully extended, 17 and 18 prone, 28 and 40 supine. Burials 17 and 18, respectively a child and an adult female, shared a common grave. No. 17 lay with the head toward the north; No. 18, apparently lying on No. 17, had the head to the south (pl. 15, *a*). No. 28 had the hands crossed over the pelvic region, with the head at the southwest end of the grave (pl. 15, *b*). No. 40, much the deepest, was badly decomposed but there seems no question as to the extended supine position. It lay with the head to the east, the grave evidently having been scooped out of the hard greenish underlying sandy clay. The bones of all four were thickly encrusted with calcareous matter. There was not the slightest evidence of wrappings, of paints, or of associated cultural materials of any sort. A few inches above each were thin unbroken beds of ash and calcined shell, indicating that the bodies had been interred in very shallow graves over which a thin layer of earth and rubbish was then piled. There is not the slightest question that the surfaces from which they were buried was much lower than that from which the upper-level graves were dug, in some cases probably as much as 6 to 8 feet beneath the latest living surface indicated.

MATERIAL CULTURE

Artifacts were surprisingly scarce at site 2, even where particular pains were taken to salvage any possible remains as in the camp site. The trenches yielded relatively little, and most of the graves contained no associated objects. The materials recovered comprised a shorter range of types than those from site 1, as well as a few which were absent at the latter. Number of specimens by types and their vertical distribution in terms of 12-inch (30 cm.) levels are indicated in the summary table.

WORK IN ASPHALTUM

There were 14 recorded occurrences of asphaltum at site 2. Four consist of small irregularly shaped lumps, which may have been analogous to the "balls" and patties at site 1. One of these is crudely spherical, 25 mm. in diameter, and has a deep dent on one side as from a stick or bone thrust into the mass while in a semiviscous state. A mass of small fragments may be from a similar but larger ball shattered during excavation. The other two lumps are small and shapeless.

Pebbles bearing a shiny coating of asphaltum and presumably used hot in waterproofing baskets were found six times.[18] As stated elsewhere, burial 78 (adult female) was accompanied by 137 such stones, filling a pocket 9 inches across by 4 inches about 7 inches from the skeleton. Another but smaller cluster including 7 specimens was in a post hole in square 106/35. The remaining four occurrences include as many single pebbles scattered through the terrace material from near the surface to a depth of about 3 feet.

Three hopper mortars, described in detail elsewhere, each bore a ring of asphaltum about the top. One was 16 inches, the others 19 inches beneath the surface.

A thin sheet of asphaltum covered with rows of small shell disk beads was recovered in square 112/43 at 18 inches depth One edge and what may have been an end is rounded and smoothed, but the exact form and appearance of the original mass has not been certainly determined. The reverse is flat, and appears to have been placed against a grained surface such as a smoothed board or similar object.

WORK IN BONE AND HORN

Awls.—These have been classified according to the scheme used at site 1. (See p. 40.) All three major groups and most of the subgroups were represented at site 2.

Type 1. As at site 1, the great majority of classifiable awls were made of whole and split mammal bones, though the actual proportion at site 2 was slightly lower (29 out of 33, or 90 percent). Subgroup A, wherein the head was left unaltered, includes but two specimens. Both were apparently made from the ulna of some medium-sized carnivore. They show little evidence of use. Specimens made from the cannon bone of the deer were absent.

Subgroup B includes two short stout awls, respectively 80 and 105 mm. long. In the longer one, split from the distal half of an antelope cannon bone, half the articular end still remains (pl. 22, *g*). The shorter and heavier one was apparently split from the proximal end of a heavier but unidentified bone (pl. 22, *h*).

Subgroup C is represented by four complete and one restored specimens. All were carefully finished. Four were made from split bones, the fifth from a whole bone. In length, four range from 90 to 133 mm. One certainly and a second possibly is smeared with asphalt about the head. To this subgroup has also been assigned a large daggerlike implement 262 mm. long (pl. 23, *a*), which has been worked in a manner identical with the smaller ones. It was held in the hand of burial 62, an adult male buried from the 32-inch level.

---

[18] Kroeber, 1925, p. 634.

Subgroup D includes two well-polished objects from which the head of the bone has been entirely removed. One measures 128 mm. and has a tapered butt (pl. 22, *u*) ; the other is 139 mm. long and has had the joint cut off (pl. 22, *v*).

Subgroup E. There are nine splinters of various sizes and shapes whose tips have been worked into awl points. The heavier specimens especially are highly polished from use, with the polish extending well up the shaft. As a rule, however, there is little modification beyond sharpening of the tip. The pieces range in length from 59 to 147 mm.

Subgroup F comprises 10 unclassifiable tips which if complete might make possible their inclusion in one or another of the preceding groups. All are sharply pointed, and seem to be from implements more carefully made than those of subgroup E. The largest, made out of the fibula of a deer or antelope, has an asphaltum plug in the narrow cavity at the broken end, suggesting that after breakage the sharp ends were treated with this substance so that the implement could be conveniently used for a time longer (pl. 23, *k*).

Type 2. Mammal-rib awls number only three, with subgroup A not present. From the edge of a large rib was fashioned the now broken specimen shown in plate 23, *q*, assigned to subgroup B. In addition there are two splintered rib fragments with ragged edges but highly polished tips. These measure 103 and 113 mm. in length; they are placed in subgroup C.

Type 3. The sole representative of this type (subgroup A) is a 68 mm. awl made, as at site 1, by cutting a bird bone diagonally near one end of the shaft and polishing this to a smooth point. The articular surface at the other end was retained unaltered for easier grasping (pl. 23, *s*). The species from which the bone was taken is unidentified.

· *Bipointed objects.*—To this category are assigned nine well-finished objects varying considerably in certain details. Most of them are pointed evenly at either end, but in four one end is somewhat blunted. The range in size and form may be judged from plate 24, *c–e, g–i*. One of the upper three in this illustration (*c*) has asphaltum smeared over about 28 mm. of the blunted end, and seems to have been set as well as lashed in this substance. It and the lower three specimens illustrated (pl. 24, *g–i*) suggest barbs for compound fishhooks. (Cf. Heye, 1921, pp. 83–86, pls. 51–53, figs. 10 and 11.) Of those shown, *c* (asphaltum-stained) is 83 mm. long; the smallest, *i*, is 30 mm. Of the remaining pieces, *e* seems too long (116 mm.) to have been so used. Not figured are three bipointed specimens 60 to 87 mm. long and fairly heavy, though not nearly so well smoothed as those illustrated. Whether they represent gorge hooks or are barbs from large compound hooks, I am unable to say.

Much the same range in form and size is recorded by Gifford and Schenck (1929, pp. 350–351 and pl. 76, *n–x*), who add as further suggestions for their use the following: as nose pins, hairpins, pin fasteners, and needles.

Horn.—Artifacts of horn were even scarcer here than at site 1. The single specimen found, and that not certainly an artifact, was the horn core of a bison noted 30 inches deep. The tip is somewhat worn, perhaps from improvisation as a flaking tool, but this is un- certain. The shaped double-ended flakers such as occurred at site 1, were wholly absent at site 2.

Pierced fish vertebrae.—From burial 8, that of a child, were taken 11 centrally perforated fish vertebrae with the edges carefully worked down (pl. 30, *f*). They average about 16 mm. in diameter, 8 mm. in thickness, and the holes are about 5 mm. across. Slight irregularities in the latter suggest that they were reamed or cut out rather than bored. The species of fish is unidentified. The verte- brae were scattered through the grave fill about the knees and legs of the skeleton.

Half of another similar but larger vertebra came apparently from the general diggings. Owing to a mix up in the catalog entries, its exact provenience is not known. In the field these objects were tentatively identified as beads. A more likely use is suggested by ethnography, however, since similarly worked salmon vertebrae seem to have been widely used by various tribes in northern California and elsewhere on the Pacific coast in playing the ring and pin game. (See Culin, 1907, pp. 542–543 and fig. 714 (Hupa); ibid., p. 553, fig. 731 (Umatilla) and fig. 732 (Shasta); Kroeber, 1925, fig. 14 (Sinkyone)). Heye (1921, pp. 11–113, figs. 20–21) found analogous forms at San Miguel Island, which he was inclined to view as beads or game pieces.

Pins.—There is some doubt as to the correctness of the name given three slender delicate bone objects, or even as to whether two were actually artifacts. One is 72 mm., with one blunt and one pointed end. Another measures 86 mm. but was once longer and may have been an awl. The third is a fish spine, 20 mm. long, very sharp and smooth. The proximal end has a small probably natural aperture which would have permitted its suspension as part of a necklace.

Sweat scrapers?—Here are included several objects made from the ribs of various mammals, all exhibiting a high degree of polish and use. The largest and most easily recognized are wide, thin, and flat, with exceedingly smooth surfaces and round edges (pl. 25, *b–d*). There are a number of other smaller variously broken frag- ments of split ribs likewise smoothed on both surfaces. Some are made from the unsplit rib. While mostly too fragmentary to be readily identified, these pieces are probably from specimens identical

with the few whole ones recovered. Their appearance is such as
to suggest that they were used in scraping greasy yielding surfaces—
perhaps the perspiring bodies of the natives after a session in the
sweat bath, though I have not been able to find published record of
such a practice for the southern San Joaquin or nearby regions
ethnographically.[19] It will be recalled that a few somewhat similar
specimens were found at site 1.

Tubes.—These number but five. Four are unbroken, undecorated,
have both ends squarely cut-off, and in general show a good polish.
From their lightness, they are probably of bird bone. In size and
proportion they fall well within the range of those from site 1;
the largest is 9 by 47 mm., the smallest 4 by 88 mm. All could have
been used as beads.

The fifth fragment is from a larger heavier tube broken at one
end. It is probably made of animal bone.

Whistles.—In contrast to their abundance at site 1, whistles at
site 2 were represented by a single example. It was 12 mm. in
diameter, with one neatly cut end, and has been broken at the vent,
a portion of which remains. There are traces of asphaltum near
the vent. It measures 52 mm. in length. In all essentials, it is
identical in type with those from site 1.

Miscellaneous.—This includes three thin, flat, well-dressed objects
for which no name suggests itself. One, possibly two, have or once
had points; they might have been awls but are much thinner than the
objects so classed in this paper. They are somewhat reminiscent
of the mat weaving needles of the eastern United States. A fourth
specimen is heavier, spatulate in outline, with a rounding well-worn
tip, and a rounded notch about 25 mm. above the tip.

Quite different is the piece shown in plate 24, *m.* It is made of
split mammal leg bone, the flat split side being down in the illustration. The rounding upper surface has a flat groove 15 mm. wide
by 3 mm. deep. The lower end is finished off square; the upper
begins to round off but has been broken so that the original conformations cannot be determined. It is unique from the site and
its use is not known.

There are two scraps of cut bone, evidently rejects, from the site.

WORK IN CLAY

A solitary example of the potter's art in our collections from site 2
was a small fusiform object 20 mm. in diameter by 16 mm. thick,
pierced at the thickest point with a 3-mm. hole. It is of soft, poorly
fired, reddish clay, and like the similar pieces from site 1, seems to

---

[19] Latta (unpublished notes) reports that the Yokuts used a curved elk-rib sweat scraper
18 inches long.

have been clumsily molded around a grass stem or wooden splint. Presumably it was used as a bead.

A faded black-on-white puebloan sherd was picked up by a watchman on the beach sands, but, because of its superficial provenience, is regarded as of no significance whatever in the aboriginal history of the site. Molded tule-wrapped objects, cylindrical forms, etc., were uniformly absent.

PIGMENTS

Red ochre in nonmetallic form, apparently prepared and made readily usable by mixing with clay, was fairly plentiful throughout the site generally. A lump of soft friable marl and a subhemispherical flat-bottomed object of allophane or white clay (amorphous aluminum silicate) may have been used as sources of white paint. There is one piece of yellow ochre.

WORK IN SHELL

As was the case at site 1, shell at site 2 was used seldom or never for manufacture of utilitarian objects. The specimens occurred as grave finds, less commonly as isolated pieces scattered about through the site. Identified species, all marine forms, include:

Olivella biplicata.	*Pachydesma stultorum.*
Megathura crenulata.	*Diadora aspera.*
Haliotis rufescens.	*Cardium quadragenarium.*
Haliotis cracherodii.	

All of these save the few bits of *Cardium* and the single whole shell of *Diadora* were represented in the artifact series.

Clamshell objects.—Small disks and short cylindrical beads comparable to those from site 1 were not found here. There are, however, four segments from large thick disks made of the shell of *Pachydesma stultorum.* Two complete enough to measure are each 10 mm. thick, and by projecting their respective arcs it is calculated the original disks were approximately 55–60 mm. in diameter. A third piece is about half of a 55-mm. disk, badly split, undecorated, with a 5-mm. biconical hole at the former center. The fourth is a sliver inadequate for reliable projection for size, but seems to have been from a specimen comparable to the others. All may have been pierced when in use. The edge of one bears simple incised decoration consisting of groups of vertical lines separated by wide (22 mm.) sections crossed by 2 converging lines (pl. 29, *i*).[20]

---

[20] Gifford and Schenck (1926, pl. 14, *i*) figure a similar but smaller disk from Pelican Island, on the north shore of Buena Vista Lake. I have excavated others of like character from a small burial mound in the Buena Vista slough region about 12 miles north of McKittrick. The latter specimens are now in the Museum of Anthropology of the University of California, Berkeley.

There is a smaller complete disk probably also of clamshell. It measures 31 by 4 mm., the thickness varying considerably, and has a conical central perforation 4 mm. in diameter. This is undecorated.

Haliotis.—No abalone disk beads were found. However, spangle disks were present—thin fragile objects from 8 to 15 mm. across with holes whose diameter about equalled the radius of the disk. One was set in asphaltum. A thicker 20 mm. piece, except for its size and weight not markedly different, was designated a ring. Found only at site 2 were two large unpierced and undecorated subcircular "disks," one 33 by 39 mm., the other 50 by 56 mm. (pl. 29, *f*, *g*). Pendants include a 35 by 27 mm. triangle with pierced apex, and two oblong or oval pieces with one end perforated. Another oval object 16 mm. long has a central hole with short incisions about the rim which, if continued, would intersect at the center (pl. 28, *g*). Beside these, there is one perforated scale of *Haliotis* and two large unworked or rejected fragments of *H. rufescens.*

Of particular interest as indicating a probable direct trade importation is a small specimen of *Haliotis cracherodii* in which three of the six siphonal openings have been plugged with asphaltum (pl. 30, *g*). The edge is chipped from wear or careless handling, but not in a manner suggesting use as a scoop. The piece measures 87 by 104 mm. It is identical with the smaller vessels of abalone shell frequently recovered in the Santa Barbara coast and island sites, where they were used as seed containers, paint receptacles, for storage of asphaltum, etc. (Wheeler Survey, 1879, pp. 115–116 and fig. 37; Heye, 1921, pp. 118–119, figs. 22 and 23, pls. 73 and 74; Harrington, 1928, pp. 146–147, pl. 24; Rogers, 1929, p. 396.) It and a necklace of beads accompanied child burial No. 36.

Keyhole limpet.—Objects made from limpet shell (*Megathura crenulata*) were appreciably more common here than at site 1. Twenty-one specimens show only moderate grinding which produced medium to large oval ornaments 37 to 68 mm. long. Nineteen of these, covered with a rusty brown scale, came from the grave of burial 84, presumably as the remnants of a necklace (pl. 29, *d*). Of the other two, both from the general digging, one shows slight but indubitable traces of red ochre (pl. 29, *e*). It bears a curious resemblance to certain painted specimens reported by Heye from San Miguel island (Heye, 1921, p. 156 and frontispiece).

In 27 other specimens the original shell has been ground away until only fragile oval rings remain, these not exceeding 27 mm. in length and some as small as 12 mm. Fifteen are from two graves, including nine from burial 106 (pl. 29, *a*) and six from burial 65 (pl. 29, *c*). The remainder came from the general diggings (pl. 29, *b*); ten were found in square 112/43, but dissociated from any grave. As a whole, the type compares with those of the Santa

Barbara region. (Wheeler Survey, 1879, pl. 13, 67; Heye, 1921, pl. 71; Harrington, 1928, pl. 25; Rogers, 1929, pl. 71.)

Olivella.—Most abundant are beads of *Olivella* shell. They include the same three types represented at site 1, viz, whole spire-lopped, perforated or punched half-shell, and small concave centrally pierced disks. Half-shell beads include numerous slightly lipped specimens somewhat smaller and more carefully perforated than those at site 1, but the larger rougher form was also present. The smaller half-shell beads intergrade with the disks, and may represent an intermediate stage in manufacture of the latter (Gifford and Schenck, 1926, p. 59). Because the line separating the two types is not always sharply drawn, the count made of each for the summary table must be viewed as an approximation only.

An interesting but rare variant of the disk, found only at site 2, is characterized by its extreme minuteness of size (pl. 27, *a*). Their diameter is under 3 mm., that of the hole not over 1 mm. Because of this pronounced reduction it is not known of what shell they were made, though they are here classed tentatively as *Olivella*. With some plausibility Gifford and Schenck speak of this type as ". . . in reality rings which are quite different from the large disks. Such rings may have been made for inlaying or bushing as on the Santa Barbara coast" (Gifford and Schenck, 1926, p. 60; Harrington, 1928, pl. 26, *h*). At site 2 the rings occurred in quantity only twice: burial 65 yielded upward of 730 averaging about 2–2.3 mm. in diameter, and burial 106 had between 1,200 and 1,500 of slightly larger size. In both instances the beads were scattered about the head and neck, while some of those with burial 65 still contained traces of a hemp (?) cord upon which they were once strung. It is uncertain from the record whether these were merely necklaces or were perhaps sewn to some sort of since-vanished headgear. In view of their close similarity to the small rings of the Channel region, it may be significant that the two burials with which they were found also were accompanied by southern type limpet ring ornaments.

The few examples of inlay work found at Buena Vista consisted of small disks averaging slightly larger than the rings just described, but in no case exceeding 4–4.5 mm. in diameter. The best example, in which disks about 3 mm. in diameter were set in rows in a sheet of asphalt, has been described elsewhere. Possibly the tiny rings were occasionally used in like manner.

WORK IN STEATITE

Worked steatite occurred to a maximum depth of 5 feet at site 2. Of 50 specimens on which this discussion is based, 42 (84 percent) were found from the surface to a depth of 2 feet, and only two are certainly from a depth greater than 3 feet. This means that fully

95 percent of this material was above the sterile alluvial stratum.

Both fine-grained and coarse varieties of stone were encountered here. Their possible sources have been considered in the description of site 1 and need not be reviewed again.

Arrow straighteners.—Three of these were found. All are oval in outline; the two largest have one flat and one convex surface so that in profile they have a roughly hemispherical form. The largest is 153 by 77 by 40 mm., with a single transverse groove on the convex surface. The second is 114 by 68 by 38 mm., with the flat under side worn smooth as though from grinding or rubbing. Its convex face shows traces of two transverse grooves, but the specimen has scaled off so badly that this point is somewhat uncertain. The third specimen is also flattened and has been broken at the transverse groove, of which about half remains. It measures 75 by 50 by 26 mm., of which the first dimension may be taken as representing approximately half the original full length. All are made of the coarser variety of steatite.

Bars.—This group includes five variable specimens. The finest is a well-finished double-pointed object 77 mm. long (pl. 37, *c*). It tapers evenly toward either end from a maximum diameter at the center of 8–10 mm. A second bipointed piece, 57 by 13 by 8 mm., has an encircling groove slightly to the side of center and bears an incision on one side between this groove and the tip. The other specimens are circular to squarish in cross section, shorter than the above, and of various sizes.

Disks.—Five complete and two fragmentary circular objects, unlike any from site 1, were found. Three of the whole ones and both fragments were pierced centrally. The largest (pl. 37, *a*) was 81 mm. in diameter with a 14-mm. perforation from which 22 irregular and unevenly spaced scratches radiated outward to the rim. The smaller pierced specimen in the same illustration, *b*, measures 52 mm. and has an 11 mm. perforation. The two fragments are from disks of about this size but have much rougher surfaces. The third pierced piece is only 33 mm. across with a 3-mm. hole, and is not as well shaped as the preceding.[21]

Two unpierced disks are 65 (pl. 37, *f*) and 56 mm. in diameter. All, including the perforated type, are from 8–10 mm. in thickness. Their purpose is unknown.

Groove-edged objects.—In contrast to their abundance at site 1, these curious forms were all but absent at site 2; only one was recognized. It may be classed as type 2 (see p. 56), characterized by a complete encircling edge groove with the convex surface subse-

---

[21] According to Latta's unpublished notes, the Yokuts suspended from their ears steatite disks 1–4 inches in diameter with center and edge perforations.

quently ground down until the remaining concave surface presents a flangelike appearance in profile. It measures 42 by 30 by 15 mm.

There were no steatite labrets at site 2.

Reellike objects.—This type was represented by four examples. The two best specimens are shown in plate 37, *d, e*. They are respectively 44 and 37 mm. long, and resemble in every respect those from site 1. A third is much narrower but has deeply notched ends, and the fourth has one upright of the H entirely ground away.

Tube fragment.—There is one fine-grained steatite fragment which appears to be part of a large tubular pipe or sucking tube. It includes part of the finished lip, was well smoothed on the outside surface, and still shows portions of the bore. Identity is uncertain owing to its very incomplete nature (pl. 37, *g*).

Vessel sherds.—As at site 1, only part of the sherds unearthed were retained for study purposes. There were no whole or restorable vessels. So far as can be ascertained from the rim sherds present, only wide-mouthed vessels and shallow bowls were made. There are two rim fragments of coarse steatite from large deep bowls in which the wall below the lip attained a thickness of 25 mm. or slightly over. By projecting the curvature of the remaining arcs it is estimated one of these bowls must have been 275–300 mm. in diameter by roughly half as much in depth. A third smaller sherd of similar coarse stone is inadequate to reconstruct the original size or form.

Fourteen sherds of finer stone are well under 15 mm. thick. Here the lip is usually rounding; in four specimens it is relieved with fine cross incisions or notches. Only two show the evenly spaced holes below the lip, so common at site 1. Mostly these seem to be from moderately deep bowls. The largest by projection is from a vessel 180–200 mm. across by perhaps 70 mm. deep. These appear in general to manifest a somewhat better finish and technology than is found in the wares at site 1.

Miscellaneous objects.—Unclassified but worked objects include about a dozen specimens. One cut triangle 50 mm. on each side and pierced in two corners may have been a pendant or weight (pl. 37, *h*). A similar use might be imputed to a thinly ground oval piece pierced at the small end and apparently twice at the opposite end (pl. 37, *j*). Otherwise, the miscellaneous group includes variously shaped cut, pierced, and scored fragments which may have been improvised as sinkers, weights, or for other purposes.

WORK IN CHIPPED STONE

The raw materials used for chipped artifacts at site 2 are about the same as those at site 1—variously colored jaspers, cherts, and some obsidian. However, the light gray chert so frequently employed at the latter for the manufacture of small projectile points is very much less common. Perhaps consonant with the smaller volume of mound material handled, chipped implements were only about a third as numerous at site 2.

In marked contrast to the profusion of small delicately fashioned leaf-shaped (NAb1) and triangular (NBa and NBb) points at site 1, site 2 yielded mainly heavier and cruder forms. Type NAb1 predominates, but the examples are much inferior to the corresponding form at site 1. They range from 35 to 75 mm. long, 15 to 28 mm. wide, and from 6 to 10 mm. thick. At site 1 even the larger knives and blades seldom approached this thickness, and projectile points proper are mostly between 3 and 5 mm. Chipping at site 2 is coarser and blades in cross section are thick and lens-shaped. Specimens of this type include 12 of obsidian and 30 of other material. The two largest, doubtless knives, each measure about 100 by 35 mm. (pl. 40, e, f); one is of obsidian, the other of dark brown chert with the base slightly asphalted. They are virtually identical with certain forms at site 1.

Type NBb is next in order of abundance among unstemmed points with a total of 19. These approach in technique and proportions the characteristic form at site 1. It is probably significant that 15 occurred in the uppermost 12 inches, where they exceed in number any other types. The largest specimen is 42 by 16 mm., whence they range downward to 18 by 9 mm. Seventeen other fragments, not counted in the summary, are either from this group, or else belong with four small NBa points. Five larger and heavier points have been assigned to type NAb. The smallest is 18 by 34 mm., the largest 52 by 24 mm. Three have "fish tail" bases, and are vaguely reminiscent, in outline only, of the Folsom point.

We may note here a piece from a large broken blade with slightly concave base and straight finely serrate edges (pl. 40, g). At present it measures 164 mm. long, 45 mm. wide at the base whence it tapers very gradually to a width of 40 mm. at the broken end. Both surfaces exhibit traces of the limestone matrix which formerly inclosed the chert vein from which the specimen was cut. It is remarkably similar in most respects to the large spearheads described from Dos Pueblos by Abbott (Wheeler Survey, 1879, p. 52 and pl. 3) and to a number of complete pieces from the Santa Barbara region now in the United States National Museum (U.S.N.M. Nos. 15189, 21629-32, 62484). Complete specimens from this locality are from 37 to 50 mm. wide at the base and from 175 to 260 mm. long, a range into which the Buena Vista piece readily fits. It seems quite reasonable to view the latter as a trade article from the south, or at any rate, as due to direct influences from there.

Stemmed points and blades form a considerably larger proportion of all chipped forms at site 2 than at site 1. Classifiable pieces number about 45. Nearly half, 20 to be exact, belong to type SAa. These vary considerably. Four are almost diamond-shaped, and there is some uncertainty whether they should not properly be separated into a group as NC. The others, however, show a rather clear differentiation of stem and blade, the latter being generally larger and heavier with more or less rounding shoulders. In size they range from 17 by 38 mm. up to about 37 by 75 mm. A larger specimen, probably a knife, measures 100 by 35 mm. (pl. 40, *f*). The larger ones tend to be fairly thick and heavy but most are thin enough to have had considerable penetrating power. Green, gray, and black chert, and red and brown jasper were the usual materials employed. Eleven other specimens have had the shoulder worked down so far that they are grouped as SAc. All are under 75 by 23 mm. and have been worked to a thinner profile than the preceding type. They could have served as spear or lance heads, or as knives. Five well-made specimens have rather pronounced barbs and fall into group SAb. The largest is 60 by 23 mm.

Other rarer stemmed types include SBb (2), SBc (2), SCa1 (2), SCa2 (1), and SCa3 (1). In addition there are a great many fragments exhibiting workmanship but too fragmentary to be classified. Probably the majority of these are from unstemmed leaf-shaped flints (NAb1) or closely similar forms, though other types were no doubt present. These broken specimens, along with miscellaneous spalls and scraps outnumber the classified pieces but because they defy classification have been omitted from the table. It may be noted that there is a somewhat higher proportion of obsidian here than at site 1, although most of it was from the upper 2 feet of deposit. There were also nine pieces of worked quartz porphyry, of which only two or three could be classified.

Crescentic flints.—Six in number, these are all of gray chert. Mostly they include about half or somewhat more of the original object (pl. 39, *w*, *x*), but one is complete save for a tiny chip off one end (pl. 39, *y*). This measured 50 by 18 mm.; three of the fragments are from somewhat larger examples. They seem to have been bilaterally symmetrical, i. e., a line drawn through the short axis or midline would divide them into two essentially identical halves. The ends are rounded, not pointed, and the curving edges between have been retouched to varying degrees of fineness. There seems to have been no attempt at producing fine serrations. In form they are vaguely reminiscent of some of the "Stockton curves" made of obsidian in the lower San Joaquin drainage (Gifford and Schenck, 1926, pl. 95, *a*, *h*), but this superficial likeness is offset by the presence in the latter of serrations, of at least one sharp tip, of frequent notches as for suspension or fastening, of nonsymmetrical proportions, and by the characteristic difference in material used. The purpose of the Buena Vista crescentics is unknown. One was found in our dirt piles, the others are from depths of 36 to 40 inches.

Perforators.—There are eight objects which may be classed as expanded base drills. Two, and possibly a third, suggest type 2a at site 1 (see fig. 7), differing in that they are broader and more nearly almond-shaped. They measure 62 to 70 mm. long and 23 to 33 mm. wide. Two others, broken, resemble type 3. The other three cannot with assurance be classified further.

In addition there are eight fragments which are either from straight drills with diamond to elliptical cross sections or, with equal plausibility, shafts from expanded base forms whose basal portions have been broken away and lost. Eight of these specimens were in the upper 12 inches; the deepest was found at 66 inches.

Saws.—These objects, 15 in number, are made of gray chert, and are similar in all respects to the sawlike specimens from site 1. All are fragmentary, with a few small enough to pass as knives. Because of their general uniformity and close resemblance to the much larger series from site 1, however, they are here grouped together. Their probable use in cutting steatite has been discussed elsewhere. At site 2, as at site 1, their vertical distribution generally parallels that of steatite.

Scraper knives.—To this group are assigned some 50 artifacts comparable to the larger collection at site 1. Only a few are as well shaped as those from the latter, however. They are subcircular or oblong with rounded corners and quite thin. The majority are little more than spalls with retouched edges. Only three bear traces of asphaltum. Most may have been improvised for temporary use and ready discarding. As a whole, they impress one as makeshift devices rather than as a well established and abundantly used type such as that represented at site 1.

WORK IN GROUND STONE

Balls.—Four spheroidal objects made of sandstone or other hard crystalline material were found. All are somewhat irregular and none rolls evenly on a flat surface. The largest (pl. 44, *h*) is 49 mm. in diameter; the smaller ones are 28 and 25 mm. (pl. 44, *f*, *g*). The smallest is flattened and has a shorter diameter of about 18 mm. Their possible use in certain games, as among the historic Yokuts, has been mentioned elsewhere.

Charmstones.—In proportion to the total number of artifacts, plummetlike forms at site 2 were relatively far more numerous than at site 1. Their abundance exists only in relative degree, however, since but eight specimens came to light at site 2. This would seem to be in line with the rarity of the general type in the Buena Vista Lake region as noted by Gifford and Schenck (1926, p. 97).

Of the eight examples recovered none was complete, although two are substantially intact save for marred tips. Five bulbous midsections are present. Most nearly complete is one of diabase 116 mm. long by 36 mm. in diameter, in which the maximum diameter appears to have been near or at the center of the specimen. One end is broken off; the other swells slightly and is crossed by a shallow notch. It is the most symmetrical and best finished of the series (pl. 44, c), and possibly conforms with Gifford and Schenck's (1926, p. 94) type WBb5. Another, of white limestone, has a much thicker somewhat lemon-shaped body 43 mm. thick; the shoulders are rounding and there is an even taper toward either end, both of which are missing (pl. 44, a). With one, or possibly two, exceptions the other body fragments suggest slender evenly tapered plummets like the first specimen described above, but all lack extremities and hence cannot be certainly classified. There is also one unclassifiable tip. None shows any evidence of ever having been perforated. All are of limestone, sandstone, or diabase, usually rather carefully (but not exceptionally well) shaped and finished. They seem to be of Gifford and Schenck's 1926, p. 94 and pl. 34) type WBb–, i. e., unperforated with plain pile (secondary curves) at both ends. Because the ultimate subtypes in this classification rest on the shape of the tips, mostly missing in our specimens, it cannot be determined whether they belong further with WBb1, WBb3, WBb4, or WBb5.

Hammerstones.—To this class more properly designated as unworked stone are assigned nine well-rounded elliptical waterworn boulders with battered ends and/or edges. Eight are of granite, the ninth of sandstone. They are generally smaller than mullers, the largest (24 oz.) being 112 by 70 mm. Further, they lack the flattened grinding surface which usually readily distinguishes the latter. They evidently represent naturally shaped stones picked up because of their convenient size and shape and for their toughness and resistance to fracture. They were found to a depth of 5 feet.

Half of an elliptical block of gritty gray sandstone bears two shallow grooves which run lengthwise of the piece. They suggest secondary or auxiliary use as an awl sharpener or other abradant.

At a depth of 10 inches was found a quartzite discoidal 77 by 67 by 38 mm. It is flattened, and each face has a shallow pit 3 or 4 mm. deep by about 45 mm. across. There is no evidence of battering or other hard usage around the edge. Its use is uncertain.

Mortars.—The comparative scarcity of these objects, as at site 1, was in keeping with the largely negative ethnographic evidence for the locality. Three whole and three broken specimens were recovered, two of the latter being discarded subsequently. Both of these were small; they came from a depth of about 12 inches. For the remaining four mortars the characteristics have been given in table 5. With them is included a sherd possibly from a sandstone bowl. From the standpoint of vertical distribution, it should be noted that two mortars were found at the 5- to 6-foot level, well below the alluvial deposit; the others were above the latter.

TABLE 5.—*Mortars and bowl from site 2*

Measurements and observations	Specimen No.				
	2–697	2–211B	2–160	2–158	2–223
Diameter	Unequal; lower smaller.	Greatest at neither top nor bottom.	Same as 2–211B.	Same as 2–211B	Irregular boulder.
Upper diameter	206 mm	196 mm. (outside of rim); 240 mm. (maximum).	108 mm. (outside of rim); 124 mm. (maximum).		222×166 mm.
Lower diameter	145 mm				
Height	183 mm	180 mm	81 mm		144 mm.; less than diameter.
Sides	Straight	Convex	Convex	Convex	Irregular.
Cavity:					
Diameter	235 mm	170 mm	Ca. 85 mm	(?)	155×118 mm.
Depth	145 mm	107 mm	Ca. 35–40 mm	Ca. 85 mm	Ca. 65 mm.
Lip	Flat, squarish; no outward slope.	Rounded and thin.	Rounded and thin.	Rounded and thin.	Rounded and thin.
Rim	Ca. 20 mm. wide; undulating and irregular, edges worn through use.				
Bottom:					
Shape	Flat	Rounded	Rounded	Rounded	Irregular.
Thickness	Ca. 38 mm	Ca. 72 mm	Ca. 40 mm	Ca. 28 mm	Ca. 80 mm.
Finished	All over	All over	All over	All over	Inside only.
Material	Basalt (?)	Sandstone	Sandstone	Sandstone	Sandstone.
Condition	40 percent missing; fracture mended with asphalt.	Complete; edge chipped and battered.	Rim badly crumbled.	Sherd only, rim to bottom.	Complete, rim much worn.
Remarks	Mortar	Mortar or bowl	Mortar	Bowl	Mortar.
Provenience:					
Square	112/39	119/34	Tr. 1 W. 65 ft	Tr. 1 W. 75 ft	Tr. 1 W. 31 ft.
Depth	14 in	12 in	66 in	22.5 in	62 in.
Reference: UCPAAE, v. 23, No. 3, 1926.	Type 2; p. 245 and pl. 50, a.	Type 4; p. 246 and pl. 50, c.	Type 4	Type 4	Type 5.

In addition to the above, there were three examples of the hopper mortar. None of these is available for detailed description but the following data concerning them have been gleaned from the field records. One (field cat. No. 2–123) was a large boulder, asphaltum-encrusted, lying right side up at a depth of 16 inches in trench 1. The second (No. 2–870), with an interior diameter of 8 inches (20 mm.) and asphaltum around the rim, was in square 109/37 at 19 inches depth. It had been smashed into three pieces. The third (No. 2–434), of white sandstone, lay inverted 19 inches underground in square 108/25. Shallower than the others and apparently made from a boulder just large enough to close the bottom of a hopper, it was completely encircled with asphaltum which here and there still bore the faint impression of coiled basketry. As might be judged from the figures given as to depth, all lay a foot or more above the alluvial stratum, and their earliest noted occurrence was thus considerably after the unasphalted mortars.

Mullers and metates.—At all depths from the surface to 9.5 feet were encountered complete and fragmentary mullers or manos, to a total number of 15. Though the sample is relatively small, significance undoubtedly attaches to the fact that they occurred to a greater depth than any other recorded artifact type. There is considerable variability in form, size, and proportions, but nearly all can be described as roughly elliptical in outline with one (or two) well-worn flat surface(s). About half the examples in the series at hand present two flattened grinding surfaces. The rest are rounding in more or less degree on the upper grasping side. With exception of a small sandstone object possibly used for rubbing instead of grinding, all the mullers are of tough granite. In size they generally fall under 130 by 110 by 50 mm., though individual specimens may exceed one or another of these measurements. The type is adequately illustrated by the specimen in plate 43, *h*; others have been figured by Gifford and Schenck (1926, pl. 31).

Three of the flat or slightly depressed mealing slabs, with which the mullers were in all likelihood used, were also found. Neither the specimens themselves nor adequate photographs are now available but they approached quite closely one figured elsewhere from the east side of Tulare Lake (Gifford and Schenck, 1926, p. 91, pl. 30). All were of sandstone, and one had been used for grinding on both sides. They were found in trench 1 at depths of 2, 2.5, and 5 feet.

A word of explanation is in order at this point relative to the vertical distribution of mullers and mealing slabs. Owing to the peculiar and very local erosive agencies at site 2 the figures on depth as they stand are misleading. In the summary table, for example, 10 mullers are recorded for the upper 4 feet. In reality, the field notes show that virtually all of these specimens were found beneath the present beach in the very hard "plum pudding" or closely contiguous soil layers. Wherever mullers occurred in the terrace, they were much deeper and consistently below the alluvial horizon (stratum 4, fig. 10). As elsewhere stated, there is a very strong likelihood that the terrace front has been subjected to considerable wave action which has pushed it back toward the hills. So far as absolute elevation above sea level is concerned, the shallower mullers were in very nearly the same plane as the deeper ones under the terrace. In other words, if the alluvial stratum be extended on its present plane some 30 or 40 feet out toward the lake all of the mullers would be found to underly it by several feet. This, I am inclined to believe, is near the truth of the matter. By the same token, the mealing slabs recorded at 2 and 2.5 feet below the present beach originally lay at much greater depths and well below the alluvial bed. They may, therefore, have as great an antiquity as the single specimen actually found, at a depth of 5 feet, beneath stratum 4 in the terrace. In short, mullers and mealing slabs probably represent an early complex in very large part antedating the break in occupation manifested at site 2 by the sterile alluvial bed (stratum 4).

Pestles.—Twelve pestles were unearthed at site 2, but in sharp contrast to the mullers, none was found at a depth greater than 39 inches. Nine are certainly of hard gray to dun sandstone, a tenth possibly so; the others are of granite. Typographical differences are slight and apparently do not correlate with depth or other significant factors.

Two especially massive pestles are subcylindrical; i. e., their greatest diameter is in the middle whence they taper slightly and about equally to either end (pl. 47, *e*). Both ends are rounded and they could have been used interchangeably. From their general appearance they were termed "roller" type in the field, but the term has no functional connotation. Both are well made. The remaining 10 are tapered, but fall roughly into two subgroups on the basis of proportions. Two are long and relatively slender, with a more or less pointed or slightly rounded handle, and have a flattish cross section. The larger is 292 by 70 mm.; the smaller and more carefully finished is 229 by 35 mm. (pl. 47, *f*). Otherwise the tapered pestles are shorter and thicker; they range between 110 and 180 mm. long, with a maximum diameter at the grinding end of about 45 to 65 mm. (pl. 47, *a*). The only specimen at site 2 which shows any specialization of the handle is illustrated in plate 47, *a*; it is of smoothed granite or diorite with slightly enlarged handle. There were no ringed or otherwise elaborated specimens and the series generally conforms closely to those previously recorded for the locality (Gifford and Schenck, 1926, p. 92).

Miscellaneous.—This includes two small flattish pebbles pitted, perhaps by man, on one and both surfaces. There is a well-smoothed object of crystalline stone with flat oval cross section and measuring 45 by 20 mm. Both ends are broken, so that the original length and shape, like its purpose, are unknown.

WORK IN WOOD

Four pieces of wood are included in the collections from site 2. The largest has one pointed end; the other end is broken and has a large cavity suggestive of the hearth of a fire-making set. However, the piece is worn smooth and has evidently been subjected to much wave action. Since it is catalogued as coming from a depth of 4½ inches it may have been washed in quite recently.

Three other fragments from depths of 2–3 feet, according to the field catalog, resemble juniper. One looks suspiciously like an aged piece of planed and sawn lumber such as might have come from a thin packing box. I am unable to explain their alleged depth if this suspicion is correct, but, nevertheless, have grave doubts that any can safely be viewed as evidence of aboriginal wood working.

SITE 3

Site 3 was situated on a round-topped hill about 2,000 feet south and a trifle east of site 1 at an elevation of 420 feet above sea level. It occupied the highest and most conspicuous point within a distance of nearly a mile from the lake shore (pl. 1, *a*). To the east and west the ground slopes away into dry gullies; northward, a saddle connects the hill with a lower knob (elev. 370 feet) directly overlooking site 1. From the village site at the lake's edge it is a comparatively easy climb via this lower ridge to the burial ground 120 feet above, the trip being made regularly by our laborers in cars after the scrub brush had been cleared away. To the southwest, another saddle connects the burial hill with the higher mass of the main Buena Vista Hills.

The burial ground was discovered after a systematic search of several days during which every knob and ridge within a thousand yards of sites 1 and 2 was tested. Surface indications were of the scantiest sort—a few weathered shell beads and a human molar, but two long cross trenches intersecting at the summit soon revealed an unexpected plenitude of skeletal remains underground. By a singular stroke of fortune, these graves seem to have been wholly untouched during all the years the two shell heaps below were being plundered by relic hunters. This circumstance made possible an unusually detailed study of burial methods and practices—an opportunity alloyed only by the lamentably fragmentary and deteriorated condition of the bones and to some extent by the paucity of diagnostic accompanying artifacts.

From 6 to 12 men were regularly employed at this site from December 22, 1933, to January 23, 1934.

The area occupied by the burials measured approximately 70 by 48 feet, with its long axis running west-northwest by east-southeast (fig. 13). In depth the remains ranged from 8 to 48 inches. They were scattered through a loose sandy fill which overlay the very much harder "country rock" (Tulare formation) of which the hills generally consist. At the east and south limits of the excavation the compact Tulare was scarcely a foot below the surface, but it dipped irregularly under the cemetery to depths of more than 6 feet on the west and north edges. Within the sandy area were occasional small pockets of coarse partly consolidated gravel and gypsum in which few burials occurred, owing, probably, to the difficulties of excavating graves into such soil with the tools available to the natives.

The condition of the skeletal remains, as already indicated, was uniformly poor. In most cases, the bones crumbled away as exposed, often showing less resistance to brushing than did the enclosing matrix. Disposition of the body could generally be inferred with reasonable certainty but relatively few satisfactory photographs were obtained. Likewise, only a few of the skulls were in condition suitable for detailed study despite the liberal use of shellac on all likely looking specimens. This advanced stage of distintegration can probably be attributed to the porous nature of the sandy deposit in which the burials lay and to the lack of proper drainage due to proximity and surface irregularity of the immediately underlying Tulare. Another factor was the frequent practice on the part of the natives of disturbing existing graves in the excavating of later pits with attendant disturbance of the skeletal arrangement and frequent fracture of bones. This habit likewise precluded a stratigraphic approach to the relative age of the various burials, since later interments were in many cases deeper than the earlier, in others shallower. Consequently no attempt has been made to separate the burials temporally on the basis of depth or position in the cemetery. The vast majority probably date from the same general period and occupancy, and, as will be brought out elsewhere, are thought to represent a lapse of not more than a century.

The summary description which follows is based on field records for 348 burials. Several of these were double, including mother and child or other combinations which would raise the total number of individuals to about 356. Owing to lack of standardized data sheets and to the lack of special training on the part of many of the workers, at least during the earlier part of the work, the records contain an unfortunately high percentage of unreliable observations. Attention has been duly called to these shortcomings as they enter into the discussion. Despite these limitations, it is believed the remaining records are sufficiently extensive and accurate to give a good insight into the burial complex at this site.

Of 356 individuals represented, 122 (34 percent) were tentatively identified in the field as adult males, 131 (37 percent) were unsexed adults (mostly females or weak males?), 17 (4.7 percent) were adolescents, and 15 (4.2 percent) were children. For 71 (20 percent) there are no reliable data, either because they were too incomplete or for other reasons. The proportion of children seems much too low, but this may be owing to the generally less durable nature of their bones and a consequent greater susceptibility to decomposition. In this event, obviously, the few children's graves listed is not a true index to the original number interred here. As will be brought out presently, there are strong evidences that site 3 was closely affiliated with the uppermost levels at site 1, perhaps representing the main burying ground for the latter. In this connection it is probably significant that the majority of graves found in the shell heap at site 1 contained the remains of infants and children, which suggests that persons deceased early in life may often not have been carried to the hilltop cemetery but were merely laid away in some convenient place nearer at hand.

Interesting, too, is the fact that at site 3, as at site 1, there were no evidences whatever of extended prone or supine burials. Of the total of 356 individuals, 50 (14 percent) are listed as "indeterminate" (i. e., were disturbed, etc.) or "no data," 27 (7.6 percent) as secondary reburials, and 20 (5.7 percent) as crania only. Thus, 97 (27.3 percent) yielded no information as to burial method. The remainder have been divided into two unequal groups on the basis of degree of flexure exhibited by the skeletons. Flexed burials are those in which the body was compactly folded into the smallest possible volume, typically with the knees against, or nearly against, the chest, the feet against the innominates, and the arms against the sides of the trunk (cf. burial 28, site 4, pl. 18, b). Semiflexed burials differ in that the knees are at a right or obtuse angle to the trunk; usually the feet here, too, are drawn against the innominates and the arms close against the body (pl. 17, b, c). Semiflexion occurs about twice as often as full flexion. The flexed or semiflexed bodies were laid in the grave in any of several further positions, as follows:

Flexed:	No.	Percent of 354	Semiflexed:	No.	Percent of 354
Upright ("seated")	5	1.4	On back	132	37.3
On back	53	15.0	Side not stated	33	9.3
On right side	2	.6			
On left side	1	.3		165	46.6
Face down	1	.3			
Side not stated	21	5.9	On back, flexion indeterminate or not stated	9	2.5
	83	23.5	All others	97	27.4
			Total	354	100.0

From these figures it is evident that partial or complete flexion (nearly 70 percent), with the body usually on the back (ca. 55 percent), was the characteristic method of interment.

As to orientation of the individual deceased, i. e., direction of head in relation to body, the gross figures indicate no very marked predilection for any one direction unless perhaps for the west. Here again there is an unfortunately large proportion of unclassifiable (because indeterminate or unrecorded) data, the total of 98 (27.5 percent) being nearly identical with the figure for burials whose mode of body flexion could not be ascertained. Also, there were many borderline cases so that the groupings here given are to some extent arbitrary. No attempt was made to record the directions in which the various skeletons faced.

Head to:	No.	Percent of 356	Head to:	No.	Percent of 356
North	25	7. 0	West	72	20. 3
Northeast	6	1. 7	Northwest	37	10. 4
East	23	6. 3	Indeterminate or		
Southeast	22	6. 2	no data	98	27. 5
South	42	11. 8			
Southwest	31	8. 7	Total	356	99. 9

Omitting from further consideration the 98 unclassifiables, we may represent diagrammatically the number and revised percentage of the remaining burial directions as shown in figure 14. From this it appears that burials were oriented to every point of the compass,

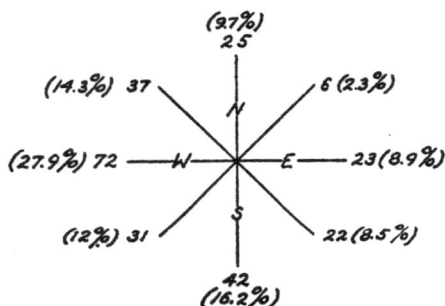

FIGURE 14.—Orientation of 258 burials at Buena Vista site 3.

least commonly toward the northeast (6 times, or 2.3 percent) and most often toward the west (72 times, or 27.9 percent). That a general westerly or southerly direction was probably intentionally sought is indicated by the fact that over 70 percent of the determinable burials were laid with their heads to the northwest, west, southwest, or south, showing a rather decided preference for this half of the circuit. In this connection it may be recalled that at site 2, the northeast quadrant (north, northeast, east) included 57.6 percent of the 92 determinable positions against less than 21 percent so placed at site 3. Also the northeast-to-south half the circle included 36 percent as against 55 percent at site 2.[22]

---

[22] Heye (1921, p. 38) states that during his excavations on San Miguel Island, "Of the undisturbed skeletons practically all were found lying on their backs, with arms and legs flexed and the skull directed toward the west. . . ." I am not certain whether this refers to all or only part of the 343 skeletons (p. 34) found. This apparently consistent orientation may be of little significance, however, as Rogers (1922, p. 377) reports the Canalino burials as having the "heads pointing in every conceivable direction of the compass." Whether the seeming preference for certain directions at the Buena Vista sites is a purely local matter, or on the other hand reflects more widespread practices at different periods is a question whose solution is not yet at hand.

Turning now to the matter of grave furniture, we note first that no less than 271 burials (76 percent) were accompanied by traces of woven textiles or tule, or both. It is not clear just how this material was used in the graves. With one or two doubtful exceptions, the tule does not appear to have been actually woven. I am inclined to believe that unwoven masses of this readily available rush may have been placed in the bottom and about the sides of the newly dug grave pit as a bed for the corpse to rest on. There was some indication that a similar layer may have covered the burial bundles, at least in a few instances. The woven textile, a soft twined brown vegetal material, may have come from bags or shrouds, or possibly both. The extremely poor preservation of these remains makes their certain interpretation impossible. It may be suggested, however, that most of the deceased, after flexion, were perhaps wrapped first in soft native woven cloths, following which they were placed on, under, or between layers of unwoven tules, to be finally covered over with sand and earth.

Two hundred and twelve burials, save for the occasional presence of textile or tule fragments, contained no artifacts. Projectile points only were found with 31, but it was generally impossible to ascertain whether these were offerings, personal possessions, or a result of arrow wounds. Materials in all likelihood interred intentionally with the corpse were thus limited to 112 instances (31.8 percent). These included chiefly work in shell, but asphaltum, ochre, steatite, and other substances were present as well. It is scarcely necessary to state that these were not mutually exclusive, i. e., that two or more materials sometimes occurred together in the same grave. Distribution of materials and the number of graves containing each may be summarized as follows:

Materials:	Number of graves	Materials—Continued.	Number of graves
Objects of shell	58	Steatite beads	15
Objects of *Olivella*	35	Basketry fragments	9
Objects of abalone	19	Wood (posts)	9
Objects of clamshell	16	Sandstone objects	6
Other or unidentified objects	13	Bone beads	4
Objects of chipped stone	53	Pebbles	4
Objects of chert and jasper	47	Bone pendants, etc	2
Embedded in bones	12	Charred roots or tubers	2
Objects of obsidian	5	Wooden "balls"	1
Ochre	28	Burnt-clay fragments	1
Asphaltum	25	Quartz pebble	1

In 22 instances projectile points accompanied one or more of the other materials. Asphaltum was nearly always present only as a smear or stain or, if in larger masses, as an adhesion to textiles or basketry. Ochre likewise occurred principally as coloring, usually intentional, on textiles, but there were also a few lumps presumably representing unutilized pigment. Curiously enough, the catalog and field notes show that a number of graves yielded only one to a dozen small shell and steatite beads, which would probably have been overlooked altogether except for their proximity to the skeletons. Such small numbers certainly do not suggest necklaces or even armlets or anklets, but they could be remains of small ear ornaments or similar trinkets. On the other hand, they may be nothing more than stray pieces which escaped destruction in the last funerary rites to which the property of the deceased was consigned.

By comparison with the richly furnished graves of the Santa Barbara region (Heye, 1921, p. 38; Rogers, 1929), those at site 3 on Buena Vista Lake yielded remarkably little. This point, if not sufficiently obvious from what has been said previously, may be further emphasized by a list of the more prolific burials and their accompanying cultural materials as shown in table 6. Probably 25 percent or more of all artifacts came from these eight graves.

TABLE 6.—*Burials and associated objects from site 3*

No.	Age	Sex	Associated objects
3	Subadult	♀(?)	Woven textile; red ochre; 25 abalone pendants; 88 *Olivella* disk beads; steatite beads.
16	(?)	(?)	Tule; 53 clamshell beads about wrist; 1 stone bead; 1 asphalted basket fragment.
20	Adult	♀	Tule and textile; 150 *Olivella* disk beads.
41	(?)	(?)	200 *Olivella* disk beads; abalone pendant; few steatite beads.
102	(?)	(?)	Tule and textile; 900+disk beads; 9 abalone pendants; 25 miscellaneous shell beads.
254	Child	(?)	Woven textile; 178 *Olivella* beads; 24 clamshell beads; 2 abalone pendants; 1 bone bead; 1 projectile point.
256	Youth	(?)	Tule and textile; large broken jasper blade; ochre; few shell beads.
302	Adult	(?)	Tule and textile; ochre; 100+disk beads; 3 abalone pendants.

Field notes and specimens for 13 burials of infants and small children are at hand. The most lavishly furnished, No. 254, has already been described. Another, No. 231, had 100 *Olivella* beads. With a small infant, No. 92a, buried with an adult female there were 8 steatite beads. No. 6 had "a number of small clamshell and *Olivella* beads," and around the neck of No. 2 were several bone beads. All of these were further wrapped in tule and/or textiles. Of the remainder two yielded one shell bead each, one a sandstone bowl fragment, the others nothing. Since children comprised only 4.2 percent of the total number of individuals found, it is probably true that the relative number of specimens accompanying such burials is somewhat higher than for adults. But the difference is not striking, and there seems scant reason to assume from our evidence that any especial regard was entertained by the natives toward their deceased offspring.[23]

[23] Heye (1921, p. 38) observes that during his excavations at San Miguel Island "more than 12,000 beads and ornaments of shell were found, and of these about ninety-six per cent accompanied the skeletons of children."

Mention has already been made of the occasional presence of one or more arrowpoints firmly embedded in the bones of various skeletons. This feature was seen in no less than 12 graves. Where sex determination was possible these individuals were found to be males. Most striking was one bearing the field catalog No. 3–206A, a normal male who, judged by skull characters and wear of teeth, must have been of middle age. Those bones directly concerned we preserved with shellac. One point lay in the spinal canal at the second and third cervical vertebrae with its shattered tip protruding into the region of the first cervical. The arches of the lower vertebrae were missing hence the path of the arrow, if actually shot into the individual, could not be traced. In the remaining bones there were no signs of injury and the point could conceivably have worked into this position after death. Not so with several additional points, however. A second was at the level of the intervertebral space between the sixth and seventh cervicals. It appeared to have entered from the left, cutting the body of the seventh cervical just above the point of attachment of the pedicle. The tip was missing. Projecting into the spinal canal, this point, while probably not inflicting a fatal wound, could have caused partial paralysis, and, given time, might have started infection. Of more serious nature was a third point shot from the left rear so that it shattered the left lamina of the second thoracic and penetrated its body, presumably severing the spinal cord and inducing paralysis. A fourth point, in itself of minor effect, was lodged in the twelfth thoracic, having grazed the left side after entering from slightly to the right rear.

It is interesting to note that the embedded projectile points, at least in this particular case, all seem to have been shot from the rear. For the other similarly stricken individuals there are virtually no data at hand, due to the fact that the carefully treated bones containing the points disappeared under mysterious circumstances from our field laboratory. It was found, however, that the points in every instance were of NBb type (triangular, with concave base), practically indistinguishable from those which characterized the upper levels at site 1. This suggests that the males who thus carried several arrowpoints to their graves were former members of the community, perhaps unsuccessful shamans sent to their last accounting by disgruntled fellow tribesmen.[24]

One other feature of the burial ground remains to be described here. Scattered about among the graves, especially in the central portions of the area, were short lengths of wooden posts, probably juniper, from a few inches to 2 feet in length (see fig. 13). In diameter they ranged

---

[24] ". . . The repeatedly unsuccessful [Yokuts] medicine man stood in danger of his own life, and it appears that violence was the end of members of the profession as often as among most California tribes . . ." [Kroeber, 1925, p. 516.]

from 2 to about 5 inches. In several instances it was observed that they stood more or less upright in proximity to one or more skeletons (pl. 17, *a*), and that the upper ends were apparently charred. According to information supplied in the field by Latta, the historic Yokuts erected juniper posts above the graves and suspended therefrom such offerings as beads, baskets, and other articles. It seems reasonable to view the timbers revealed by our excavations as the stumps of markers or supports used in some such fashion. Their partial carbonization may have been due to burning of the post and associated objects during or after the mourning rites.[25]

Generally absent at site 3 were extended burials, cremation, clear evidence of dug grave pits, and any trace whatever of glass or metal attributable to European or American trade contacts.

Work in Bone

Of the small tubular bone beads found with a few of the skeletons there is not the slightest trace in the collections which reached the United States National Museum. It is possible they vanished from the field laboratory along with the human bones stuck with arrowpoints.

Otherwise, the sole specimen of worked bone was a thin triangular pendant accompanying burial 258. At its widest part this measures 39 mm. Its present length is 125 mm. but since the tip is broken off the original measurement may have been 10–20 mm. more. The corners are rounded; one corner and the center of the top (short side) have each a 2-mm. perforation. The opposite corner is undrilled. All three edges as well as both larger surfaces have been carefully smoothed. At what must have been the approximate middle of the unbroken specimen, it is crossed on one surface by three irregular rows of small holes pricked into the bone. Between these and the wide end are three zones of similar dots forming cross-hatched (lozenge-shaped) and vertical chevron designs. These zones are separated from each other by double rows of dots, with a single row bordering the broad end of the object as well. The lines of dots are not very regular, and there is no evidence that the holes were ever filled with paint (pl. 21, *b*). The reverse bears no decoration.

This particular decorative technique, which was found on no other specimens from the Buena Vista locale, is strikingly reminiscent of that reported on certain objects of bone and shell from San Miguel Island (Heye, 1921, pl. 67, *c*, and fig. 16; pls. 70, 106–110).

Work in Shell

Beads and ornaments of shell, besides occurring in more graves than any other category, were also the most numerous by far.

---

[25] Walker, E. F. (1935, pp. 145 and 148, reports similar juniper stubs at a post-European native burial ground, probably Yokuts, in the Elk Hills, some 6 or 7 miles north of our site 3.

Olivella biplicata seems to have been preferred. Whole spire-lopped shells included but seven specimens, only one of which was under 15 mm. long. Half-shell beads were absent. Disks ranged from 5 to 12 mm. in diameter, some of the larger examples being deeply concave with suggestion of a slight lip. Unlike those from sites 1 and 2, beads from the cemetery were usually in poor state of preservation. Their crumbling and partially disintegrated character makes classification and description difficult, and often it is well-nigh impossible to differentiate between *Olivella* and clamshell disks. Some of the sets obtained, perhaps representing necklaces (pl. 30, *e*), seem actually to have included both the thin-cupped *Olivella* and the thicker flat clamshell disks. Clamshell was certainly used for such beads as have a thickness equal to or in excess of their diameter (pl. 30, *d*). In no case is the length more than twice the diameter; the maximum dimensions represented are 17 mm. in length and 8–9 mm. in diameter. These cylindrical or tubular beads occurred in several graves along with the more common disks.

Haliotis shell is present in the form of pendants of various shapes and sizes. As at site 1 these include both circular and rectangular (or oblong) forms. None have central perforations. Circular and subcircular pieces range from 25 to 40 mm. across, usually with one, two, and three edge perforations. Where there is more than one hole, they may occur on opposite edges. Oblong to subrectangular pendants vary from 20 by 11 mm. up to 60 by 45 mm. A few of the larger ones are relatively narrow, including especially a series of 25 from burial 3 (pl. 28, *j–l*). One of the latter has a milled edge. Characteristically, there are two 2-mm. holes at one end; two or three have holes at both ends. None is painted or otherwise ornamented. There is also a slender curving fragment 50 mm. long, evidently cut from the lip of an abalone shell, with a 1-mm. perforation for suspension near the intact rounding upper end. Its former length is, of course, conjectural. Like its analogues from the shell heap at site 1, it recalls one of the types so common on the Santa Barbara coast.

An oval edge-pierced pendant with red ochre stains has been cut from the shell of *Pinctada fimbirata*.

There are no limpet shells or circlets made therefrom from site 3.

WORK IN STEATITE

From 16 graves were taken small gray to black beads made of serpentine or some similar-appearing fine-grained soft stone. For the most part these accompanied burials which also had shell, textiles, or other cultural material. The largest set from a single burial included eight specimens, according to the field count. Possibly half those found have since been lost or mislaid, so that only about 25 are available for description. The smallest is 3 mm. in diameter by 1 mm. thick, with a hole about 1 mm. across, thus comparing favorably with the tiny shell rings from site 2. The others are from 4 to 6 mm. across by 2–3 mm. thick. All are nicely circular, with squared edges, but in several the two flat surfaces are not exactly parallel when seen in profile. Only two or three have rounded sides, i. e., tend to be somewhat barrel-shaped.

There is one larger stone ring 10 by 4 mm. which may not be steatite.

Of different type are the two small pulley-shaped and perforated objects shown in plate 31, *h, i.* The smaller is 4 mm. thick by 7 mm. across; the larger measures 13 by about 5 mm. Both are biconically pierced a little off center. The encircling groove in both specimens, seen in profile, is a slight rounded   , from 1 to 1½ mm. deep; it is not so well polished nor so dark in color as the surfaces which would be subjected to the most handling. One each occurred with burials 15 and 222.

WORK IN CHIPPED STONE

At site 3 chipped-stone artifacts were confined almost entirely to projectile points. About 97 complete and fragmentary specimens were obtained from 44 graves. There is some discrepancy here between the catalog and the field data, as the latter distribute chipped flints, either exclusively or along with other objects of shell, bone, etc., among 53 graves.

Thirty-one pieces, nearly all tips, defy classification. The overwhelming majority of the remainder, to the number of 64, are of NBb type—mostly evenly tapered with more or less finely serrate edges and concave base. An exceptionally graceful slender but otherwise good example of this type is shown in plate 38, *k; j, l, m,* and *n* are representative. Eight are of obsidian, the rest of chert or, rarely, jasper. They are essentially identical in size, form, technique, and variability of basal concavity with the same type from site 1. In fact, the two lots are so similar that were they mixed together, it would be wholly impossible to separate them without recourse to the catalog numbers. This near identity and the decided preponderance of the type at sites 1 and 3 tend to link the burial ground (site 3) with the upper portions of the midden at site 1.

The other points include one leaf-shaped NAb1 specimen with broken tip, which also finds congenial company at site 1 in the type occurring second in order of abundance there. There is also one NBa of quartz porphyry, and the basal portion of an SAa of the same material with notched or bifurcate stem.

Probably the unclassified tips, judging from their shape and workmanship, are from other small unstemmed NB– points.

The large fragment of chipped blade found with burial 256 deserves further comment. It is of very dark gray banded chert or jasper. Presumably it was broken elsewhere than in the grave as the missing tip was never recovered. The remaining piece (pl. 40, *d*) has a rounding base from which straight edges converge evenly toward the fractured end. At present it is 180 mm. long, but judging from the degree of taper this would represent only about half the former length. It has a width at the base of 45 mm.; at the break, of 33 mm. Maximum thickness is about 13 mm., with a thick lenticular cross section. As may be seen in the illustration, bits of asphaltum adhere to the base, and on the side shown, these bear faint impressions of a cord wrapping or lashing. Along the edges on both surfaces are smears of bright red ochre as much as 8 mm. wide, which continue onto the asphaltum only to the edge of the string imprints. The flaking is generally good, at least by comparison with most of the larger chipped objects from the locality. The edges are carefully retouched and sharp, showing little evidence of usage.

All things considered, it is difficult to regard this specimen as utilitarian in function. It is possible that it, like other items at Buena Vista Lake, was manufactured elsewhere and reached the valley through trade. Here again we may look toward the south. There are in the national collections a number of similar narrow blades from the Santa Barbara region with rounded base and straight edges, which range in width from 27 to 37 mm. and in length from 165 to 250 mm. Most of these taper gradually to within a few centimeters of the tip, where the edges curve toward each other rather abruptly. If the piece from Buena Vista was finished in like fashion, it may well have fallen within the range of sizes here represented. Interestingly enough, there are traces of string-impressed asphaltum on the base of one of the broken examples from Santa Barbara, which is 193 mm. long, 35 mm. wide at the base, and 30 mm. at the break (U.S.N.M. No. 62480). Several of these "ceremonial" blades from Dos Pueblos have been illustrated elsewhere (Wheeler Survey, 1879, pls. 1, 5–7) and from the accompanying description it is clear that the type is essentially identical with the lone piece from Buena Vista site 3.

WORK IN GROUND STONE

During the earlier phases of work at site 3 a well-finished pestle was found in one of the exploratory trenches near or at the ground surface. This was about 200 feet south of the burial ground proper and may never have been directly associated with the graves. It is of very hard crystalline stone, 185 mm. long. The flat working end is 58 mm. across and tapers evenly to a handle about half as large.

OBJECTS OF UNWORKED STONE

These were three in number. One is a smoothly worn flattish oval pebble, too hard to be scratched with a steel knife blade. It measures

130 by 55 by 23 mm. The broad end shows some traces of use for battering or pecking. It was found on the chest of a disturbed burial, No. 302. Another somewhat similar limestone object, 70 by 48 by 23 mm., accompanied a male burial, No. 15. The ends are battered. There is also a small subspheric object of calcareous sandstone about 25 by 23 mm.; owing to confusion in the catalog entries its exact provenience is not known.

TEXTILES AND BASKETRY

Textiles, cordage, and basketry fragments were encountered at sites 1, 2, 3, and 4. Except for an occasional impression or piece preserved in asphaltum or clay, however, such substances were but scantily represented at the two habitation areas. With a single infant burial (No. 22) at site 1 were detected traces of fabric; six burials out of 108 at site 2 (Nos. 88, 98, 100, 103, 104, 106) yielded similar evidence. By contrast, the cemeteries, perhaps because of their higher drier elevation, their more recent use, or for other reasons, gave much more freely. As already stated, at site 3 no less than 271 interments seem to have been wrapped in tules and/or woven shrouds, and at site 4 at least 38 out of a total of 64 were apparently treated in like fashion. The materials recovered at site 3 comprise much the largest series, and appear to be representative of the finds at the other sites. Accordingly all woven textiles and textilelike items will be considered in this section. An unusually complete basket from site 4, which was preserved intact in a plaster and burlap cradle, will be described elsewhere with the other materials from that cemetery.

Tule.—Many of the graves opened contained masses of fibrous material at first thought to be shredded juniper bark. Ultimately, as more and better information accumulated, it was decided that this was actually tule, which after partial decomposition and whitening seems to assume a superficial resemblance to bark. Its manner of occurrence with reference to the burials has already been described. Despite careful examination in the field, it was wholly impossible to detect any crossing or intertwining of elements. The few samples preserved for further analysis in the laboratory likewise defy attempts to establish the nature of the weave, if indeed the material ever was worked into a true textile. A single exception is a small mass from burial 7 which appears to have twined wefts. Possibly the advanced stage of decay has obliterated such traces in other instances, although the writer has excavated from other mounds in the Slough region specimens about equally rotten wherein twined weft elements could be unmistakably discerned. All in all, it seems safe to assume that the tule was placed, unwoven, in the grave under and around the corpse to protect after a fashion the corpse and other contents.

Soft twined textiles.—The inner body wrapping, occurring sometimes alone but usually along with the tule, is of markedly different character. It is much like textile fragments commonly obtained by amateur excavators in the burial mounds of the Buena Vista and Tulare Basins, and may be the same as that somewhat noncommittally designated by Gifford and Schenck as "brown vegetable fibre." Positive identification of the archeological specimens seems difficult to obtain. Three representative samples from site 3 were submitted to the National Bureau of Standards, with the following results under date of December 11, 1934:

The specimens of woven material from archeological finds in California were examined microscopically.

Samples marked 2 and 3 are woven entirely of a plant material which resembles the raffia commonly used by horticulturists and florists and in certain art work. Raffia is not fibrous in the strict sense of the word, but is a surface material produced by stripping the epidermis of the leaves of palms of the genus *Raphia*, native in Africa, Madagascar and Brazil. According to Dodge (Useful Fiber Plants of the World, U. S. D. A. 1897) epidermal strips similar to raffia may also be produced from the leaves of many other species of palm.

The only palms known to be native in California are *Washingtonia robusta* and *Erythea edulis*, the latter commonly supposed to be found wild only on Guadelupe Island, but recently reported elsewhere in Southern California (Dr. Miriam Bomhard, Forest Service). The Washingtonias have a very narrowly restricted range in the canyons around the base of San Jacinto Peak in Riverside County extending northward into San Bernardino County to Corn Springs and southward to Carrizo Creek in San Diego County (L. H. Bailey, Cyclopedia of Horticulture).

It is also possible that this material could have been obtained from the leaves of the yuccas, of which Mr. L. H. Dewey of the Bureau of Plant Industry tells us there are at least four species common in Southern California.

The specimen marked No. 1 is woven of this same material but contains occasional threads of black animal fiber. It appears also to have been lined with a thinner fabric woven entirely of this hair. The badly crumbled condition of this black material makes it impossible to identify, but we are convinced that it is probably horsehair or human hair. It is much too coarse for rabbit hair or wool, and has some slight characteristics of alpaca.

San Jacinto Peak lies far to the southeast of Buena Vista Lake, a journey by foot of probably more than 180 miles. The abundance of native textiles in the San Joaquin would seem to argue strongly for a nearer source of raw materials. Of the two possibilities suggested in the report above, yucca would appear to be much the more likely, since the plant grows abundantly within a short distance of Buena Vista Lake. Ethnography offers several other possibilities. Kroeber says that the fibers of the common milkweed (*Asclepias*) were commonly used by the Yokuts for making string, and suspects that wild hemp (*Apocynum*) may also have served.[26]

---

[26] Kroeber, 1925, p. 534. Latta's unpublished notes also mention milkweed fiber string. Local collectors refer to the grave textiles as of "wild hemp."

With an abundance of these materials close at hand it is not likely the earlier natives would have gone far beyond the mountains in search of exotic fibers.

Detailed piece by piece analysis of all textiles recovered has not been attempted here, but a general examination leads to the conclusion that with a very few scattering exceptions the material is of simple weave and without much variety. The fibers vary in color from light to dark reddish-brown. They have been twisted on each other, usually but not exclusively to the right, into a moderately fine 2-ply string. This was used for both warp and weft in the preparation of woven articles. Characteristically, these are in plain soft twined technique, running from 9 to 15 warps and 10 to 20 wefts per linear inch (pls. 48, 49). Some of the coarser and more open weaves seem to be the result, at least in part, of the disappearance of some other fiber or substance, probably human hair. So far as noted, the only exceptions to the characteristic plain twined weaving are found in a number of pieces containing bands or small zones of wrapped twining, apparently for decorative effect (pl. 50, *a*). I am not aware that this particular technique has been recorded heretofore for the southern San Joaquin Valley.

Despite the lamentably fragmentary condition of all woven fabrics found, which precludes anything save conjectures as to size, form, and selvage of the original articles, it has been possible to reconstruct small portions of decorative zones in a few examples. These were usually achieved in one of three ways. Most frequent was the use of a black weft, probably human hair, worked into the fabric in a variety of serrate, stepped, triangular, diamond, and narrow line designs. Black was also used in plain twining either as paired wefts, or as a single element in conjunction with a brown unit. In the latter alternative, brown and black surfaces appear successively on any given side of the fabric. Less common was the use of black elements in wrapped twining. Much less frequently, weft elements were dyed red or pink before weaving; or bands of red ochre were applied to the finished fabric. In the case of dyed yarns, these seem to have been paired with undyed so that the finished design is in pink and natural brown colors. I have not found any evidence of dyed or naturally black string other than human hair. The third type of ornamentation resulted from the occasional use of undyed brown elements in wrapped twining (pl. 50, *a*), usually in combination with black units.

In figure 15 are shown nine design motifs woven into twined bags and/or other fabrics from site 3. Some of these, especially such relatively intricate patterns as *f*, *g*, and *h*, are approximations only, reconstructed as accurately as the material permitted with use of a hand lens. The motifs, as illustrated, were developed in black against a brown background. In the first two examples, the black and brown zones were separated by narrow stripes of red. Areas left plain in the drawings represent the natural brown background. They are shown in the correct proportions so far as specific warp

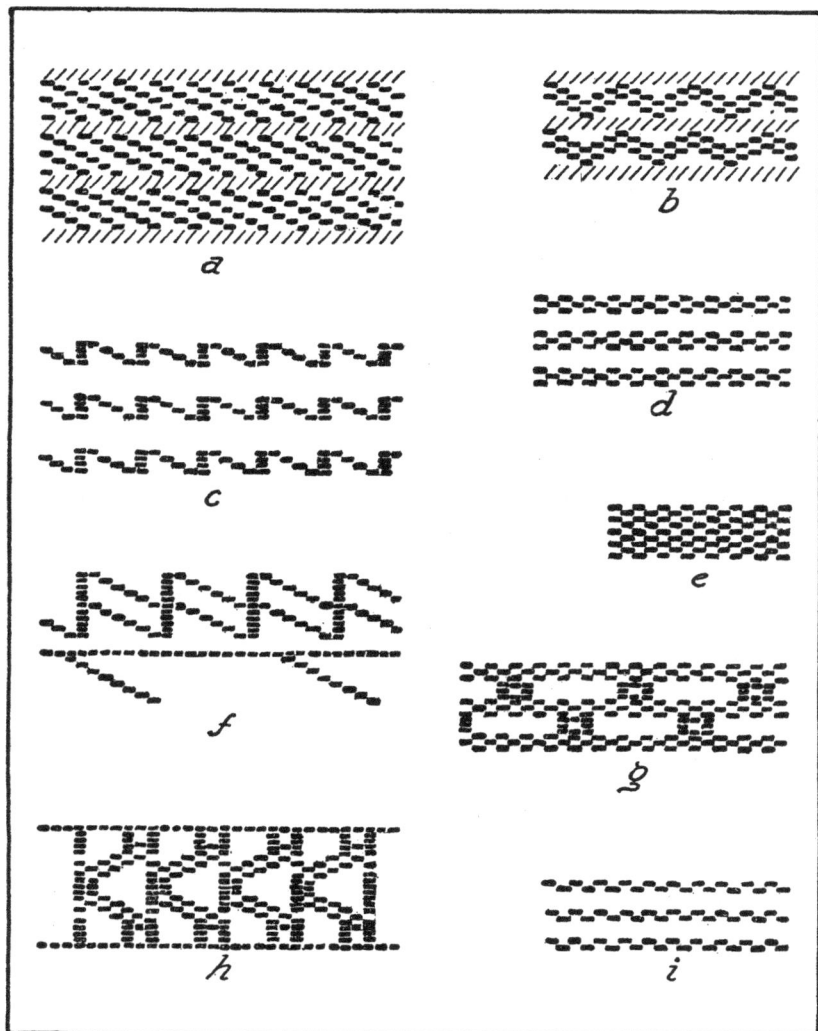

FIGURE 15.—Black and red (hachured) designs in soft twined textiles from Buena Vista site 3: *a*, U. S. N. M. No. 380594; *b*, *c*, *d*, U. S. N. M. No. 380598; *e*, *f*, 3–248 (field No.); *g*, U. S. N. M. No. 380591; *h*, U. S. N. M. No. 380596; *i*, U. S. N. M. No. 380592.

and weft units are concerned, but the actual proportions differ slightly from those in the originals. That is to say, figure 15, *f*, for example, is somewhat narrower vertically in the reconstruction than is actually the case in the fabric itself. Nevertheless, they may afford some slight archeological evidence as to the decorative art of the prehistoric Buena Vistans as reflected in their textiles.

As to the articles into which these fabrics were made there is little evidence. In materials, technique, decoration, and perhaps other details the specimens under consideration closely resemble some of the twined bags and other objects described by Gifford and Schenck.[27] The latter specimens were excavated by Nelson at a burial ground in the Elk Hills 6 or 7 miles north of site 3, and are in much better preservation than ours. A few fragments from site 3 have radiating parallel warps and probably represent bags similar to the Elk Hills specimens. Others may be remnants of shrouds, shawls, blankets, or other large pieces.

There are a few examples of twisted 2-ply cordage and several of braided black hair. The latter suggest unwoven material, or conceivably were intended for use as fringes. There was no tule rope or cordage.

Basketry.—In striking contrast to the profusion of soft-twined fabrics at site 3, only three or four small bits of basketry were recovered. All owe their preservation either to a degree of carbonization or to a protecting smear of asphaltum or other mucilaginous matter. Though treated in the field with shellac, they are so crumbly that positive determination of structure is exceedingly difficult and identification of materials used impossible. Two fragments have been identified as coiled ware (pl. 50, *c*) seemingly with a foundation of grass stems. Examination under a hand lens shows no examples with rod foundation. The sewing element appears to have been either a coarse grass or strips of bark. I have not been able to ascertain whether the stitches merely interlock or whether they also pass through the bundle above, but the former seems the more likely alternative. It is utterly impossible to even guess at the shape of the original vessels.

One and perhaps several other small bits of basketry were evidently made by plain weaving, using a twisted 2-ply warp foundation. While the weave is identical with that in the soft fabrics, both warp and weft consist of much heavier elements (pl. 50, *d*). As a result, the finished product was considerably stiffer and coarser than the bags (?) and shrouds (?). This technique was more clearly evidenced by a number of pieces at site 4, in which section appear further relevant details.

WORK IN WOOD

From burial 55 were taken two flattish wooden objects with circular outline and apparently artificially shaped or at any rate fin-

---

[27] Gifford and Schenck, 1926, pp. 102–103. For illustrations of design motifs resembling those at Buena Vista site 3 compare our fig. 15, *h*, with their pl. 7, fig. 15, *c*, with their pl. 10, and fig. 15, *d* and *i*, with their pls. 8 and 9.

ished off by human agency (pl. 51, *a*, *b*). The smaller is about 50 by 37 mm., having a shape much like that of a hulled black walnut. It has split into two pieces since excavation, and the surface is rough and crumbly. The other is about 62 by 40 mm. with an irregular surface. Where the surface is broken away the grain is seen to be very gnarled, the piece evidently having been made from an (oak ?) burl. Possibly the smaller is likewise a natural excrescence, though the grain is much more regular. Their purpose is uncertain, but it seems possible they represent shinny pucks, wooden forms of which have been reported from the Yokuts in historic times (Kroeber, 1925, p. 538; Latta, 1929, and unpublished notes). Perhaps they are too small to have been so used.

Of particular interest is an irregular wooden slab 7–10 mm. thick bearing traces of red paint and of shell disks inlaid in asphaltum. Its shape and general appearance can best be judged from the illustration (pl. 51, *c*). Both sides have essentially the same decorative features. Just below the rounded and red painted upper end is a strip of asphaltum in which was set a row of pierced disks averaging about 4 mm. in diameter. A similar row follows down the curving side whose edge was also painted red. A larger disk 9 mm. in diameter was set on the surface 25 mm. from the top and an equal distance from the splintered edge (right edge in the illustration). From this disk two lines of bead-impressed asphaltum radiate to either side. The areas between the inlaid strips generally have traces of red ochre, and on the surface shown the upper zone still has a few adhering disks. For the most part, the asphaltum bears only circular impressions the disks having become unseated and lost. The specimen is probably not complete, nor is it possible to say what its original size, shape, and purpose may have been.

Somewhat similar to the above, at least insofar as they involve the technique of inlaying asphaltum strips with small disks, are several circular shell ornaments figured by Heye from San Miguel Island (Heye, 1921, pl. 112).

SITE 4

From the hill located farthest to the east on our key map (fig. 2), the observer may enjoy one of the finest views to be gotten anywhere in the vicinity—or at any rate, could prior to reclaiming of the lake bottoms. Toward the north, east, and south the ground slopes away to the lake 75 feet or more below. Hence, the eye could travel eastward across the waters of Buena Vista and Kern Lakes to the distant snow-capped Sierras, while toward the southeast the Tehachapis and San Emigdios formed a soft blue backdrop to a broad expanse of flat grass lands. The sweeping panorama thus afforded was exceeded in extent but scarcely in impressiveness by the outlook from the slightly higher hill to the west whose summit was occupied by site 3.

On the east slope of this hill, where a slightly lower point directly overlooks the ancient habitation area at site 2, was situated the second major burying ground to be examined. It lay at an elevation of 355 feet above sea level, about 50 feet higher than and approximately 550 feet west of the main excavations at site 2 (pl. 9, *b*). Airline, this point was about 2,600 feet almost due east of site 3. The approach from site 2 was not a difficult one, involving at the worst a climb of some 35 feet in about 50 yards and a more gradual ascent for the remainder of the distance. Easier but longer paths were also available if desired.

The area occupied by graves measured about 37 feet east to west by 32 feet, within which were found 64 burials ranging in depth from 5 to 56 inches (fig. 16). The fill by which they were surrounded consisted of two rather well-defined strata overlying the hard yellow clayey country rock (Tulare formation). At the crest of the knoll, from the ground surface to a depth of about 38 inches was a stratum of dark ashy sand and gravel containing many small fire-blackened pebbles. Below this was a 10- to 12-inch water-laid stratum of loose yellow sand and gravel. In this sand and in thin layers on parts of the country rock were irregular deposits of crystallized gypsum. At several points thin deposits of asphaltum followed the upper surface of the Tulare, apparently having seeped downward from the soils above while in a fluid state. Only a few traces of charcoal and no definite firepits were noted.

As regards the vertical placement of graves, about 80 percent were in the upper stratum and the rest in the sandy wash. According to the observers in direct charge of the digging, they were further divisible into three levels, respectively, the top gravel from 5 to 17 inches deep, a second level from 19 to 33 inches, and a third in or just on the yellow sand from 36 to 56 inches. The last burial found, No. 64, was in a pit dug out of the hard yellow country rock; the body lay in the pit with the skull resting against and on the consolidated Tulare. There appears to be no particular significance to this presumably chance occurrence of skeletons in "levels."

As at site 3, condition of the skeletal remains at site 4 was nearly always very poor; only two skulls and parts of one skeleton were deemed worthy of preservation for laboratory analysis. Just why the bones from the hilltops should be so ill preserved is difficult to understand. The usual explanation—that they were subjected to alternate periods, seasonal or otherwise, of excessive wet and dry conditions—does not harmonize with the fact that textiles on the whole have survived the passage of the years rather well. Seasonal temperature fluctuations in the locality are not great enough to have had any marked effect on underground remains. Possibly chemical rather than physical agencies are to be sought—either positive factors in the surrounding soil which would act unfavorably on osseous material or else negative factors which might extract from

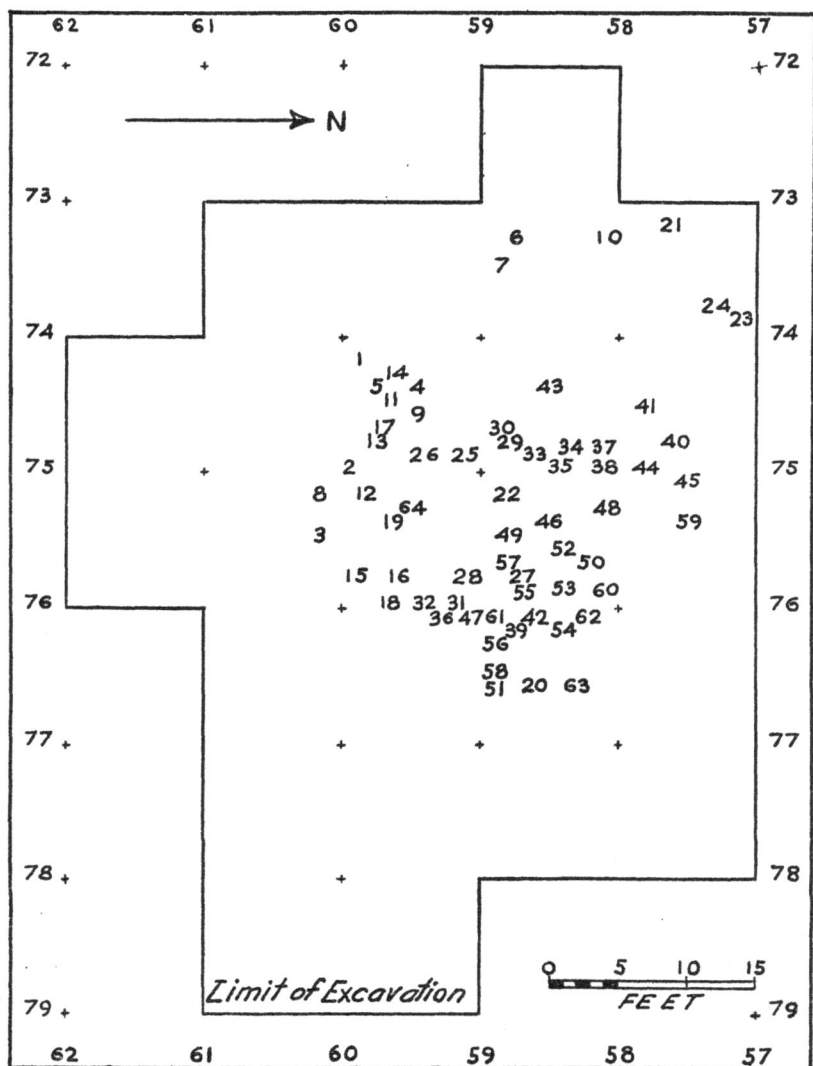

FIGURE 16.—Distribution of burials at Buena Vista site 4.

the latter such minerals as would otherwise make the bones durable. I leave to the soil chemist of the future the elucidation of this problem.

The 64 burials were tentatively sexed in the field as follows: 28 males, 3 females, and 33 unidentified. Possibly the majority of those unidentified should be regarded as females and immature individuals. The field records attribute 54 burials to adults (one accompanied by a child), 2 to adolescents, 7 to children and infants; one is undetermined. As regards posture of the corpse, 38 (59+ percent) were flexed (pl. 18, *b*), 15 (23.4 percent) were semiflexed (pl. 18, *c*), and 11 (17+ percent) could not be classified. The percentage of partly or wholly flexed (82+ percent) is thus higher by about 12 points than was the case at site 3, where on the other hand unclassified individuals were relatively more numerous. At site 4, twenty-five (39 percent) lay on the back, the rest on the right or left side. The hands were usually folded over the abdominal or chest region; in 3 instances they are reported as on the shoulders or under the chin.

The head was oriented, with reference to the body, in the following directions and proportions:

Head to:	No.	Percent of 64	Head to:	No.	Percent of 64
North	13	20. 3	West	9	14. 0+
Northeast	5	7. 8	Northwest	5	7. 8
East	5	7. 8	Indeterminate	9	14. 0+
Southeast	5	7. 8		—	———
South	9	14. 0+		64	100. 0
Southwest	4	6. 3			

If now we drop the nine unclassifiables, the remaining 55 with their respective revised percentages distribute themselves as follows:

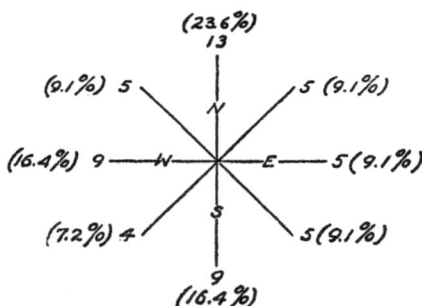

FIGURE 17.—Orientation of 55 burials at Buena Vista site 4.

As at site 3, heads were directed toward every point, with a slight preference for the north (23.6 percent); the west and south were next with 16.4 percent each. Beyond these three cardinal directions and perhaps a slight favoring of the northwest quadrant (west, northwest, north: 49.1 percent), there seems to have been no overwhelming predilection for any particular orientation. The eastern quadrant (northeast, east, southeast), as also at site 3, shows fewer occurrences than any other three successive rays of the wheel.

Thirty-eight (ca. 60 percent) of the burials were accompanied by traces of woven textiles and/or tule. In those from the uppermost "level" this was generally lacking, but between 15 and 33 inches, where most of the interments occurred, the use of such wrappings seems to have been general (pl. 18, *a*). Asphaltum was encountered relatively more often than at site 3. In a few graves this was found as an irregular mass spread between the outer tule layer and an inner wrapping of soft twined textile. Asphaltum-smeared basketry encased or adhered to portions of three skeletons. In one the legs and feet were contained in what appeared to have been a large basket. Another had the hands liberally bedaubed, while in the third the tarry stuff closely surrounded jaws and teeth.

Among the 53 adult burials only 7 (13.2 percent) were accompanied by beads or ornaments. Burial 3 had 3 shell beads; No. 22, 12 shell and 5 steatite beads; No. 26, 3 abalone pendants; No. 34, 3 *Olivella* beads; No. 50, 256 *Olivella* beads; No. 51, 2 shell beads; and No. 52, 1 shell bead. By contrast four of the eight children and infant burials yielded such materials. Thus, No. 2 had 705 *Olivella* beads; No. 25, 2 of shell, 1 of steatite, and a shell ornament; No. 37 (mother and child?), 5 abalone and 2 clamshell pendants; No. 39, 208 *Olivella* beads. Not only is the proportion of furnished graves higher in the case of children, but the gifts themselves were somewhat more freely bestowed than those with adults.

Two skeletons were found with projectile points shot from the side or back so as to remain lodged in the spinal column. Both were identified with reasonable certainty as males. Like similar individuals at some of the nearby sites, especially site 3, these are perhaps to be regarded as unsuccessful shamans or other undesirable persons put out of the way by members of their own community group.

As at site 3, this cemetery was also characterized by absence of extended or cremated burials, of clearly defined pits (except in No. 64), and of European or American trade articles. A blue glass bead was entered in the catalog as coming from the grave area, but it was found on the surface and hence is probably of no significance whatever in dating the burials. Absent also were juniper grave markers or posts such as were encountered at site 3. Generally speaking, burial practices at the two hilltop locations were essentially identical, although minor differences obtain in artifact types and materials.

In one respect site 4 was unique for the Buena Vista group. Mention has already been made of an ashlike admixture in the upper grave-bearing fill, of fire-blackened pebbles, and asphaltum spread here and there over the uneven surface of the underlying Tulare. E. F. Walker, under whose direction this particular phase of the work was carried out, expressed the opinion in his field report that the great area having a black stain to a depth of several feet indicated the former presence of large fires due to ceremonial or mortuary rites (cf. Kroeber, 1925, p. 500). Asphaltum melted and perhaps burned by these fires then theoretically soaked into the ground to accumulate ultimately on the impervious Tulare. He further inferred that the fires thus denoted were too extensive for the relatively few burials on the hill and, therefore, may have served also in rites for those interred elsewhere, as at site 2. If this interpretation is correct, it seems a little odd that no comparable evidence was forthcoming at the much larger and probably more recent site 3. The present writer has no convictions on this score.

In square 77/58 just beneath the surface was found a pile of rocks and steatite bowl fragments. Some of these had been broken, others cut. There was no evidence of fire and the deposit was not near any burials. It was conjectured that this may have represented an altar or possibly a symbolic offering in connection with the postulated mortuary rites. If so, the size, shape, and general appearance of the steatite sherds suggests that many of those from the village sites may have come from vessels ceremonially broken whose remnants were later re-employed for other utilitarian purposes.

BASKETRY AND TEXTILES

The soft-twined fabrics from site 4 are in all respects like those already described from site 3, hence nothing further need be said concerning them here. No further light was obtained on the types of finished articles, as the remains generally were no better preserved. Basket fragments were relatively more abundant, however, and techniques were more adequately represented.

Only one specimen of basketry even approximated completeness. This was uncovered at a depth of 11 inches in square 75/61, a few feet south of the main burial area. Its form and the general appearance can best be judged from plate 14, *b*, from a view taken as the specimen lay in situ. The weave is in the usual plain twining with a 2-ply twisted warp. Warps average about 6, wefts 9 or 10, per linear inch. The basket is thickly encrusted inside and out with pitch, the interior coat being the heavier. Most of the fabric on the underside, as the specimen lies in the illustration, has rotted away, and I am unable, therefore, to arrive at a satisfactory conclusion as to its original shape and size. Provisionally identified as a water bottle, it now looks more like a deep pouch-shaped affair in which the bottom was represented by the rounding whole end shown at the lower left in plate 14, *b*. This form would resemble the softer twined bags from the Elk Hills (Gifford and Schenck, 1926, p. 102). In this event, the opening would have been at the upper end, and if of some size, must certainly have left traces of a selvage. Since there seems to be no such evidence, the opening may have been at the side (cf.

Kroeber, 1925, pl. 50, *c*), where the edges have long since been obliterated through decay. The basket at present measures about 360 by 280 mm. Cradled in burlap and plaster, it was sent to the United States National Museum but full restoration has not been possible. From the few accompanying broken bits, it does not appear likely that further information on the original form will ever be obtained.

In addition to the foregoing, bitumen-covered basket fragments from site 4 accompanied no less than 10 burials, with 4 other seemingly dissociated scraps. Still others tentatively cataloged as woven material have since proved to be lumps of asphaltum mixed with grass or with debris, or, if once basketry, are now too far gone to give usable information. Nine burials yielded stiff twined basketry with twisted 2-ply warp foundation. As in the soft fabrics, both right and left twist were recognized. Usually, the pitch has been so generously applied that the exact nature of the base is hidden except on a freshly broken surface. By comparison with the soft cloth, the weaving elements in what I have chosen to call basketry are much heavier. Generally, either of the two elements of which the warp is made up much exceeds in thickness the 2-ply warp used for the soft bags. The raw materials used can not be identified.

What appears to be finely coiled basketry on a grass bundle foundation was found with burial 35. The material is pretty completely disintegrated, though the asphaltum has retained a few traces. For this reason, the identification is not positive.[28]

Burial 59, besides twined basketry, contained a few bits of coarse braided tule cordage.

PIGMENTS

Lumps of soft friable red, yellow, and white mineral substances, undoubtedly used as sources of pigment, were found throughout site 4. The red, which leaves a bright streak on the skin, has been identified as anhydrous iron oxide. A large mass of gravel and clay was thoroughly permeated with this coloring, but it is not certain whether this represents a prepared cake or only a chance mixture by nonhuman agencies. Except for the coarser gravel and less regular outlines it is not unlike the molded cakes commonly found in the Channel region.

Yellow occurs as hydrous iron oxide or limonite (Fe_2O_3), which was also mixed with clay and can be rubbed off easily with the fingers.

White marl, soft fine-grained limestone, or some similar substances worn or ground into rounded shapes, probably served as white pigment.

---

[28] Admitting the inconclusive nature of our evidence, such as it is it seems to parallel Kroeber's (1925, p. 532) findings among the Yokuts that, "Twined baskets were more poorly made, but filled a greater variety of needs and perhaps outnumbered coiled pieces in the normal household. . . ."

WORK IN SHELL

Most of the items of personal adornment at site 4 were made of *Olivella* shell. Whole shell beads from which the spire had been ground for stringing came from two graves. Burial 2, a child, had 572 of these, while No. 9, an adult male, had 2. All were under 10 mm. in length. Half shells of decidedly ragged form occurred in three graves, one of which, No. 50, yielded 370. Five others were distributed among burials 34 and 52 and the general diggings. There is considerable diversity in size, many of the smaller ones resembling the disks except for their indifferent workmanship. Some of the larger specimens have a rather marked lip at one end. The perforations tend to be smaller than at site 1, seldom exceeding 2 mm. in diameter. *Olivella* disk beads from 5 to 12 mm. across were found in five graves, but here again the great majority were from two child interments. Burial 39 yielded 208 large disks; burial 2 had 145, all falling near the lower limit of the size range. This, it will be recalled, is the grave which also yielded nearly all of the whole *Olivella* beads. Nine other disks came from burial 27, and the rest were scattered here and there in graves and in the surrounding fill.

Limpet rings were represented by a single specimen with burial 25.

With burial 22 were 80 tiny shell rings 2 to 3 mm. in diameter by 1 to 2 mm. thick. Four others came from the general diggings.

Pendants, mostly of unidentified shells, were quite scarce. Five oblong to subrectangular specimens each had two perforations at one end or at one edge. Three smaller objects averaging 12 by 16 mm. have either one or two central holes.

WORK IN STEATITE

The few steatite specimens unearthed at site 4 were in no instance directly associated with individual graves. Curiously enough, they include no ornaments or other nonutilitarian forms.

From square 77/58, at a depth of 30 inches, came the arrow straightener illustrated in plate 43, *a*. This is of fine steatite and well finished, but seems to have been damaged by fire. It measures 93 by 70 by 50 mm., with a flat base and convex upper surface. The latter is cut transversely by a highly polished U-shaped groove 15 mm. wide by 17 mm. in maximum depth. On either side of the groove and running at right angles, or nearly so, to it, are fine parallel scorings. Those to the left in the plate, 23 in number, cover a band 38 mm. wide and fade out at the end of the stone. On the other side they are much more carelessly done, sometimes running into or even crossing one another, but apparently not representing a continuation of the lines on the other side of the groove.

Except for the scorings, the above specimen does not differ materially from others found during our excavations in the vicinity. The lines were probably for ornamentation, although Gifford and Schenck (1926, p. 67 and pl. 170) have suggested that a similar feature noted on a straightener from the Tulare Lake region "seems more likely to have been of service in abrading arrows during the straightening process."

Outside the burial area proper, just to the north, at a depth of 12 inches, were found two fragments of a carefully finished steatite olla. About 150 mm. of the margin of the larger and 70 mm. of the smaller show cut edges but these do not match. It is quite probable, though, that the sherds are from the same vessel. Made of coarse steatite, the walls averaged 15 to 18 mm. in thickness. The surfaces are better finished than on the bowls from sites 1 and 2, the interior being especially well smoothed. The lip is thin and rounding, and the orifice was not flanged. The shape must have been markedly unlike all others indicated for the Buena Vista sites, since it was very evidently a large globular small-mouthed olla of southern Caliofrnia, i. e., Channel type (cf. Gifford and Schenck, 1926, pl. 24; Rogers, 1929, pls. 44, 67, 68). The dimensions, so far as I have been able to estimate them by projection, were probably in the neighborhood of 370 mm. for greatest diameter, with an orifice of about 217 mm. Whether this jar was a direct importation from the coast across the mountains or a local product by some one familiar with coastal types cannot be stated, though the difficulties inherent in transporting a piece of such bulkiness would favor the latter alternative. If not from a vessel made at or near Buena Vista Lake, it is possible that only the sherds were carried in from elsewhere.

One other smaller and thicker rimsherd is from a vessel roughly fashioned of coarse steatite. About 10 mm. below the lip are three holes bored from both sides, each 3–4 mm. in diameter, and spaced at 30–35 mm. intervals. All are intersected by a deep groove which apparently encircled the entire bowl, in a manner similar to that already noted in sherds from site 1. The sherd thus conforms in all respects to local types, and probably came from a moderately deep wide-mouthed vessel whose greatest diameter was at or just below the rim.

WORK IN CHIPPED STONE

Chipped artifacts consisted principally of projectile points. Most common were those of unnotched triangular NAb1 type. Eight were of chert and one of obsidian, these including several long graceful well made pieces with very finely serrate edges. In size they ranged up to 60 by 18 mm. A second obsidian point is of SBb type; a third has coarsely serrate or notched edges. Three NAb1 and one (drill fragment?) of nine broken and intermediate pieces show asphaltum stains at the base, probably from hafting. There are also portions of two larger flint objects which may have been knives; one is very thin and has two finely retouched edges, the third side being broken.

Projectile points, in three instances made of obsidian, occurred in six burials. One of the obsidian points was of the usual triangular form, though crude; another was of SBb type, and the third described above as serrate, was unique in form. Their occurrence, so far as the data go, was as follows in table 7:

TABLE 7.—*Projectile points found with burials in site 4*

| Burial No. | Sex | Number of points | | Where found |
		Field count	Cata- log	
5	Adult male	3	1	In scapula, in base of skull, and in arm.
9	----do	--------	1	
52	----do	7	4	In spine, in rib, and loose in torso.
56	Adult	3	2	Against vertebrae.
58	Adult male	1	1	

A large chopper or hand ax of brecciated gray chert was found with burial 28 in such position as to suggest that it had probably been laid on the chest of the deceased at time of interment. It may be seen as it lay in situ in plate 18, *b*, lying between the upper end of the sternum and the sternal extremities of the clavicles. The material appears to be the same as that of which the "saws" or "steatite-cutters" at sites 1 and 2 were made, as well as two similar but smaller choppers at the former mound. Between the lamina there are thin somewhat irregular and discontinuous sheets of calcareous material, and the chert tends to split along these planes. Part of the surface shown in the burial photograph has since broken off. The specimen measures 150 by 116 by 44 mm., is quite irregular in shape, and has a strong chipped cutting edge (pl. 41, *d*). Held in the padded hand, it would have made a very effective tool for chopping, smashing, or similar heavy usage. There is no evidence whatever of hafting or lashings.

WORK IN GROUND STONE

Here are included two very coarse-textured blocks of grayish white calcareous sandstone. In superficial appearance the material is reminiscent of a poor grade of sidewalk cement. The larger piece is 120 by 47 by 18 mm., tapers slightly toward one end, and has one flat and a faintly grooved side. The other piece, 110 by 40 by 27 mm., has one side rounded and the other with a groove running lengthwise. They show little sign of wear, are crudely shaped and rough, but, while poorly matched, were probably intended for use together. Placed against each other groove to groove they suggest the generally better-made paired arrowshaft buffers widespread throughout the plains and the western United States.

ARTICLES OF UNWORKED STONE

These included chiefly small to medium-sized pebbles and boulders scattered, perhaps fortuitously, throughout the area of excavation. They may or may not represent artifacts or objects used by the natives.

In square 78?/59, about 10 feet east of the burial area proper, at 36 inches depth was found a slightly flattened subspheroidal granite object 81 by 72 mm. It is well smoothed save on one side where a small area is pitted and roughened as though from weathering. Though not perfectly symmetrically it could have been used as a gaming stone or ball. Another note says the object was with burial 9, which would place it in square 74/59. Three smaller, rougher, and still less uniformly shaped pebbles are cataloged as "boiling stones," though I know of no sound basis for such a designation. They are of sandstone or other hard rock. The largest is about 53 by 65 mm., the smallest about 43 mm. in diameter. The three were found together at a depth of 12 inches. A fourth stone with equally rough surface but more nearly approaching the spheroid in shape came from our dirt pile; it measures about 47 mm. through. Part of its surface is black as though stained by bitumen or by fire.

Near the north edge of the cemetery 4½ feet underground was a flat circular object of sandstone about 18 mm. thick by 110–120 mm. in diameter. Its surface has a feel much like fine sandpaper; it may have been used as a handstone or rubbing implement. Ten feet to the southwest, 24 inches deep, was a subrectangular stone with rounded corners. It measured 136 by 78 by 28 mm., and may have been a muller.

Aside from the foregoing, there are half a dozen or so elongate and somewhat irregularly shaped limestone and diabase pebbles from the burial area. Four of these may have served as pecking stones since the ends exhibit some evidence of wear or battering. Another, 105 mm. long with both ends worn off in rounding fashion, might have been used as a pestle for grinding paint. Other than their worn ends, none of these seems to have been altered from its original natural form.

SITE 5

During the search for burials on the hills behind sites 1 and 2, evidences of aboriginal activity were found on another small point some 80 yards northeast of site 4 and about the same distance west of trench 1 at site 2. These lay very close to the 345-foot contour. The evidences consisted of a few shell beads, and dark supposedly fire-stained patches of soil visible over the surface of the ground. Here and there partially filled pits showed where earlier parties and relic-hunters had dug. Extensive trenching, however, revealed only one incompletely flexed adult burial, at a depth of 14 inches, with which was found a single shell bead. Several sandstone rubbing or grinding stones were found on the surface nearby, as well as a few indecisive fragments of chipped flint. Lumps of yellow ochre occurred to a depth of about 2 feet. A few inches beneath the surface, about 5 feet from the grave, was a pestle 7 inches long, both ends bearing traces of red ochre.

From the surface likewise came several sherds attributable to pottery of southwestern type. These are believed to have been dropped in recent years by visitors or curio-seekers, and had no bearing on the archeology of the site itself.

It was conjectured by E. F. Walker, who supervised the work at site 5, that the knoll was perhaps utilized not as a regular cemetery but for mourning ceremonies in conjunction with interments at sites 2 and 4. This was based on the presence of asphaltum-stained gravel, of irregular masses of bitumen which had soaked into the ground and solidified, of numerous fire-cracked stones and artifacts, and upon the commanding location.

OTHER EXCAVATIONS IN THE VICINITY

As already stated, a thorough reconnaissance was made of virtually the entire area included in the key map (fig. 2) in an effort to discover burial grounds other than those at sites 3 and 4. All hilltops, knolls, and other likely spots were tested by trenching. In each case, trenches were dug in the form of a cross, the arms varying in length from 30 to 60 feet according to the size, height, and general promise of the particular location. Depth of these tests varied from 1 to 4 feet; the width averaged 3 feet. In all, 28 separate points were thus examined. At one or two, bits of burned and weathered human bone were noted on the surface, but the evidence from the trenches was uniformly negative as regards graves. This, of course, does not prove conclusively that isolated or even small groups of burials may not occasionally have been missed. Nevertheless, it is presumptive evidence that other large burying grounds which might have been utilized by the occupants of our sites 1 and 2 probably do not exist in this immediate vicinity.

Such remains as were brought to light by the tests included occasional charcoal deposits, bitumen, flint scrapers, broken projectile points, and scraps of steatite. These prove nothing except that, as would be expected, the refuse from the communities along the lake shore is not entirely limited to the immediate areas of occupation as we have defined them.

The only artifacts worthy of note were an incomplete quartz charmstone found at a depth of 18 inches on a hill some 500 yards southwest of site 1, and a carelessly made limestone ring 30 mm. thick from a depth of 8 inches about 300 yards farther west. None of these doughnut-shaped stones were found at any of the sites where detailed investigation was carried on.

CULTURAL RELATIONS

SUMMARY OF CULTURES AND CORRELATION OF SITES

From the data presented in the foregoing descriptive sections, it is evident that the cultural remains on the southwest shore of Buena Vista Lake vary more or less from site to site and also perceptibly from level to level within each of the two village sites. It thus becomes necessary to define, so far as our evidence permits, the archeological assemblages manifested, to show them in proper time perspective, and to correlate with the postulated periods all of the mounds and burial grounds. Before we undertake this synthesis, however, it will be advisable to point out certain limitations inherent in the evidence, both archeological and otherwise.

In the first place, such interconnections as are suggested between the two inhabited areas, sites 1 and 2, must be recognized as existing usually in a broad sense only. In the field it proved utterly impossible to establish a direct and positive relation between any of the soil strata or occupational horizons at site 1 and similar features at site 2. The single possible exception, noted elsewhere, involves layer 2C at the former and stratum 4 at the latter, but this is at best only inferential evidence based on probabilities. None of the archeological materials present have the degree of sensitivity of a pottery subtype, e. g., which in other areas frequently permit direct equating of specific strata at different sites in which similar wares are found. In other words, efforts to link the sites by cross dating methods were generally futile.

Again, to repeat a point previously touched on, the bedding or "pseudo-stratification" which appeared in portions of the profiles, varied greatly and often over comparatively short horizontal distances. This applies particularly to the shellheap at site 1. Here, though the profiles from three cross sections 100 feet apart showed certain general similarities, very few single layers could be correlated except by careful tracing through intervening areas, and then only with considerable difficulty. For this reason, arbitrary 12-inch levels were used in the further excavations, and these frequently did not exactly conform to the shell and other layers deposited during the normal accumulation of the mound mass. It is entirely conceivable that this procedure may have obscured certain subtle cultural phenomena of which no record was obtained. At site 2, where aboriginal habitation took place on a steadily rising flat instead of a round-topped mound, the natural strata were much more consistent with the layers in which the material was excavated. For both sites, such differentiations as are here made, derive from consideration of the gross data in the belief that major if not specific minor distinctions will be demonstrable.

One final word of caution with regard to the vertical variations which we shall set forth. Of the total quantity of artifacts and worked materials recovered, probably 80 percent or more were found in site 1, and perhaps upward of 95 percent of all finds from sites 1 and 2 came from their upper portions. At site 1 only a few specimens and no burials were recorded at a depth exceeding 5–6 feet, and the frequency table shows in nearly every case a progressive increase in types and in number of artifacts of each type toward the top. While this probably reflects an actual enrichment in material culture during the later period of occupancy, it must be remembered that the relative quantity of mound material handled in excavating varied roughly in inverse ratio to its depth below the surface. That is to say, several times as much soil was scrutinized in the upper 3 feet as in the 6- to 9-foot levels, for the simple reason that the latter was far more difficult to get at. Similarly, at site 2 somewhere in the neighborhood of 20,000 square feet were turned over to a depth of 36 inches, but less than a third of this was further examined between the depths of 36 and 72 inches. On theoretical grounds, one may well wonder what the final effect on our results would have been had the "camp site" here been as extensively tested below the sterile alluvial stratum (stratum 4) as it was above. In partial answer, it may be pointed out that samples from the cross trenches and other deeper cuts in general conform, as to vertical variations, with the larger quantities recovered by the more extended work in the upper levels. Below the 6-foot level [29] at site 1 and the 3-foot level at site 2 our trenches generally showed a very decided falling off in number of artifacts as well as a probably sig-

---

[29] Use of the phrase "6-foot level" in connection with site 1 may require further clarification. Because this was a shell heap built up on an essentially flat surface, the thickness of the loose shell and refuse layers in which most of the artifacts occurred perforce varied from 1 foot or even less at the mound edges to a maximum of about 6 feet at the point of greatest accumulation. Thus, the "6-foot level" insofar as it refers to the bottom of the shell layers is a misnomer, since this bottom actually varied from 1 to 6 feet below the mound surface. As used throughout this entire report, therefore, the "6-foot level" must be thought of as a more or less arbitrary line which conforms in reality to the *zone of contact between the unconsolidated shell and refuse layers above and the gray hardpan below* (cf. fig. 5). All remains *above* this zone of contact are, for our purposes, considered to be above the "6-foot level," while specimens found in the hardpan, regardless of their actual depth below the mound surface, are referred to as below the "6-foot level."

nificant change, at least at site 2, in the types. Though repeatedly checked by deep pits and tests, this picture seemed much the same everywhere. Viewed in light of certain attendant soil changes, it therefore appears likely that the distinctions we are about to make on archeological grounds are valid.

Confining our attention for the present to site 1, we may remark first that all of the general categories of material—asphaltum, bone, clay, shell, steatite, chipped and ground stone, etc.—were represented here. Moreover, with a few exceptions, the items inventoried in table 8, were all found to depths of 2 feet or more below the surface of the shell heap. Their further vertical distribution, however, and the time of their earliest appearance differ from item to item. Charmstones, e. g., were found only in the upper 2 feet and but sparingly there; reel-shaped steatite objects occurred down to 4 feet; mullers ranged from the surface to a depth of nearly 10 feet. The general decrease in abundance of specimens is even more striking. Below 5 feet occurred only one or two examples each of bone tubes, sweat scrapers, worked steatite, asphaltum (on basketry), *Olivella* and clamshell beads, leaf-shaped and stemmed points, mortar fragments, pestles, and several mullers. Below the 6-foot level, where the gray hardpan begins, only mullers and a drill fragment were found.[30] Flexed burials and stone fireplaces went down to 5–6 feet, but here again the great majority were appreciably less than 5 feet beneath the surface of the mound.

The cultural phenomena summarized above correlate quite accurately with changes in structure and appearance of the soil zones. These have been detailed elsewhere, hence it is necessary only to reiterate here the fact that material remains below the 6-foot level, i. e., in the hardpan, included no asphaltum, baked clay, shell, steatite, chipped stone, or obsidian, and that flexed (or other) burials and stone-filled hearths were likewise absent. Present were mullers and a few earth fireplaces, sufficient to establish definitely the occasional occupancy of the site by man prior to deposition of the shell heap proper.

At site 2 there is a comparable change in material culture according to relative depths, but the break between the major periods is a little less sharply indicated. Generally speaking, the sterile alluvial layer (stratum 4) will serve as a cleavage marker. Above are loosely deposited shell, ash, village debris, and soil, not unlike the materials composing the shell heap proper at site 1. And, as at the latter, so here also the great bulk of the work in asphaltum, bone, shell, stea-

---

[30] In this connection, it should be noted that at site 1, 5 out of 11 mullers in the material at hand were found at depths from 5 to 10 feet; one of 23 pestles was in the 5–6 foot horizon, the rest in the upper 4 feet. This is in line with the stratigraphically demonstrated priority of the muller-metate over the mortar-pestle complex in the Santa Barbara region (Olson, 1930, p. 12).

tite, and stone, as well as all flexed burials, stone fireplaces, and roasting pits were in these upper layers. Where certain items are indicated in the summary (table 8) as occasionally extending below this, the general 3–4 foot level, some of the specimens should be viewed with caution. From the evidence at hand we can not categorically deny their right to be here, since the artifact sample from the lower levels is, from the comparative standpoint, rather meager. In a few instances, however, it appears that specimens from above the alluvial stratum may have fallen or been carried through it by way of post holes, rodent burrows, or other former openings with which the profile showed this layer to be honeycombed. Others may have been lying in roasting pits or burial cists dug from a higher living surface, so that their actual provenience must have been above stratum 4. At any rate, below it according to our records were found only an occasional bit of worked bone and steatite, poorly fashioned leaf-shaped and stemmed projectile points, rare scraper knives, perforators, flexed burials, one example each of mortar and pestle,[31] and all or nearly all of the mullers and mealing slabs. The flexed burials were in every case those of individuals interred from above stratum 4. Below the 5- to 6-foot zone artifacts included a single leaf-shaped blade and four mullers, in addition to all of the four extended burials.

From the standpoint of the cultural evidence, sites 1 and 2 are thus seen to exhibit the same general developmental features. At both there is an older horizon characterized by compact unstratified, or at best very poorly bedded, deposits; by the presence of virtually no artifacts save mullers and mealing slabs; by a few fireplaces; and, in the case of site 2, by extended full-length lime-encrusted burials. Overlying these, and therefore patently younger in each site, are looser middens in which occur a comparatively wide variety of objects of asphaltum, bone, clay, shell, steatite, etc., flexed burials, stone-filled firepits, and circular post-mold groups probably representing habitations. Moreover, this latter and later array of cultural elements seems to appear rather suddenly at each site and from the manner in which it was found evidently indicates a much more intensive occupation than the meager one which preceded it.

Beneath the superficial or generic resemblances which the upper level assemblages from the two sites bear to one another, there may be discerned certain interesting and significant dissimilarities in matters of detail. These involve the relative abundance or scarcity of specific artifact types and, in lesser measure, of certain raw ma-

---

[31] For comparison with site 1: at site 2 pestles were all above 3–4 feet, 12 out of 13 above 3 feet; 9 of 15 mullers were below 3 feet (see also explanatory remarks in descriptive section on "Mullers and metates" under site 2, p. 103).

terials. For instance, common items at site 1 which were rare or absent at site 2 include the following: Awls of type 1A; bone tubes and whistles; shaped antler flaking tools; baked-clay objects; beads and ornaments of abalone shell; groove-edged and reellike objects of steatite. If the collections at hand are representative, we might add asphaltum and the use of steatite generally, both much less common at site 2. At the latter, moreover, leaf-shaped and stemmed points predominated over triangular forms, and *Olivella* half-shell beads in proportion to disks were considerably more numerous than at site 1. These seemingly inconsequential differences loom rather large when viewed against the background of two archeological manifestations as simple and as nearly contiguous spatially as those herein portrayed. They take on added meaning in light of observations made previously by Gifford and Schenck (1926, p. 110) in the same general area. Working almost wholly with surface collections gathered by amateurs from sites in the Tulare and Buena Vista Basins and in the intervening slough region, these investigators outlined two artifact complexes respectively characteristic of the Tulare Basin and of the Buena Vista Basin. Among the 14 traits comprising their list,[32] nine at least of the entries for the Alpaugh region (Tulare Basin) harmonize with our site 2. These have been starred in table 10 reproduced below. Four, including "boat-shaped" stones, ground crescentic and perforated stones, and "snake heads" are not duplicated in our materials. Plummetlike objects (i. e., charmstones) were plentiful at site 2 only by comparison with site 1—eight specimens against two. Our site 1, by contrast, finds much more congenial company with the (Buena Vista-Kern) Lake region list. In light of these considerations it would appear that our generic upper-level manifestation is further divisible into two phases: one represented at site 2, wherein a simple perhaps basic valley complex is indicated, the other a richer aggregation of traits

---

[32] Under Table 10, Occurrence of Principal Artifacts, Gifford and Schenck enumerate the following (traits harmonizing with our site 2 marked with asterisk):

	Alpaugh region	Lake region
Clay (pottery)	*At site 12 only (rare)	At site 3 only.
Shell	*Very little abalone	Abalone relatively plentiful.
	*Very few olivella disc beads	Olivella disc beads relatively plentiful.
Steatite	*No disc beads	Disc beads.
	"Boat-shaped" stones	No "boat-shaped" stones.
	*No plugs	Plugs.
	*Few sherds	Sherds exceedingly plentiful.
Stone (chipped)	*Very few in schistose	Schistose material definite.
	*Leaf-like points predominate	Triangular points predominate.
Stone (ground)	Crescentic stones	No crescentic stones.
	Perforated stones	No perforated stones.
	*Plummet-like stones very plentiful	Plummet-like stones scarce.
	"Snake heads"	No "snake-heads."
Textiles	*None preserved	Woven, braided, twined.

which undoubtedly owes much to external influences from another direction.

As to the hilltop cemeteries, it seems safe to infer first of all a relatively recent date though, like the two habitation sites, both appear to antedate the period of local contact with white men. Unfortunately, aside from textiles the burials yielded little cultural material but such as it was it pretty clearly indicated a correlation with some general manifestation like that found at the upper levels at sites 1 and 2. This inference rests on the fact that the shell ornaments and and other items of grave furniture were substantially identical with types found in the upper village horizons. It is strengthened by the observation that flexed burials only were found, which was also the exclusive practice at the village sites. At site 3 particularly the finding of quantities of perishable native textiles and basketry and also of wooden stumps suggests no great antiquity. The last named item, indeed, seems to stand as a near-link with the historic period since both ethnography and archeology attest the recent use of such grave markers or supports (for trinkets, etc. to the dead) in the southern Yokuts area. (Latta, unpubl. notes; Walker, E. F., 1935.) So far as specific identities to village site materials are any proof of connection, it is noteworthy that 64 out of 66 identifiable projectile points scattered throughout the grave area were of the triangular NBb type. This, it will be recalled, was the most common type by far at site 1, in the uppermost 2 feet of which it was overwhelmingly predominant. Since burials in this shell heap were far too few to account for the implied number of its former occupants; since no other nearer burying ground was found to which the dead might have been consigned; and since there are some points of similarity in artifact types between the two, I am led to conclude that site 3 should be regarded as the final resting place of the aborigines whose domestic and other activities were responsible for the middens comprising the shell heap proper at site 1.

For site 4 the evidence is less satisfying. The burials differ in no important respect from those at site 3, or for that matter from those at site 2. However, of 10 projectile points found, 9 were leaf-shaped, which type though generally of poorer workmanship, predominated at site 2. Large rough *Olivella* half-shell beads were common here, and they resembled the type relatively more plentiful at site 2 than at site 1. Limpet ring ornaments were too scarce to offer much help, but here again the evidence favors site 2. A more practical consideration is the relative distance to the two village areas—from site 1, the corpse would have had to be carried upward of 1,300 yards, or about twice as far as the distance to site 3, whereas from site 2 there would have been a carry of not much over 150 yards to site 4. All things considered, I should be inclined to ascribe the burials found at site 4 to the upper levels at site 2. That they may have antedated those at site 3 is suggested by the absence of wooden posts—not necessarily conclusive evidence, of course.

The correlations attempted in the foregoing paragraphs may be more easily understood by reference to the chart shown herewith (fig. 18). This has been condensed from table 8, of which it represents essentially a graphic summary. No effort has been made to depict the relative frequency of the various items in each level since this may be readily determined from the table. The chart and table must be used together since the interpretations rest in part upon the number of specimens of each type whereas the bars in the graph show only presence or absence.

Further explanations are necessary. The 5- to 6-foot level at site 1 has been equated with 3- to 4-foot horizon at site 2, because both represent in a general way zones of cleavage between the sparsely evidenced lower-level manifestations and the much richer upper middens. At this point, too, there are well-defined changes in the structure and composition of the culture-bearing deposits—compact and poorly stratified below, loose and stratified or lenticular above. Such upper level types as appear from the chart to have penetrated below this zone have been duly noted in the foregoing discussion.

The upper 3 feet at site 1 are thought to be later than the top of site 2 because they contain in relative abundance most of the types and materials found sparingly, and others not at all, in the upper levels at site 2. These have been noted above in connection with the observations of Gifford and Schenck for the Alpaugh and Lake regions. Particularly noteworthy in this respect are the use of fired-clay artifacts and the much more pronounced emphasis on steatite working at site 1. It is interesting to see that certain types found but rarely in the topmost levels at site 2 continue in growing profusion in the subsequent portions of site 1. Here we may enumerate only a few of the more noteworthy examples, viz, steatite reels, bone tubes and whistles, delicate leaf-shaped and especially triangular (NBb) projectile points, scraper knives and saws, mortars, use of asphaltum, and most shell ornament types (especially those of abalone). In contrast to the increasing use of the above is the marked relative decrease in such other types as bone sweat scrapers and bipointed objects (compound fishhook parts ?), large steatite and clamshell disks, charmstones, and roasting pits. These items were all present at site 2, and, as cannot be adequately shown in the chart, they may signify the brief presence of a particular cultural complex not compatible with any clearly marked period at site 1.

Whether the phenomena as charted have the chronological connotations implied in the foregoing discussion is another matter, though I am inclined to believe they do. There is no good reason, so far as I can see, for questioning the general contemporaneity of the 5- to 10-foot levels at site 1 with the 4- to 10-foot levels at site 2. What there was of cultural material herein as well as the less objective observations as to soil differences, all argue for the view that the remains probably date from a general period, doubtless of long duration, wherein the material phases of local culture were of the poorest. At the other end of the sequence, it seems very probable that site 2 as the habitat of a sizable village community was finally abandoned before site 1, as is implied by the chart. For one thing, during the excavations no traces whatever of European or American glass or metal were found, whereas at site 1 several glass beads and a scrap of iron were noted down to about 18 inches. While I am inclined to view most or all of these with suspicion as possibly intrusive, their spurious nature as archeological evidence cannot be positively asserted. Therefore, for the uppermost 1 or 2 feet at site 1, they hint at a possible recency of which there was not the slightest indication anywhere at site 2. The wider diversity of artifact types and the greater frequency of objects of steatite, asphaltum, baked clay, and other materials at site 1 suggest a complex basically like that in the upper portions of site 2 and quite possibly an externally stimulated outgrowth of something akin to that represented there. Moreover, a number of types late in both sites and especially common in the upper part of site 1 are apparently close to historic Yokuts. This similarity is heightened somewhat if site 3 is accepted as belonging to the late occupation at site 1, as postulated. As an incidental item, we may cite also the absence of charm stones, except for two fragments, from site 1, whereas they were several times as frequent at site 2. Archeologically common in California, the manufacture of the type ceased in prehistoric times, and the modern Indians used only such specimens as could be picked up. Their virtual absence at site 1, along with the other evidence cited, may afford further proof of the lateness of site 1 as compared with site 2. As a final point, it may be noted that the entire upper 4 or 5 feet of the midden at site 1 are appreciably looser in texture and show much more whole-shell beds than anything at site 2 excepting perhaps the topmost 12 inches or so of shell, ash, and dirt on the camp site.

In summary, it appears from the chart that a general two-fold stratigraphic sequence can be recognized at each of the two village-midden sites excavated by us on Buena Vista Lake. With the upper and more adequately indicated can probably be correlated all of the hilltop burial grounds found nearby—site 3 with site 1, sites 4 and 5 with site 2. Furthermore, there is a strong likelihood that dissimilarities in certain details as between site 1 and site 2 upper-level complexes connote slight temporal as well as cultural divergences. Lastly, while it is evident that the cultural history of the two sites followed generally congruent paths throughout, site 2 probably ceased to be intensively inhabited before the final abandonment of site 1.

AGE OF SITES AND LENGTH OF OCCUPANCY

Formidable indeed are the difficulties confronting any attempt at estimating in terms of years the probable age and duration of occupancy of the sites discussed in the present paper. While the depth of accumulated human refuse seems somewhat impressive at first glance, it must be stated at the outset that we know nothing as to the number of persons who lived on the two village sites at any given time or the stability of occupancy or population numbers, or as to the amount of refuse which a single individual or a community might leave over a specific period. There is no point at which the aboriginal occupation can be convincingly tied in with the datable European or American penetration. Except as surface finds, glass beads and metal were found only at site 1, and even there their occurrence is partly clouded with uncertainty. The central portions of the site had been haphazardly dug over to a depth of 2 feet or more prior to our activities, and there is a distinct possibility that our contact finds came from such local disturbances. In other words, there is no positive proof that the site or any of the archeological features described postdated the Caucasian penetration of the Buena Vista region. It does seem probable, though, that abandonment must have occurred not long before arrival of such influences, since the later cultural manifestation at site 1 bears a strong resemblance to the material culture of the historic Buena Vista Yokuts. How long before Fages (1772) these trade influences may have appeared is uncertain but the very purpose of his trip—"pursuit of the deserters"—indicates that as might be expected he had already been preceded into the region by white men. One suspects that such objects of trade as have occasionally been found underground in the Buena Vista region may date for the most part after the middle of that century. If this view is correct, I should be inclined to suppose that site 1 ceased to be permanently inhabited some time during the first half of the eighteenth century, that is, between 1700 and 1750. A slight upward revision may be necessary if future work establishes the postcontact nature of the topmost levels, here viewed as improbable.

From time to time Nelson, Gifford, Schenck, and other students of California archeology have sought some reliable basis for estimating the rate at which shell heaps would accumulate under native conditions, and to determine therefrom the approximate age of various refuse mounds. (Nelson, 1909, p. 345; Gifford, 1916; Schenck, 1926, p. 208; Schenck and Dawson, 1929, pp. 320, 409.) Estimates have varied widely, the earlier figures generally being much larger than the more recent. My own efforts along this line at Buena Vista are presented below, also as a suggestion rather than as anything approaching a proved fact.

At site 1 it is estimated that roughly 35 to 40 percent of the total mound mass was dug over by our party, including much of the thickest deposits. Thirty-five burials were found, most of them scattered and separately buried. Neither our excavations nor those made previously disclosed any evidence of burial plots. Proportioning the 35 burials seen, most of which were infants, and assuming that there are no community cemeteries, it seems likely that not more than 100 individual interments occur throughout the mound. This estimate ought to include all adults present at any rate; infants of the tender age of those found would have contributed virtually nothing to the accumulating refuse. The implication, as already pointed out, is that the deceased were interred elsewhere, probably on the hilltop burying ground designated site 3. This yielded about 350 skeletons, mainly subadult to adult. Allowing for isolated and undiscovered graves nearby, for additional individuals not recognized in the more disturbed portions of the burial area, and for possible decayed skeletons, we may raise this figure to 450 interments on this one hilltop. Persistent search on all hills and points within a radius of about three-fourths of a mile yielded only negative evidence, save for sites 4 and 5 which probably are to be linked with site 2. Combining sites 1 and 3 we then have a total of about 385 observed or 550 estimated bodies.

Zalvidea in 1806 reported 218 Indians living in the village of Buena Vista, of whom 144 were women and 36 were men. The sites under consideration had probably been deserted by this date, so that there are no figures available for their one time population. Perhaps a safe estimate for the average size of the settlement represented at site 1 would be 100 to 150 persons. Assuming an annual death rate of 3 percent (Hooton, 1930, p. 333), a community averaging 100 souls would require 128 years to deposit the observed burials or 183 years to bury those we exhumed and the additional ones postulated. If the site was abandoned soon after 1700, the occupancy which resulted in deposition of the upper levels must then have begun after 1500 and perhaps even as late as 1600. A population average of 200 would halve the above figures, reducing them to the span of 2 or 3 human generations, and bringing the remains of this level entirely within the seventeenth century or even later. Conversely, a group averaging under 100 would require a proportionately longer time to build up the refuse heap and bury so many dead.

Site 2 yielded 104 burials (exclusive of 4 deep-level interments) but because of the extremely irregular and ill-defined site limits, it is far more difficult to estimate the proportion worked. However, since graves were much more frequent here, it seems not unlikely that 2 or possibly even 3 times as many may have been scattered about through the mass originally. The associated hilltop cemetery nearby, site 4, gave up 64 dead, and site 5 yielded one. Again allowing for additional undiscovered and unrecognized graves in the vicinity, we may estimate a maximum of 100 bodies for the burial plots located outside the village limits. To this we add, say 300, for the village itself. Observed bodies at sites 2, 4, and 5 then total 169; estimates of additional dead not found would raise this to a maximum of 400. Again assuming an average population of 100, the time required to bury 400 dead would be about 130 years, roughly 4 or 5 generations. It is quite possible that this site was inhabited by a consistently somewhat smaller group than site 1, in which case the time would have to be lengthened. Perhaps it is equally true that our estimate of 400 bodies is too generous. Seventy persons over a period of a century and a half would presumably bury about 300 of their number—nearly twice the observed total at sites 2 and 4. If these calculations be viewed in conjunction with those at sites 1 and 3, which were probably used at a somewhat later date, it may be suggested that the overwhelming bulk of upper-level materials at Buena Vista village sites 1 and 2 were deposited since 1400.

Since, among other omissions, the mass of the Buena Vista shell heaps was not accurately computed on the spot, there are further difficulties in determining their possible rate of accumulation. However, we may essay the problem for one of the mounds at any rate. Earlier in this paper a rough estimate of 250,000 cubic feet was given for site 1. If this material was laid down by a total of 550 persons each with a life span averaging 33 years, the total per person would have been about 455 cubic feet. The annual rate per person would thus have been close to 14 cubic feet, which seems conservative. It is of passing interest to note that Schenck, using Nelson's data at Ellis Landing shell mound on San Francisco Bay, independently estimated a rate of 14.6 cubic feet per person (Schenck, 1926, p. 211).

The writer hastens to point out his own reluctance to accept these calculations as in any sense final; there are too many unknown and uncontrolled factors involved. There is no assurance that all of the dead present are allowed for, nor do we know how many of the people may have been buried in distant places while on hunting, gathering, or trading trips, on raids, etc. There is no proof that the population at either village averaged or even approximated 100, but this argument cuts both ways—it may have been substantially more for some or much of the time involved. The sites may have been inhabited only intermittently at the beginning and again at the close of their general period of occupancy. Perhaps, too, a considerable part of site 2 has been destroyed by wave action, so that the basis of the above computations may not be a fair one. Even the average annual death rate used may not apply.

Despite these strictures, and there are doubtless others not mentioned, one fact seems to be strongly indicated by the figures. I refer to the comparatively short period apparently required for the growth of these village middens. Before actually attempting the above calculations I had guessed that they might represent a lapse of 3 or 4 centuries each, although the loose unconsolidated character of the upper levels and the fresh appearance of some of the shell strata scarcely supported such a view. Now it seems more likely that the earlier guesses may have been much too generous; certainly there is no reason whatever for lengthening the interval. In other words, the upper 3 feet at site 2 and the upper 6 feet at site 1, wherein occurred nearly all the steatite, obsidian, asphaltum, and work in bone, shell, and stone, in their entirety may fall within the period of 1400–1700. I emphasize again the fact that these dates are given only to illustrate the probable order of time involved, not because they represent established points in the local chronology.

At the moment there is no basis whatever for even guessing at the antiquity of the deep-level remains at Buena Vista. At both occupational areas, sites 1 and 2, these levels are rather clearly set off from the upper. At site 1 the chief difference is in the hard compact and generally structureless character as contrasted with the loose ashy upper portion with its easily turned shell beds and soil strata. In site 2 the distinction is heightened by the presence of the sterile alluvial horizon, stratum 4, below which the various layers lose the recent appearance of those above. It is possible that the general lack of clearly marked shell beds, ash lenses, and such features in the lower levels is due to their frequent or long continued immersion beneath the waters during a high stage or stages of the lake. Conceivably, calcareous matter leached from the shells and human occupational debris might in time help to cement the surrounding soils, but we know nothing as to the length of time necessary. It is quite plausible, too, to view the present 4 to 7 feet of lower-level deposits as the compacted residue of middens once substantially deeper and looser in texture. All in all, it seems evident that the lower-level deposits may considerably antedate the upper; that there may have been a period of complete or almost complete abandonment of the sites between the two periods; and that the lower materials besides being older may have accumulated very much more slowly than the upper. The problems involved are as much geological and sedimentational as archeological, but up to the present no student of the earth sciences has contributed much help on the matter. The possibility of a cultural connection with the Oak Grove people of the Santa Barbara coast will be pointed out in the next section. Valid or not, I see no justification as yet for assigning the lower-level Buena Vista remains an antiquity even approximating that suggested by Rogers for the Oak Grove complex (Rogers, 1929, p. 353; cf. also pp. 257–259 and pl. 30). Until competent geologists, physiographers, and soil experts have weighed the evidence and had their say, any estimate in terms of years is the sheerest conjecture. My own guess would be that nothing so far revealed at our sites 1, 2, 3, 4, and 5 on Buena Vista Lake has an antiquity much, if any, in excess of 1,200–1,500 years.

RELATIONSHIPS WITH OTHER LOCALITIES

Few sites or localities in California have been subjected to excavation and analysis on a scale comparable to that used at Buena Vista Hills, and fewer still have been described in the literature in sufficient detail to permit ready and precise comparisons. As Kroeber (1936, p. 108) has pointed out,

> . . . In part this is due to most of the earlier explorations having been conducted without sense of genuine scientific problem, as in the first stages of work in so many other regions. But in even larger measure the delay in discovering positive time changes is the result of difficulties inherent in the archaeological data of the area. Mostly there is no pottery at all. The historic cultures being simple, their artifact inventory is fairly limited and lacking in specialized types. Except in the Santa Barbara region, the numerical yield of specimen data is low for volume of soil moved. . . .

Against such a background it is easy to understand why the same authority as recently as 1925 (p. 931) was constrained to remark that ". . . relatively little transformation and but slight succession of civilizations occurred in prehistoric California."

In light of subsequent researches in certain localities this view is now seen to stand in need of modification. In the Santa Barbara region not over 50 miles airline southwest of Buena Vista Lake and also in the San Joaquin-Sacramento Delta approximately 250 miles to the northwest, the past decade has witnessed the accumulation of a very considerable mass of new information based on careful excavation. As a result the first hesitant gropings of a handful of scholars prior to 1929 in quest of the elusive time factor have now grown into what promises to be true cultural sequence (Gifford and Schenck, 1926, p. 110; Schenck and Dawson, 1929, p. 402; Rogers, 1929; Olson, 1930; Lillard and Purves, 1936; Kroeber, 1936; Heizer and Fenenga, 1939).

In attempting to correlate the lower cultural levels at Buena Vista with "early" periods as now recognized or postulated elsewhere, several difficulties obtrude. In the first place, the data themselves are extremely scanty at Buena Vista, where the older levels exhibit as positive traits little save extended lime-encrusted burials, the mano and mealing slab, red ochre, and perhaps the occasional presence of crude stemmed and leaf-shaped flints. To build high on such a meager foundation seems especially hazardous when it is remembered that the intervening districts in every direction are as yet too imperfectly known to permit satisfactory tracing of cultural influences and gradations between the more intensively worked localities. Recognizing these limitations, we may nevertheless profitably look afield for such similar or comparable phenomena as the available evidence offers.

The first of our two principal lower-level culture items—extended burials—has been reported by Rogers (1929, pp. 342–355) in the Oak Grove horizon, recognized by him as the earliest in the Santa Barbara region. Along with flexed burials and occasional cremations, it is also listed by Lillard and Purves (1936, p. 19; cf. Heizer and Fenenga, 1939, p. 385) for the "Early" level in the Deer Creek-Cosumnes District of the lower Sacramento. In the Stockton-Lodi locale (lower San Joaquin Valley) extended interments predominate (Schenck and Dawson, 1929, p. 340), but from the published record it is not at all clear whether they characterize all periods or any one in particular. Extended burials in these localities contrast with the usual California practice of flexing (Kroeber, 1936, p. 111).

The general priority of the metate-mano complex over the mortar and pestle in southern California has been affirmed by several writers. Rogers (1929, p. 349) links the mano and mealing slab with prone and supine inhumations in the Oak Grove culture, antedating the mortar and pestle of the Canaliño period. Olson's stratigraphic tests on the islands and mainland of the same general region conclusively demonstrated this particular succession (1930, pp. 20–21), but his published summary is silent as regards any change in burial types. In the alluvial Delta region, where the environment militated against use of stone mortars, such objects and pestles are generally uncommon, but Lillard and Purves (1936, p. 16) say that

We cannot state positively that we have recovered a single mortar or pestle in the Early level. Nor have we, so far, recovered what is undeniably a mano. But we have found crude metates in this level.

Heizer and Fenenga (1939, p. 389) list the metate for the Early horizon in the Delta.

From these findings it thus appears that the metate-mano-extended burial association preceded the mortar-pestle-flexed burial assemblage on the Santa Barbara coast and in the extreme southern end of the San Joaquin Valley, and that a similar tendency is suggested for the Delta. In the Delta, stemmed and leaf-shaped blades seem also to be early or at least to have appeared before the finely chipped triangular and notched forms, but at Buena Vista these occurred definitely later than the extended burial-metate-mano group. Here the similarity with Early Delta ceases. Perforated charmstones, quartz crystals, and other Early northern diagnostics are wanting at Buena Vista. So also are *Olivella* and abalone beads, bone beads and ornaments, baked-clay objects, bead appliqué with asphaltum, and even the use of bitumen itself, though all of these are present in our upper-level manifestations. The oldest levels at Buena Vista show a much smaller number of positive traits than does the Early Delta, but it is not now apparent whether this is owing to the impoverished nature of the material culture borne by these earlier peoples, to a predilection for artifacts of more perishable nature, to the possibly considerable length of time that has elapsed since their passage, to our relatively limited sample, or to some other fact. My own impression is that the Early Delta horizon is a later and considerably more developed phase than that suggested by the lower-level remains at Buena Vista.

Southward the connections seem to be a little stronger, particularly if Rogers' Oak Grove People are actually to be regarded as an early manifestation. In addition to extended burials, metates, and manos, this horizon has yielded masses of red ochre in the graves, which also are frequently covered with stones, crude chipped blades, and bone bodkins or hairpins. Olson's Early Mainland period, as defined in his summary (1930, p. 16), includes such nonearly Buena Vista elements as use of asphaltum, steatite, the mortar and pestle, and charmstones. None of these occur in the Oak Grove horizon, but as a complex they approach the plane of culture represented by the Early Delta. It thus appears that the Oak Grove People may be viewed as representing an earlier cultural substratum than any detected by Olson in the Santa Barbara region. As between the simple Oak Grove People on the one hand and on the other the relatively rich and varied Early Delta manifestation, I should be inclined to choose the former as probably more closely related generically and temporally to the even less clearly defined lower-level "complex" at Buena Vista Hills. It is regrettable that the preservation of the deep burials here was such as to preclude any somatological comparisons with the Oak Grove and Early Delta dolichocephalic populations.

Resemblances between the upper-level artifacts and burials at Buena Vista and materials elsewhere seem a little clearer. We have already discussed the grounds for postulating two phases which may have existed at slightly disparate intervals. The earlier, represented by site 2, exhibits a number of minor traits absent or relatively much rarer at site 1. These would include charmstones; bone sweat scrapers and bipointed objects; small crescentic flints; ornaments and rings of limpet shell; roughly finished *Olivella* half-shell beads; large disks of steatite, abalone, and clamshell; tiny ring beads; roasting pits, secondarily used for burial, and dug (?) cist graves; bird wing-bone necklaces and perforated objects of fish vertebrae. Conversely, this phase lacks other traits plentiful at site 1, particularly with regard to the relative emphasis placed on work in steatite and fired clay. The simpler inventory at site 2 seems to equate with that at various sites in the Tulare Basin to a more marked degree than does the related but more varied material at site 1. Presence of the charmstone here— ". . . the one thin guiding thread backward into the prehistory of most of California . . ." (Kroeber, 1936, p. 114)—suggests a general contemporaneity with the Delta Transitional and perhaps also with Olson's Intermediate Mainland-Early Island horizon.

Since most of the elements comprising the latter have not been adequately segregated and illustrated in the literature available to me, no further attempt at more precise synchronization of periods is here made.

For much the same reason it has been thought inadvisable to set forth a detailed trait by trait comparison of the material from site 1 with the Late horizon in the Delta. An adequate comparative series of index types from the latter region is not to be found in the national collections. From such lists as have been made available and from published illustrations of artifacts, it is evident that there exist many points of similarity as well as some significant differences. In both localities objects of bone, shell, and stone were abundant and varied. Types common to both include bone awls, sweat scrapers, whistles, and bipointed forms; whole, half-shell, and disk beads of *Olivella;* clamshell disk beads; certain forms of abalone ornaments; steatite disk beads and labrets; use of asphaltum and obsidian; coiled basketry; and flexed burials. At Buena Vista there was a better developed steatite industry, and perhaps a more pronounced use of asphaltum, tule, and native textiles—all founded on utilization of raw materials obtainable close at hand and in unlimited quantities. The Delta, on the other hand, seems to show a much stronger development of work in baked clay and obsidian. Such specialized types in the Late Delta as the following were not found by us at Buena Vista: Large banjo-shaped abalone ornaments, certain techniques of shell decoration (e. g., milled edges), long tubular pismo clam beads, bone dice, antler projectile points, slate pendants, incised bird-bone tubes, barbed fish spears, perforated antler shaft straighteners, magnesite beads and tubes, tubular stone pipes [33], "Stockton curves," and probably others. Conversely, hopper mortars, wooden grave markers, receptacles of abalone shell, pitch-coated basketry and yucca (?) fiber brushes, saws, scrapers and knives hafted in asphaltum, steatite reels and other forms, to mention only the most obvious, occurred at Buena Vista but apparently not in the Delta. The differences in cultural inventories from these two regions as thus roughly indicated are doubtless due to several factors—facility with which certain types of raw material could be gotten, cultural influences from mutually separate sources and directions, and to local specializations of material culture at this general stage in California prehistory.

Whatever the degree of relationship ultimately demonstrated between Buena Vista and the Delta, there can be little question that with respect to material culture the former was profoundly influenced by the peoples of southern California. Traits at Buena Vista which stand as a link with this general area include coiled basketry on

---

[33] Two doubtful fragments at Buena Vista.

bundle foundation, hopper mortars of flat and globular form, transversely grooved arrow straighteners, (asphaltum-handled) fiber brushes, and perhaps pottery. Most of these are widely distributed throughout the southern part of the state and some at least may extend also eastward into the Great Basin. In themselves they do not constitute evidence of direct borrowing from any one locality. More specific connections are implied in the soft twined milkweed string bags of the Diegueño, which Kroeber (1925, p. 722) says "are unparalleled in California except for some ancient specimens found in the southern San Joaquin Valley . . ., and for somewhat similar wares made by the Mohave and Yuma . . .;" and in a whole host of features whose appearance is unmistakably Santa Barbaran. Here are a well-developed and varied steatite working industry; extensive use of bitumen for adhesive, waterproofing, inlaying, and other purposes; spheroidal and other prepared objects of the same substance; long slender curved abalone pendants with one pierced and one pointed end; abalone shell receptacles with asphaltum-plugged breathing pores; limpet-shell ornaments painted red and others ground to thin rings and ovals; tiny ring beads of shell; thick clamshell disks, with and without incised edges; compound fishhook barbs and bipointed objects of bone; perforated fish vertebrae; long heavy bone daggers or hair ornaments; finely pricked decoration on bone; scrapers or scraper knives set in wooden handles with pitch; long narrow carefully chipped chert and jasper blades with concave to convex base and ranging from 150–260 mm. long; thin exquisitely made triangular, "swallow-tail," and lanceolate projectile points. In many of these, type by type comparison of the Buena Vista materials with those from Santa Barbara in the national collections has shown an astonishing similarity which seems best explained as due to direct trade contacts. Some of the more widely spread traits previously enumerated are likewise shared by the Channel peoples with those of Buena Vista Lake, viz, coiled basketry, hopper mortars, arrow straighteners, and fiber brushes with asphaltum grip.

Diffusion of the steatite industry from the Santa Barbara Islands to the adjacent mainland and thence to the interior has been outlined by Kroeber.[34] Direct comparisons have not been instituted to determine whether our steatite is of Channel type, but from local collectors we learned that it could have been obtained at several places in the valley. It appears to be coarser in texture than that from the islands. Moreover, such complete and restorable vessels as came to light were not of Channel type, and the same can be said of a number of other artifact types represented at Buena Vista. From this it would appear

---

[34] 1925, p. 629, ". . . Inland the vessels penetrated at least sporadically as far as the Yokuts of Tulare Lake if scant archeological records may be trusted. It is not sure that this entire area was served from Santa Catalina . . ."

that the germ of the trait, perhaps also certain techniques, but rarely or never the raw material itself, were imported. Otherwise, the list of parallels above includes elements in several distinct phases of material culture—subsistence, personal adornment, warfare, decorative arts, etc.

The traits ascribed to southern, particularly Santa Barbaran, influences above were not strictly limited to site 1, where they were, however, much more numerous, varied, and evident than elsewhere. Here they ranged throughout the upper 5 or 6 feet of middens; in lesser quantities they were present at site 2 and also at sites 3 and 4. From the survey by Gifford and Schenck it would appear that coastal influences did not extend far down the San Joaquin valley—or if they did, they weakened rapidly after leaving the Buena Vista Basin. As to the time involved, it may be noted that they were most feebly represented at site 2 in our diggings. Since the manifestation here generally was simple and colorless like that found previously in the Tulare Basin farther north, it would seem probable that here was a southward thrust of what more nearly betokens the true indigenous culture of the southern San Joaquin Valley. This was subsequently enriched, as at site 1, by an influx of coastal elements which just spilled over into the extreme southern tip of the interior plain. In this event, the quickening impulses possibly dated in large measure from the last century or two of occupancy jointly represented by the upper levels at sites 1 and 2. If our calculations as to the age of these deposits are at all near the truth, this may well have taken place in post-Columbian times, but the evidence argues for the arrival of steatite working and other elements before contacts had been established locally with Caucasians. Gifford and Schenck (1926, p. 77) suggest that ". . . the large mass of [steatite] sherds in the Lake region perhaps came with the influx of coast Indians after the advent of Caucasians. . . ." If this is correct I am at a loss to explain the presence of such material in levels definitely free from European objects. Even fugitives from the coast missions would be expected to have brought along some beads and other trinkets of non-Indian manufacture.

For reasons already given, it seems improbable that general abandonment of the shell heap at site 1 is to be dated after the middle of the eighteenth century. Thus, its heyday would have preceded the rush of fugitives from the coast who arrived in a continuous stream after 1800, and who must have left a very strong imprint on the local picture. All things considered, I would view the Channel influences at sites 1 and 2 as owing primarily to steady increase in volume of trade between coast and valley rather than to a direct mass invasion from the former. Pressure from the Spanish may have been a contributing factor but perhaps only an incidental one at this particular period. Final judgment on this point must be held in abeyance until ethnologically and historically identified nineteenth century sites in the Buena Vista Basin have been explored and the cultural manifestations therein analyzed. Then we may be in position to evaluate correctly the problem of late precontact trait transmission between coast and valley.

HISTORICAL CONNECTIONS

An important consideration in selection for detailed excavation of the sites at the base of Buena Vista Hills was the feeling that it might be possible here to link a documented early nineteenth century Yokuts village site with a definite archeological manifestation. Specifically, we had hoped that site 1 at any rate would prove to be identifiable with the village of Buenavista recorded by Fages (1772), Zalvidea (1806), Martinez (1816), and Estudillo (1819). In this, I think, we failed. Even if there were no doubts concerning the authenticity of the contact materials recovered, they were too few in number to be considered proof of trade relations between Europeans and a community of 200 or more Indians during the period given. Fages says that "This village, because it is on a fair sized elevation, overlooks a great plain along the course of the River San Francisco [the San Joaquin]," and that 7 leagues to the south across the plain one came to a pass leading from the valley (Bolton, 1931, pp. 213–214). The latter remarks might apply to the location at the tip of the Buena Vista Hills, but the first does not. Neither does the description by Martinez. The historical evidence, as a matter of fact, is inconclusive, and archeology has not up to the present been able to verify the several opinions which place this native town on the southwest shore of Buena Vista Lake. (Bolton, op. cit., p. 219 and oppos. p. 216; Walker, W. M., 1935; Stirling, 1935.) In view of the largely negative findings in this regard, I am of the opinion that the Buenavista of the Spanish chronicles was situated not at the southwest but probably at the northwest edge of the lake nearer its outlet into the San Joaquin Valley proper. In this general locality, Kroeber has tentatively located the village of Tulamniu; and here, too, near the end of the Elk Hills, recent archeological work has revealed indications of large historic native cemeteries with extensive shell heaps nearby (Walker, E. F., 1935, pp. 145–150). From the preliminary report, this would seem a promising spot for further examination by a combination of historical and archeological methods.

Since written history is silent as regards the identity of the people who in late precontact days inhabited sites 1 and 2, it may be of interest to see in how far the archeological evidence parallels the ethnographic record from the recent Yokuts of the region. Such a comparison is by no means easy to make. The ethnographer deals with a much wider range of data, the greater portion of which comprises such nonmaterial aspects of culture as social and political institutions, religion and shamanism, mythology and ritual, etc. In the nature of things, these are represented but scantily or not at all in the excavator's findings. The archeologist is, therefore, driven to rely heavily, sometimes too heavily perhaps, on the minutiae of material culture. The finer distinctions which he sets up in the search for relationships elsewhere often do not lend themselves to satisfactory collation with the less detailed, at times almost casual, observations of the general ethnographer. Then, too, where the "concrete basis of life" was as simple as among most California inland peoples, and as lacking in distinctive implement types, the threads connecting archeological with ethnic entities become woefully thin.

In point of fact, the ties between the shell heaps described herein and historic Yokuts culture consist of only a few items if we confine ourselves to traits which may with some assurance be regarded as characteristically Yokuts. Pottery is one; juniper grave "markers" may be another; and it is possible that when fuller distributional data are available, such steatite objects as "reels" and large subrectangular bowls may prove distinctive. There are, to be sure, other similarities between the archeological remains and their historical sequel, but these have not the definitiveness which may characterize those suggested. They indicate only that the precontact peoples made use of certain artifact types which were still employed, but not necessarily exclusively, by the modern Yokuts. These would include: [35] Occasional use of portable stone and hopper mortars; small paint (?) mortars; coiled and twined basketry, sometimes pitch-coated; transversely grooved shaft straighteners, and by inference cane arrows; tightly flexed wrapped burials; [36] elk rib sweat scrapers; stone balls for gaming; wooden shinny pucks; nose sticks of bone; steatite disks for suspension from the ears; molded fusiform clay beads; bead inlay in asphaltum; and asphaltum handled brushes. From location of the sites it is also a virtual certainty that the subsistence economy was much the same as that of the valley Yokuts, centering about the natural resources of the lakes, swamps, and adjacent plains. If the archeological data are correctly interpreted as evidencing a late prehistoric occupation of the shell heaps in question, and if it is true that the Yokuts have been masters of the Buena Vista Basin since long before the Spanish invasion, there is little reason to doubt that we are dealing with a phase of Yokuts culture. It is even possible that some group of the Tulamni division may have been resident here, though absolute linguistic identification is not expedient. Perhaps,

[35] From Kroeber, 1925, pp. 519–543; and Latta, 1929, and unpubl. notes.
[36] Latta (unpubl. notes) was informed this custom developed shortly before the coming of the Spanish.

when the later and apparently documented native sites on the northwest shore of Buena Vista Lake have been thoroughly studied, they will be found to stand temporally between the Yokuts of ethnography and the shell heaps at Buena Vista Hills.   Then, if not now, the prehistorian may look with a measure of confidence upon the latter as a pre-Spanish manifestation of Yokuts civilization.

SUMMARY OF CULTURAL DEVELOPMENT

To what extent the succession of events revealed at the sites studied was paralleled elsewhere in the Buena Vista Basin and farther down the San Joaquin is not now clear.   However, from the evidence adduced in the foregoing pages it is possible to reconstruct for these particular remains the following story of culture growth.   Occupancy throughout was by relatively simple peoples whose subsistence economy revolved about the natural resources with which the lake and its immediate environs abounded.   The earliest groups, whose physical appearance and linguistic affiliations are wholly unknown, seemingly possessed an extremely rudimentary material culture, at any rate insofar as the archeological record is to be trusted.   Little is known about their customs and way of life beyond the fact that they used the mano and mealing slab to the exclusion of the mortar and pestle, and that they buried their dead in the fully extended position in shallow graves near their camping places.   The nature of their weapons, utensils, habitations, and ornaments is entirely conjectural.   There is no evidence that they were acquainted with the use of steatite, asphaltum, obsidian, or baked clay, though the first two materials were unquestionably available then as later at no great distance.   The camps on the lake shore may have been primarily for hunting and fishing, perhaps even being entirely abandoned during certain seasons or for periods of years at a time.   At what early date these primitives first arrived on the scene and whence they came are matters on which we can only speculate, but there are some slight grounds for suspecting connection with early groups to the south.   The interval represented by their accumulations of refuse may involve a span of several centuries, but how many is problematical.   It may be significant that at site 2, where these deposits are deepest, they lie mainly at or below the 300-foot contour, so that during high stages of water in Buena Vista Lake human occupancy would have been impossible.   At site 1, the danger of overflow was virtually nonexistent since even the earliest refuse lies slightly above the high-water level.

It has been remarked on several occasions that the rather abrupt cultural change between the lower and upper levels of occupancy appears to go hand in hand with marked differences in the character of the deposits generally. Thus, the older horizons at both sites are much more compact and resistant to the shovel, and give a decided impression of having been laid down long before the superincumbent materials began to accumulate. At site 2 this feeling is accentuated by the presence of a noncultural alluvial sheet (stratum 4) which roughly separates the two periods of occupation. Whether this should be interpreted as evidence of a long interlude of nonresidence by man or, alternatively, as indicating a shorter term of excessive precipitation is not now apparent. There is at least a hint here that a prolonged wet period with exceptionally high lake stages may have occurred during, and was perhaps in part responsible for, the presumed interval of nonhabitation.

With resumption of active residence on the sites the picture changes materially. It also becomes appreciably clearer in many particulars. Again we are unable to state whence the people came, though the limited skeletal remains available for study indicate a physical type like that characteristic of the prehistoric San Joaquin Valley generally. It is possible that this second occupancy began shortly before deposition of the outwash material (stratum 4) at site 2, but the most intensive phase certainly followed later. The remains are all above the 300-foot contour, well out of reach of inundation from the lake. Thus occupancy could have been, and inferentially probably was, fairly continuous. In addition to fish, shellfish, and waterfowl from the lake, the natives relied heavily on large and small land mammals and on wild vegetal products from the surrounding hills and plains. The bones of such forms as the pronghorn (especially immature individuals), deer, elk, and jackrabbit were particularly abundant. In the specimens returned to the National Museum these forms were exceeded in quantity only by those of the domestic dog. Interesting is the suggestion that these people may have known the bison, as shown by finding of two horn cores. Whether this animal once ranged into the locality or whether the horns alone were perhaps traded in is, of course, unknown. As to weapons, the bow and arrow may be inferred. For fishing, as among the historic lake peoples, baskets and nets as well as spears and straight or compound bone hooks may have been utilized. There is direct proof of coiled and twined basketry, and also of soft textiles woven from milkweed (?) fiber. Houses were flimsy, circular, dome-shaped structures of poles and rushes, occasionally perhaps daubed with mud. We may guess from what is on record for the recent period that tule was extensively utilized for house covering, rafts, textiles, grave wrappings, fuel, and other purposes. Circular roasting pits, leaf-shaped and stemmed arrowpoints, and charmstones were common for a time but then gradually diminished in importance. The earlier mano and mealing slab gave way but not completely to the mortar and pestle.

This may signify a change in food habits or emphases—from hard small seeds to larger fruits such as acorns—or it may be due only to the superseding of one type of pulverizing implement by another more suited to a special need. Another early period custom, extended burial, likewise was succeeded by something else—interment in tightly folded wrapped bundles either in the village area or on nearby hilltops.

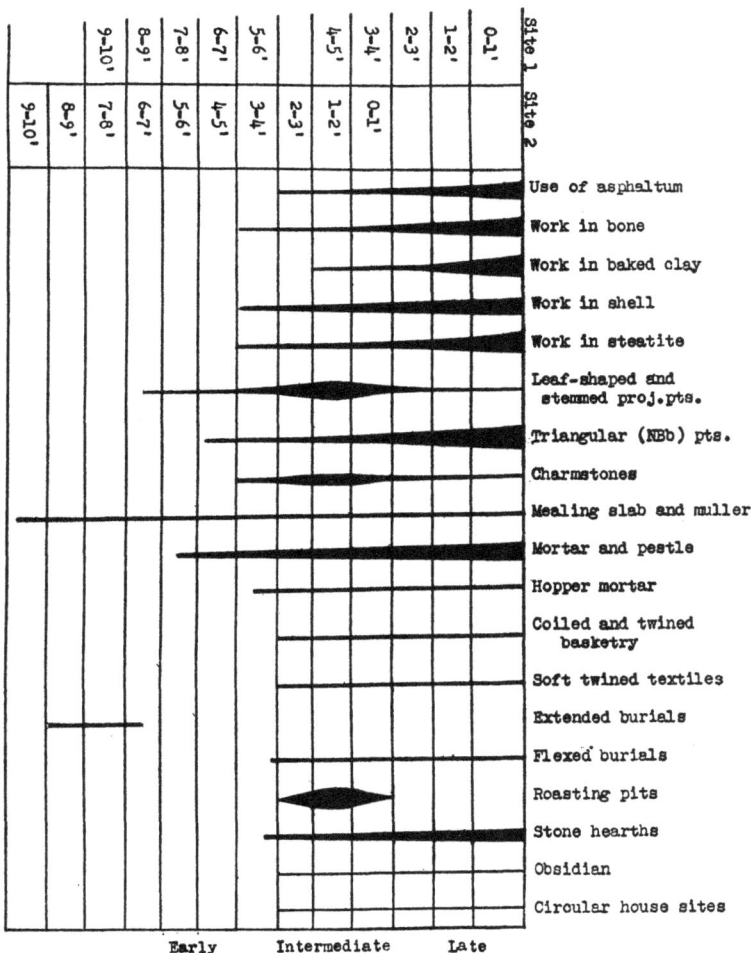

FIGURE 19.—Tentative reconstruction of cultural development at Buena Vista Lake, based on correlation of site levels through the distribution and relative frequency of various artifact types and other features. The terms "Early," "Intermediate," and "Late" are assigned with the local phenomena only in mind, and are not necessarily equivalent in time or cultural content to similarly designated periods recognized elsewhere in California.

In many respects, these people must have been sharers in a simple civilization which flourished for a time farther north beyond the Buena Vista Basin. Marked change came only with the introduction of foreign traits and ideas, mainly from the south. Most of these can probably be ascribed to the much more advanced peoples inhabiting the Santa Barbara coast. From comparatively early times, marine shells must have been traded inland to the tribes of the Central

Valley for the manufacture of ornaments; later came the idea of making tools and utensils of steatite, of certain forms and techniques for utilization of asphaltum, obsidian, shell, bone, and horn. It is difficult to appraise the influence which may have been exerted on the nonmaterial side of valley life by the ideas which must occasionally have accompanied these importations. Probably of local production at about this time was pottery, but dating from the general period are occasional objects of baked clay strongly reminiscent of forms from the Delta and lower San Joaquin. Asphaltum and steatite were locally obtainable, but obsidian and perhaps certain other rarer materials must have come in by trade from the Sierras or beyond. Nothing recovered during our investigations suggests direct contacts with or an indirect outgrowth from any puebloan or earlier southwestern culture horizon, unless the early use of the mealing slab be so interpreted.

In conclusion, I should like to emphasize again that I am not prepared to say to what extent the archeological manifestations at Buena Vista Hills comprise unique or localized elements which would set the remains as such apart from others in southern California. It is not unlikely that, aside from the three or four particular artifact types previously noted, the most distinctive feature of the material culture was the inferred heavy reliance on tule and products derived therefrom. Otherwise, there is scant indication of originality, and one is tempted to view the congeries of concrete traits as either wholesale borrowings from elsewhere or as a local focalization of elements generally southern Californian. In this respect archeology, because of the decidedly one-sided nature of its revelations, would thus credit the native peoples of the southern San Joaquin with a much less distinctive culture than the fuller ethnographic data indicate (Kroeber, 1925, p. 542). On the basis of our findings, it appears that the Buena Vistans owed far more to the Santa Barbara culture center and to southern California generally than to such foci as may once have existed in the Delta, on San Francisco Bay, in the San Joaquin, or anywhere to the east or west.

TABLE 8.—*Summary of vertical distribution of artifacts by 1-foot levels*

Traits	Site 1									Site 2									Site 3	
	0-1	1-2	2-3	3-4	4-5	5-6	6-10	(?)	Total	0-1	1-2	2-3	3-4	4-5	5-6	6-10	(?)	Total	No. specimens	No. burials
Asphaltum:																				
Balls	1	4						1	6											
Coated basketry			1			1			2											
Coated brush			1						1											
Coated pebbles		2	1						1			1								
Inlaid with beads																				
Inlaid with teeth				1					3											
On mortars	1	1																		
Miscellaneous	4	5	4	1	1				14											
Bone and horn:																				
Awls:																				
Type 1A	2	4	3					1	10	2								2		
Type 1B	2	2	1	1					8	1			1					2		
Type 1C	2	4	1	1					8	1	2	1	1					5		
Type 1D	3	3	4	3				1	14		2							2		
Type 1E	4	6	4	2	2			1	19	4	5							9		
Type 1F		1			1				2	3	5	2						10		
Type 2A																	1	1		
Type 2B			1	1				1	2		2							2		
Type 2C														1				1		
Type 3A																				1
Type 3B																				
Total	13	20	14	8	3			5	63	13	12	2	5	1			1	34	1	
Bipointed objects	1	2	2	1					6	6	9							16		
Cut bone	6	5	3	5	2	1		2	23		2							2		
Horn flakers	3	2	1	1	1				8											
"Needles"	4								4											
Pierced fish vertebrae	2	2	3	2	2				11	1		11						12		
"Pins"	2	2			1	1			5											
Sweat scrapers	11	13	4	4	3	1		1	37	6	7	2						15		
Tubes	7	2	1	3	1	1		1	15	3	1		1					5		
Whistles																	1	1		
Pendant, decorated	1								1											
Wedge (horn)	1								1											
Pierced bird claw				2					2											
Drilled turtle shell																				
Half-grooved object											1							1		
Misc. worked fragments	3	5	5	1					14	1								1	1	

TABLE 8.—Summary of vertical distribution of artifacts by 1-foot levels—Continued

Traits	Site 1									Site 2									Site 3	
	0-1	1-2	2-3	3-4	4-5	5-6	6-10	(?)	Total	0-1	1-2	2-3	3-4	4-5	5-6	6-10	(?)	Total	No. specimens	No. burials
Clay:																				
Beads	3		1						4		1							1		
Decorated pellets		1	1						2											
Fillets	3	1	1						5											
Molded tule-wrapped object	1	3	4	1	1	1			11											
Molded plain circular object	3		2						5											
Molded cylinder fragments	1	3	4						8											
Potsherds	1	1	3	3					8											
Miscellaneous		2	2	2		1			7											
European:																				
Glass beads		3							3											
Iron fragment			1						1											
Pigments:																				
Red ochre	5	6	2	1		2			16	6	1	1	1					9		
White			1						1	1	1	1						3		
Yellow ochre										1						1		2		
Shell:																				
Clamshell disk beads	64	54	47	21	11	5			202	4								4		
Clamshell disks, large	1								1											
Clamshell disks, decorated	1	1							2											
Clamshell tubes										2	12	34						48	37	4
Keyhole limpet rings	1	1							2											
Keyhole limpet, painted											1							1		
Olivella disk beads	313	486	425	238	369	133			1,964	196	15	70	5					286		
Olivella half-shell beads	8	7	23	12	9	1			60	57			1					58		
Olivella whole-shell beads	12	4	7	2	3	1			29	9	3	1					1	14		
Minute ring beads											47							47		
Minute cylinder beads																				
Haliotis disk beads	51	44	25	18	7	2			147	1							1	2		
Haliotis disk, large	4								4								1	1		
Haliotis spangle disks	3	2							5											
Haliotis rings	1		3						4			1						1		
Haliotis rim pendants	1								1											
Haliotis receptacle	1								1											

	1	2	3	4	5	6	7	8	9	10	11	12	13
Pendants of *Haliotis* and/or unidentified shell:													
Circular to oval, 2 or 3 edge perforations	2											3	3
Circular to oval, edge, and center perforations	1												
Elliptical, end perforations		2	1										
Elliptical, one end perforation		1											
Rectangular, small ends perforated	4	4		2						10			
Rectangular to oblong, 2 or 3 end perforations							1				37		
Rectangular, small, 2 or 3 edge perforations		1	1							2			
Square, central, and edge perforations		1	1							2	3		1
Oblong or rectangular, 2 side perforations											3		
Rectangular, 1 or 2 central perforations													
Triangular, apex perforated		1			1					1			
Steatite:													
Arrowstraighteners:													
Sherds	4	2	3							10	1		
Others	7	2	2		1			2		2		30+	9+
"Bars"	3	6	4		1			1		17		2	2
Beads, disk	1	2	2	1						7	1	5	2
Beads, disk, edge groove	5	7		1				3		13	2		
Beads, tubular													
Biperforate objects						1							
Bipointed objects													
Disks, large imperforate					2								
Disks, perforated				2	1			1					
Groove-edged:													
Type 1	7	13	9	5	2		3	2		39	1		1
Type 2	11	14	5	3	1		3	1		36			
Type 3	2	2		1				1		6			
Type 4	5	3	2				2	2		12			
Plugs	5	2	1				1	2		8		4	
Reellike objects	51	19	16				2			92		1	
Tube fragments										1			
V-shaped objects	2					2				2			
Vessels and sherds:													
Wide-mouthed bowls		1	2		1	1		1		5		4	4
Globular olla fragments												1	1
Rimsherds:													
6-15 mm. thick, imperforate	1	4	2	1			1	10		10	1	14	
Ditto, drilled rim	9	13	6	4				1		33		1	
16 mm. or over, imperforate	2	4	3	6	1		1	2		16		3	
Ditto, drilled rim	5	4	6	3			2			22			
Miscellaneous	50	29	28	7	2	2	2	5		118		11	11

Table 8.—Summary of vertical distribution of artifacts by 1-foot levels—Continued

Traits	Site 1									Site 2									Site 3	
	0–1	1–2	2–3	3–4	4–5	5–6	6–10	(?)	Total	0–1	1–2	2–3	3–4	4–5	5–6	6–10	(?)	Total	No. specimens	No. burials
Chipped stone:																				
Arrowpoints:																				
NAb1	27	20	20	8	6	2		3	86	14	26	5	2	2	2	1	5	55	1	1
NAb2	1								1		1	1	1					3		
NAb3										3	1		1				1	3		
NBa	6	6	8	3	1				24	15	1	1	1	1			1	4	1	
NBb	100	51	36	11	12			5	215						1			19	64	
NBb1	11	4	2	1					18											
NO										5	1	6						8		
SAa	1	2	1	3					3	6	5	1	1	1			1	20		
SAb			2					1	1	2	4	2						3		
SAc	5	2		3	1	1			14	5	4	2		1			1	12		
SBb										2	1							1		
SBc			1			1			2	2	1		1					4		
SCa1										1	1							3		
SCa2			1						1	1	2							2		
SCb3										1	1							1		
Total									366									135	66	53
Unclassified												4	1				1	6	31	
Cresentic flints	1						1		1											
Knives:																				
Disk, small		1							1											
NAa	5	2	1			1			8				1		1			1		1
NAb1	6	2	3						14											
Unclassified								2	14											
Perforators:																				
Type 1	2	2	2		1				5		1		1		1			3		
Type 2a	2	1							3											
Type 2b	1								1											
Type 2c	1	1							2											
Type 2d									1					1	1			2		
Type 3																				
Type (?)	6	3	1						10	2	3		1							
Saws	29	12	8	2	2				53	10	9	3	1					2		
Scraper knives	50	39	20	10	3				122	32	11	4	8					15		
Scraper knives, asphaltum-smeared	10	22	9	11	2	1	1		55	2	1							57		

																	Total
Ground stone:																	
Arrow straighteners	2	2			1						1					4	
Balls	1	4	1	2											2	8	
Charmstones	2	1										1				3	
Knives																5	
Mealing slabs [1]												1				15	
Mortars, dressed	1	3	1		1		1	2	1		1	2				13	
Boulder and/or hopper	1	4		2		1	7	4			3				6	13	
Mullers		2			1	1	1	11			3					6	16
Pestles	7	5			1		23		4		3	1		4	+	+	271
Miscellaneous and/or unworked				4			3				3	4					
Textiles: [3]																	
Basketry, coiled														+			2
Basketry, twined																	
Cordage, braided																	
Human hair, decoration														+		+	
Soft twined fabrics																	
Wrapped twined fabrics														+		+	
Tule, in graves																	
Tule, braided																	16
Tule, twined																	
Tule and soft twined fabrics																	271

[1] See descriptive section, p. 103.
[2] Five in upper 2 feet.
[3] + indicates presence.

TABLE 9.—*Summary of burial traits*

	Site 1	Site 2	Site 3	Site 4	Site 5
Burials:					
In mound or camp site, adult	5	61			
In mound or camp site, subadult	30	37			
In hardpan, lime-encrusted		4			
On hilltops, adult			253	54	1
On hilltops, subadult			32	10	
In cists or roasting pits		85			
Wrapped in tule and/or textile	1 (?)	6	271	38	
Supine		2			
Prone		2			
Semiflexed	2	11	165	15	
Flexed	11	73	83	38	
Oriented with head to:					
North or northeast	4	33	31	16	
East or southeast	4	24	45	10	
South or southwest	5	23	73	14	
West or northwest	4	12	109	12	
Indeterminate	18	16	97	12	
Accompanied by asphaltum	3	4	25	18	
Accompanied by bone artifacts		7	4		
Accompanied by ochre	1	3	28	5	
Accompanied by shell artifacts	1	13	58	11	
Accompanied by steatite	1	1	15	2	
Accompanied by chipped stone	3	4	53	4	
Accompanied by wooden markers			35+		
Total number of burials	35	108	354	65	1

TABLE 10.—*Size and provenience of artifacts illustrated* [1]

Plate	Diameter		Thickness		Provenience	Field No.	U.S.N.M. No.
	Inches	Centimeters	Inches	Centimeters			
19, *a*	1 17/32	3.9	1 7/16	3.65	Site 1, sq.83/35,d.12–24 in	1–2651	379601
b	1 1/2	3.8	1/2	1.25	Site 1, sq.83/33,d.0–12 in	1–2109	379607
c	2 1/8	5.4	2	5.0	Site 1, sq.83/34,d.12–24 in	1–2203	379600
d	3 5/16	8.4	1 3/8	3.5	Site 1, sq.82/37,d.0–12 in	1–2847	379606
e	1 3/4	4.4	1 5/16	3.3	Site 5, d.18 in	5–8	380649
f	2 5/8	6.7	2 3/8	6.0	Site 1, sq.94/36,d.24 in	1–1881	379599
g	2 1/8	5.4	1 1/16	2.5	Site 1, sq.84/31,d.24–36 in	1–1606	379754
h	1 3/8	3.5	1 3/16	3.0	Site 1, sq.79/39,d.0–12 in	1–1748	379732
i	2 1/8	5.4	1 15/16	4.9	Site 1, sq.87/37,d.36–48 in	1–2024	379729
j	4 3/8	11.1	2 1/2	6.2	Site 1, sq.74/37,d.24 in	1–2842	379728

Plate	Length		Width		Provenience	Field No.	U.S.N.M. No.
	Inches	Centimeters	Inches	Centimeters			
20, *a*	2 3/4	7.0	1 31/32	5.0	Site 1, sq. 95/38, d. 36–38 in	1–768	379722
b	2 5/32	5.5	1 31/32	5.0	Site 1, sq. 95/38, d. 36–38 in	1–768	379722
c	1 3/4	4.45	1 1/4	3.2	Site 1, sq. 94/40, d. 0–12 in	1–264	379724
d	1 11/16	4.3	1 1/4	3.2	Site 1, sq. 85/38, d. 36–48 in	1–1817	379725
e	2 5/8	6.7	12/16	1.9	Site 1, sq. 86/38, d. 12–24 in	1–1257	379721
f	2 11/16	6.8	1 1/16	2.7	Site 1, sq. 85/38, d. 0–12 in	1–1276	380216
g	5/8	1.5	13/16	2.0	Site 1, sq. 86/37, d. 60–72 in	1–2762	379708
h	1 1/4	3.2	13/16	2.0	Site 1, sq. 96/36, d. 0–24 in	1–2180	379719
i	1 7/16	3.7	7/8	2.2	Site 1, sq. 98/39, d. 9 in	1–985	379709
21, *a*	5 1/2	14	2 3/4	7	Site 1, sq. 73/36, d. 6 in	1–3043	379611
b	4 7/8	12.4	1 1/2	3.8	Site 3, Burial 258	3–181	380524

[1] Key to abbreviations: bur., burial; d, depth; e, east; sq., square; surf., surface; tr., trench; U.S.N.M., U. S. National Museum; w, west; cm., centimeters.

TABLE 10.—*Size and provenience of artifacts illustrated*—Continued

Plate	Length		Type	Provenience	Field No.	U.S.N.M. No.
	Inches	Centimeters				
22, *a*	7 7/8	20	1A	Site 1, sq. 83/33, d. 0–12 in.	1-1688	379612
b	3 1/8	8	1A	Site 1, sq. 98/38, d. 28 in.	1-1320	379616
c	6 5/8	16.8	1A	Site 1, sq. 87/38, d. 12–24 in.	1-1203	379613
d	2 13/16	7.2	1A	Site 2, sq. 111/37, d. 0–12 in.	2-536	380258
e	3 1/2	8.9	1A	Site 1, sq. 87/34, d. 24–36 in.	1-2393	379614
f	4 7/16	11.3	1A	Site 1, sq. 80/32, d. 0–12 in.	1-1672	379615
g	4 1/8	10.5	1B	Site 2, sq. 109/27, d. 42 in.	2-537	380259
h	3 1/8	8	1B	Site 2, sq. 112/34, d. 54 in.	2-884	380260
i	7 1/16	17.9	1C	Site 1, sq. 92/38, d. 16 in.	1-463	379619
j	3 9/16	9.1	1C	Site 2, sq. 104/34, d. 12 in.	2-667	380261
k	4 11/16	11.9	1C	Site 1, sq. 79/40, d. 24–36 in.	1-1120	379622
l	4	10.2	1C	Site 2, sq. 116/34, d. 12–24 in.	2-380	380262
m	3 7/8	9.8	1C	Site 1, sq. 84/35, d. 0–12 in.	1-2490	379620
n	4 1/2	11.4	1C	Site 2, sq. 112/29, d. 18 in.	2-545	380263
o	3	7.7	1C	Site 1, sq. 89/42, d. 12 in.	1-207	379621
p	5 3/16	13.2	1C	Site 2, sq. 115/42, d. 48 in.	2-542	380264
q	2 13/16	7.2	1C	Site 1, sq. 93/38, d. 0–12 in.	1-592	379623
r	6 3/16	15.7	1D	Site 1, sq. 84/30, d. 24 in.	1-954	379626
s	2 11/16	6.9	1D	Site 1, sq. 86/34, d. 12–24 in.	1-2313	379625
t	3 15/16	10.0	1D	Site 1, sq. 89/35, & 36, d. 12–28 in.	1-232	379624
u	5	12.8	1D	Site 2, sq. 111/35, d. 36 in.	2-585	380265
v	5 7/16	13.9	1D	Site 2, tr. 1, d. 12 in.	2-79A	380266
w	2 3/16	5.6	1E	Site 1, sq. 86/34, d. 36–48 in.	1-2468	379630
23, *a*	10 5/16	26.2	1C	Site 2, sq. 115/42, d. 32 in. (bur. 62)	2-432	380267
b	5 3/4	14.6	1E	Site 1, 92/35, d. 12 in.	1-1635	379631
c	2 1/2	6.4	1E	Site 1, 86/35, d. 24–36 in.	1-3051	379632
d	5 11/16	14.5	1E	Site 2, 109/33, d. 18 in.	2-849	380268
e	2 5/16	5.8	1E	Site 2, 109/34, d. 16 in.	2-851	380269
f	4	10.1	1E	Site 1, 82/31, d. 0–12 in.	1-1346	379633
g	4 1/2	11.5	1E	Site 2, tr. 1. d. 12 in.	2-79B	380266
h	3 1/2	8.9	1E	Site 2, sq. 112/35, d. 22 in. (bur. 85)	2-806	380270
i	6	15.4	1F	Site 1, sq. 81/39, d. 12–24 in.	1-1264	379635
j	1 15/16	4.9	1F	Site 1, sq. 83/35, d. 12–24 in.	1-2443	379636
k	5 9/16	14.1	1F	Site 2, sq. 106/34, d. 11 in.	2-701x	280273
l	2 5/8	6.8	1F	Site 1, sq. 85/37, d. 0–12 in.	1-2168a	379637
m	5	12.65	1F	Site 1, sq. 82/39, d. 36–48 in.	1-1734	379634
n	5 1/2	14	1F	Site 1, sq. 84/34, d. 54 in.	1-2122	379763
o	4 5/8	11.7	2A	Site 1, sq. 77/34, d. 48–60 in.	1-3066	379641
p	7 7/8	20.1	2A	Site 1, 62/37, d. 12–24 in.	1-2891	379642
q	4 1/8	10.5	2B	Site 2, sq. 110/28, d. 0–12 in.	2-458b	380277
r	4 3/8	11.1	2C	Site 2, sq. 106/24, d. 36–48 in.	2-501	380278
s	2 11/16	6.8	3A	Site 2, sq. 113/29, d. 24–48 in.	2-584	380276
t	4 3/8	11.1	3A	Site ı, sq. 83/34, d. 36–48 in.	1-2070	279643
u	8 5/8	21.9	3A	Site 1, sq. 77/30, d. 24–36 in.	1-2871	279644

Plate	Length		Width		Provenience	Field No.	U.S.N.M. No.
	Inches	Centimeters	Inches	Centimeters			
24, *a*	5 3/4	14.7	3/8	1.0	Site 1, sq. 86/33, d. 24–36 in.	1-2191	379649
b	2 11/16	6.9	5/16	.8	Site 1, sq. 85/32, d. 0–12 in.	1-1690	379650
c	3 1/4	8.3	5/16	.8	Site 2, sq. 113/40, d. 6 in.	2-491	380283
d	3 13/16	8.65	5/16	.8	Site 2, sq. 111/34, d. 24 in.	2-386	380282
e	4 9/16	11.6	5/16	.8	Site 2, sq. 111/35, d. 24 in.	2-538	381281
f	2 7/16	6.2	5/16	.8	Site 1, sq. 94/34, d. 18 in.	1-2428	379651
g	2	5.1	5/16	.8	Site 2, sq. 121/40, d. 0–12 in.	2-358a	380285
h	1 3/8	3.5	3/16	.5	Site 2, sq. 112/26, d. 0–12 in.	2-375	380286
i	1 3/16	3.0	1/4	.7	Site 2, sq. 112/38, d. 24 in.	2-598	380287
j	2 11/16	6.8	5/16	.8	Site 1, sq. 79/41, d. 12–24 in.	1-379	379688
k	2 5/8	6.7	3/16	.5	Site 1, sq. 69/41, d. 12–24 in.	1-386	379686
l	5 5/16	13.5	5/32	.4	Site 1, sq. 85/40, d. 12–24 in.	1-352	379689
m	2 1/16	5.2	1 1/16	1.8	Site 2, sq. 107/20, d. 18 in.	2-237	380288
n	1 9/16	3.9	1/2	1.9	Site 1, sq. 81/39, d. 0–12 in.	1-1047	379693
o	1 1/4	3.2	1 3/8	3.5	Site 1, sq. 82/39, d. 36–48 in.	1-1288	379694
p	7/8	2.4	7/16	1.2	Site 1, sq. 86/35, d. 12–24 in.	1-3049	379692
q	1 3/32	2.8	7/16	1.1	Site 1, sq. 86/34, d. 24–36 in.	1-2698	379691
r	1 13/16	4.5	5/16	.8	Site 1, sq. 81/40, d. 12–24 in.	1-1372	379687
25, *a*	10 5/16	26.2	------	------	Site 2, sq. 115/42, d. 32 in. (bur. 62)	2-432	380267
b	7 1/8	18.1	1 1/4	3.2	Site 2, sq. 108/33, d. 25 in.	2-889	380289
c	3 3/16	8.1	1 1/4	3.2	Site 2, pit 2 near tr. 1, d. 2 ft.	2-115	380290
d	5 13/16	14.8	7/8	2.2	Site 2, sq. 108/21, d. 0–12 in.	2-202	380291
e	3 3/4	9.6	29/32	2.3	Site 1, sq. 21/35, d. 0–24 in.	1-1586	379696
f	4 1/4	10.8	3/8	1.0	Site 1, sq. 86/39, d. 12–24 in.	1-2000	379699
g	4 1/4	10.8	7/16	1.1	Site 1, sq. 85/34, d. 12–24 in.	1-2146	379700
h	5 1/4	13.4	1/2	1.3	Site 1, sq. 86/33, d. 36–48 in.	1-2002	379698
i	4 1/16	10.3	1 3/8	3.5	Site 1, sq. 70/33, d. 12 in.	1-3018	379697

TABLE 10.—*Size and provenience of artifacts illustrated*—Continued

Plate	Length		Width or diameter		Provenience	Field No.	U.S.N.M. No.
	Inches	Centimeters	Inches	Centimeters			
26, *a*	7 1/2	19.3	7/32	0.9	Site 1, sq. 83/34, d. 36–48 in.	1-2138	379660
b	2 9/16	6.5	3/8	1.0	Site 1, sq. 89/(?), d. (?)	1-313	379661
c	2 15/16	7.5	5/16	.8	Site 1, sq. 89/37, d. 54 in.	1-33	379662
d	2 7/16	6.2	5/16	.8	Site 1, sq. 85/34, d. 0–12 in.	1-2348	379663
e	2 1/16	5.2	1/4	.65	Site 1, sq. 83/37, d. 0–12 in.	1-2431	379664
f	2	5.0	1/4	.65	Site 1, sq. 86/38, d. 24–36 in.	1-1537	379665
g	3 1/16	7.7	3/8	1.0	Site 1, sq. 84/39, d. 36–48 in.	1-962	379666
h	1 3/8	3.5	7/16	1.2	Site 1, sq. 84/35, d. 12–24 in.	1-2495	379675
i	1 1/2	3.8	3/8	1.0	Site 1, sq. 90/36, d. 24 in.	1-3021	379681
j	3/4	2.0	23/32	1.85	Site 1, sq. 89/(?), d. 12–27 in.	1-209	379676
k	1 9/16	4.0	3/16	.5	Site 1, sq. 75/41, d. 12–24 in.	1-382	379677
l	1 1/4	3.2	5/16	.8	Site 1, sq. 92/38, d. 0–12 in.	1-2397	379678
m	1 15/16	4.9	5/16	.8	Site 1, sq. 80/32, d. 0–12 in.	1-1593	379679
n	15/16	2.3	5/16	.8	Site 1, sq. 89/(?), d. (?)	1-314	379680
o	2 7/8	7.4	3/8	1.0	Site 1, sq. 89/37, surf.	1-3023	379667
p	3 13/16	9.7	1/2	1.3	Site 1, sq. 96/33, d. 6 in.	1-2121	379668

Plate	Diameter				Provenience	Field No.	U.S.N.M. No.
	Maximum		Minimum				
	Inches	Centimeters	Inches	Centimeters			
27, *a*	3/32	0.25	------	------	Site 2, sq. 113/40, d. 53 in. (bur. 65)	2-711	380336
b	------	------	1/8	.3	Site 2, sq. 104/36, d. 67 in. (bur. 106)	2-920	380343
c	1/4	.6	5/32	.4	Site 2, sq. 104/36, d. 67 in. (bur. 106)	2-920	380343
d	15/32	1.2	1/4	.6	Site 1, sq. 87/28, d. 0–12 in.	1-653	379766
e	15/16	2.4	3/4	1.8	Site 2, surface of sandspit	2-31 A, B	380306
f	13/16	2.0	11/16	1.7	Site 1, sq. 86/34, d. 36–48 in.	1-2476	379782
g	11/16	1.7	------	------	Site 1, sq. 89/40, d. 48–60 in.	1-80	379795
h	5/16	.8	------	------	Site 1, sq. 86/32, d. 0–12 in.	1-1701	379800
i	13/32	1.0	7/32	.55	Site 1, sq. 87/28, d. 12 in.	1-715	379824
j	15/32	1.2	------	------	Site 1, sq. 85/28, d. 0–12 in.	1-558	379806
k	5/16	.8	9/32	.75	Site 1, sq. 80/31, d. 12–24 in.	1-1333	379804
l	11/16	1.7	9/32	.7	Site 1, sq. 84/37, d. 0–12 in.	1-2067	379807
m	7/16	1.1	------	------	Site 1, sq. 86/37, d. 48–60 in.	1-2627	379812
n	15/32	1.2	------	------	Site 1, sq. 86/39, d. 0–12 in.	1-700	379808
o	3/4	1.9	------	------	Site 1, sq. 76/42, d. 17 in.	1-277	379809
p	19/32	1.5	------	------	Site 1, sq. 81/40, d. 0–12 in.	1-445	379811
q	17/32	1.4	------	------	Site 1, sq. 83/31, d. 0–12 in.	1-1322	379810
r	7/8	2.2	------	------	Site 1, sq. 84/32, d. 0–12 in.	1-1639	379840
s	11/16	1.7	------	------	Site 1, sq. 86/28, d. 12 in.	1-723	379839
t	1 1/32	2.6	3/8	1.0	Site 1, sq. 86/34, d. 36–48 in.	1-2670	379838
u	7/16	1.1	3/8	1.0	Site 1, sq. 86/33, d. 12–24 in.	1-1885	379765
v	3/4	1.8	------	------	Site 2, sq. 104/35, d. 67 in. (bur. 106)	2-928	380344
w	3/4	1.8	3/8	1.0	Site 3, burial 102	3-119	380541
x	3/4	1.8	17/32	1.3	Site 1, sq. 86/34, d. 24–36 in.	1-2699	379831
y	7/8	2.2	7/16	1.1	Site 1, sq. 86/35, d. 24–36 in.	1-2832	379832

TABLE 10.—*Size and provenience of artifacts illustrated*—Continued

Plate	Length		Width		Provenience	Field No.	U.S.N.M. No.
	Inches	Centi-meters	Inches	Centi-meters			
28, a	3 11/16	9.1	3/8	1.0	Site 1, sq. 82/30, d. 24–36 in	1–1193	379848
b	3/4	2.0	---	---	Site 2, sq. 104/37, d. 30 in	2–909	380328
c	7/8	2.2	11/16	1.8	Site 1, sq. 86/35, d. 12–24 in. (?)	1–2825	379834
d	1	2.5	7/8	2.2	Site 1, sq. 86/38, d. (?)	1–2295	379835
e	1 7/32	3.1	15/16	2.4	Site 3, burial 254	3–174a	380546
f	1 1/4	3.2	1 1/16	2.7	Site 2, sq. 112/38, d. 18 in	2–613	380329
g	5/8	1.6	1/2	1.2	Site 2, sq. 112/35, d. 36 (bur. 88)	2–861	380341
h	1 1/8	2.9	1	2.5	Site 3, burial 68 and 73	3–6	380536
i	15/16	2.4	7/8	2.2	Site 3, burial 68 and 73	3–6	380536
j	2 5/16	5.8	7/8	2.2	Site 3, burial 3	3–18	380525
k	2 1/4	5.6	7/8	2.2	Site 3, burial 3	3–18	380525
l	2 5/16	5.8	1 5/8	4.2	Site 3, burial 89	3–226	380537
29, a	1 1/32	2.6	3/4	1.9	Site 2, sq. 104/36, d. 67 in. (bur. 106)	2–919	380342
b	7/16	1.1	11/32	.9	Site 2, sq. 111/36, d. 12 in	2–535	380320
c	5/8	1.55	9/16	1.35	Site 2, sq. 113/40, d. 53 in. (bur. 65)	2–735	380334
d	2 3/16	5.5	1 5/8	4.0	Site 2, sq. 113/41, d. 59 in. (bur. 84)	2–862	380339
e	1 7/8	4.7	1 9/16	4.0	Site 2, sq. 106/20, d. 20 in	2–304	380318
f	1 9/16	3.9	1 5/16	3.3	Site 2, sq. 111/40, d. 10 in	2–811	380323
g	2 1/4	5.6	2	5.0	Site 2, tr. 2, d. 72 in	2–708	380324
h	2 1/16	5.3	1 3/16	2.1	Site 2, sq. 109/28, d. 14 in	2–896A	380322
i	1 7/8	4.8	7/16	1.1	Site 2, sq. 111/40, d. 12 in	2–805	380321

Plate	Length		Average diameter		Provenience	Field No.	U.S.N.M. No.
	Inches	Centi-meters	Inches	Centi-meters			
30, a	23	58.5	---	---	Site 4, sq. 76/58, d. 8 in. (bur. 50)	4–99	380619
b	13 1/2	34.3	---	---	Site 4, sq. 77/58, d. 54 in. (bur. 39)	4–147	380621
c	11	28.0	---	---	Site 4, sq. 75/59, d. 29 in. (bur. 2)	4–162	380617
d	5 1/2	14.0	---	---	Site 3, burial 102	3–94	380539
e	34	86.4	---	---	Site 3, burial 347	3–278	380552
f	---	---	1 1/16	1.8	Site 2, sq. 109/32, d. 27 in. (bur. 8)	2–167	380350
g	4 3/32	10.4	3 7/16	8.7	Site 2, sq. 109/24, burial 36	2–632	380332

Plate	Length (or diameter)		Width (or thickness)		Provenience	Field No.	U.S.N.M. No.
	Inches	Centi-meters	Inches	Centi-meters			
31, a	7/16	1.2	3/16	0.5	Site 1, sq. 83/33, d. 24–36 in	1–1870	379987
b	7/16	1.2	3/16	.5	Site 1, sq. 83/33, d. 36–48 in	1–1861	379988
c	1/2	1.3	3/16	.5	Site 1, sq. 86/31, d. 12–24 in	1–1625	379989
d	11/32	.9	1/4	.7	Site 1, sq. 80/32, d. 0–12 in	1–1594	379990
e	3/4	1.9	5/16	.75	Site 1, sq. 87/37, d. 80 in	1–3028	379991
f	5/8	1.6	3/8	1.0	Site 1, sq. 94/34, d. 24 in	1–1876	379992
g	5/8	1.6	13/32	1.15	Site 1, sq. 89/34, d. 48 in	1–199	379993
h	1/2	1.3	7/32	.6	Site 3, burial 222	3–263	380562
i	9/32	.7	3/16	.5	Site 3, burial 15	3–139	380561
j	19/32	1.5	7/32	.6	Site 1, sq. 84/38, d. 36–48 in	1–2429	379994
k	1/2	1.3	5/16	.8	Site 1, sq. 86/30, d. 24–36 in	1–1214	379995
l	3/4	1.9	1/2	1.3	Site 1, sq. 97/41, d. 24–36 in	1–156	379996
m	1 3/32	2.8	1/2	1.3	Site 1, sq. 91/36, d. 6 in	1–3020	379951
n	1 9/16	4.0	9/16	1.4	Site 1, sq. 85/32, d. 12–24 in	1–1847	379952
o	1 1/8	2.9	1 3/32	2.8	Site 1, sq. 93/40, d. 0–12 in	1–375	379953
p	1 17/32	3.9	5/8	1.6	Site 1, sq. 98/39, d. 24 in	1–1118	379949
q	7/8	2.2	13/32	2.05	Site 1, sq. 86/34, d. 36–48 in	1–2478	379950
r	1 19/32	4.1	3/4	1.9	Site 1, sq. 85/38, d. 48–60 in	1–1905	379948

TABLE 10.—*Size and provenience of artifacts illustrated*—Continued

Plate	Length		Width		Provenience	Field No.	U.S.N.M. No.
	Inches	Centimeters	Inches	Centimeters			
32, a	1 7/8	4.8	1 5/32	3.2	Site 1, sq. 87/28, d. 12 in.	1-692	379882
b	2 7/8	7.3	2 1/4	5.7	Site 1, sq. 83/29, d. 36 in.	1-876a	379895
c	1 3/4	4.45	1.0	2.6	Site 1, sq. 91/35(?), d. 0-24 in.	1-2242	379886
d	6 1/2	16.5	4 9/32	10.9	Site 1, sq. 89/35, d. 36 in.	1-25	379880
e	4	10.2	2 9/16	6.5	Site 1, sq. 83/34(?), d. 12-24 in.	1-2319	379881
f	2 1/8	5.4	1 7/16	3.6	Site 1, sq. 87/32, d. 12-24 in.	1-2093	379885
g	2 3/8	6.05	1 23/32	4.3	Site 1, sq. 82/31, d. 12-24 in.	1-1400	379884
h	2 7/8	7.3	1 15/32	3.75	Site 1, sq. 85/33, d. 12-24 in.	1-2236	379883
i	4 7/32	10.7	2 9/16	6.5	Site 1, sq. 84/39, d. 12-24 in.	1-703	379896
j	3 3/16	8.1	2 17/32	6.4	Site 1, sq. 83/33, d. 0-12 in.	1-2107	379897
k	2 5/8	6.7	1 11/16	4.3	Site 1, sq. 86/30, d. 12-24 in.	1-1179	379898
l	1 29/32	4.9	1 1/16	2.7	Site 1, sq. 89/36, d. 24 in.	1-24	379901
m	2 11/32	5.95	1 19/32	3.9	Site 1, sq. 87/33, d. 0-12 in.	1-2562	379899
n	2 5/16	5.85	2 9/32	2.3	Site 1, sq. 86/37, d. 12-24 in.	1-2198	379900

Plate	Length		Width (or thickness)		Provenience	Field No.	U.S.N.M. No.
	Inches	Centimeters	Inches	Centimeters			
33, a	1 29/32	4.9	1 9/32	3.3	Site 1, sq. 95/35, d. 0-24 in.	1-2224	379866
b	1 11/16	4.3	1 5/16	2.4	Site 1, sq. 85/39, d. 0-12 in.	1-1373	379867
c	2 29/32	7.4	1 9/32	3.3	Site 1, sq. 79/32, d. 0-12 in.	1-1721	379865
d	1 1/2	3.8	3/4	1.9	Site 1, sq. 89/42, d. 12 in.	1-204	379943
e	1 11/32	3.4	2 3/32	1.85	Site 1, sq. 83/33, d. 0-12 in.	1-2110	379944
f	1 5/16	3.45	1 7/32	1.35	Site 1, sq. 84/40, d. 0-12 in.	1-423	379945
g	5/8	1.6	1 1/32	.9	Site 1, sq. 83/34, d. 48-60 in.	1-2268	379947
h	1 5/8	4.1	1/2	1.3	Site 1, sq. 87/34, d. 12-24 in.	1-2578	379946
i	1 7/8	4.8	1 11/16	4.3	Site 1, sq. 86/39, d. 0-12 in.	1-766	379941
j	1 5/16	3.3	1	2.56	Site 1, sq. 85/91, d. 12 in.	1-685	379942
k	2 3/32	5.3	1 5/8	4.1	Site 1, sq. 67/40, d. 12-24 in.	1-2775	379935
l	1 7/16	3.6	1	2.56	Site 1, sq. 87/34, d. 24-36 in.	1-2715	379936
m	2 7/32	5.6	1 5/16	2.4	Site 1, sq. 78/28, d. 0-12 in.	1-684	379937
n	1 9/32	3.25	1 9/32	1.5	Site 1, sq. 82/39, d. 0-12 in.	1-938	379939
o	1 1/16	2.7	3/4	1.9	Site 1, sq. 78/30, d. 24-36 in.	1-1018	379938
p	2 5/8	6.7	1/2	1.25	Site 1, sq. 83/34, d. 12-24 in.	1-2400	379934
q	2 7/8	7.3	1 5/16	3.3	Site 1, sq. 84/40, d. 36-48 in.	1-606	379932
r	2 23/32	6.9	7/16	1.2	Site 1, sq. 80/41, d. 12-24 in.	1-348	379874
s	3 1/16	7.8	1 5/16	2.4	Site 1, sq. 84/33, d. 36-48 in.	1-1966	379933
t	5 3/16	13.2	3 1/16	7.8	Site 1, sq. 94/40, d. 0-12 in.	1-263	379929
u	2 9/32	5.5	1 13/16	4.6	Site 1, sq. 84/34, d. 48-60 in (?).	1-2503	379940
v	2 5/16	5.8	1 29/32	4.8	Site 1, sq. 83/40, d. 24-36 in.	1-665	379864
w	2 1/4	5.7	1 7/16	3.6	Site 1, sq. 91/35(?), d. 0-36 in. (?)	1-1939	379931
x	3.0	7.6	2 3/16	5.55	Site 1, sq. 81/28, d. 0-12 in.	1-627	379930

Plate	Length		Width		Provenience	Field No.	U.S.N.M. No.
	Inches	Centimeter	Inches	Centimeter			
34, a	2 1/8	5.4	1 5/32	2.6	Site 1, sq. 86/30, d. 12 in.	1-976	379954
b	1 5/32	2.6	1 3/16	2.1	Site 1, (dump).	1-3038	379955
c	1 1/2	3.8	1.0	2.5	Site 1, sq. 85/38, d. 0-12 in.	1-1443	379956
d	1 11/32	3.4	3 1/32	2.45	Site 1, sq. 85/37, d. 24-36 in.	1-2511	379957
e	1 1/8	2.85	1 7/16	3.6	Site 1, sq. 63/37, d. 6 in.	1-3000	379958
f	1 3/16	3.05	1 5/32	2.6	Site 1, sq. 87/31, d. 24-36 in.	1-1705	379959
g	1 3/8	3.5	1 9/32	2.8	Site 1, sq. 86/40, d. 0-12 in.	1-475	379960
h	1 11/16	4.3	1 7/16	3.6	Site 1, sq. 86/32, d. 0-12 in.	1-1718	379961
i	2 1/16	5.25	1 13/16	4.6	Site 1, sq. 81/31, d. 12-24 in.	1-1598	379962
j	1 15/32	3.4	7/8	2.2	Site 1, sq. 89/32, d. 12 in.	1-73	379963
k	1 7/32	3.1	1 15/32	3.7	Site 1, sq. 86/34, d. 12-24 in.	1-2519	379964
l	1 7/8	4.8	1 15/16	4.9	Site 1, sq. 92/41, d. 12-24 in.	1-91	379965
m	2 1/4	5.7	3/4	1.9	Site 1, sq. 82/28, d. 0-12 in.	1-492	379966
n	1 29/32	4.9	1 5/16	2.4	Site 1, sq. 80/32, d. 0-12 in.	1-1591	379967
o	1 3/16	3.0	1 1/2	3.8	Site 1, sq. 79/39, d. 0-12 in.	1-1383	379968
p	1 15/16	4.9	1 5/16	3.4	Site 1, sq. 75/41, d. 12 in.	1-42	379969

TABLE 10.—*Size and provenience of artifacts illustrated*—Continued

Plate	Length Inches	Length Centimeters	Width Inches	Width Centimeters	Depth Inches	Depth Centimeters	Provenience	Field No.	U.S.N.M. No.
35, a	15 1/16	38.2	12	30.5	3 1/2	8.9	Site 1, sq. 70/32, d. 63 in. (bur. 5.).	1-2869	380038
b	6 1/4	16.0	6	15.3	2 11/16	6.9	Site 1, sq. 70/32, d. 63 in. (bur. 5).	1-2868	380039
c	15 5/8	38.3	12 3/8	31.0	7 1/2	19.0	Site 1, sq. 111/36, d. 30 in.	1-2732	380040
36, a	12 3/4	31.2	11 1/4	28.6	5 1/8	13.0	Site 1, sq. 87/29, d.14 in.	1-1677	380042
b	13 3/8	33.7	13 1/8	33.3	5 3/8	13.6	Site 1, sq.111/36, d.30 in.	1-2733	380041

Plate	Length (or diameter) Inches	Length (or diameter) Centimeter	Width (or thickness) Inches	Width (or thickness) Centimeter	Provenience	Field No.	U.S.N.M. No.
37, a	3 1/4	8.1	1 3/32	1.1	Site 2, sq. 107/35, d. 0-12 in	2-478	380373
b	2 3/32	5.2	3/8	.9	Site 2, sq. 111/29, d. 8 in	2-628	380374
c	3 1/32	7.7	1 3/32	1.1	Site 2, sq. 106/25, d. 20 in	2-426	380370
d	1 3/4	4.45	1 7/32	3.1	Site 2, tr. 1, d. 6 in	2-269	380378
e	1 7/16	3.7	1 1/8	2.8	Site 2, sq. 107/20, d. 15 in	2-238	380377
f	2 5/8	6.5	3/8	.9	Site 2, sq. 104/33, d. 6 in	2-796	380372
g	1 15/16	4.95	1 9/32	3.25	Site 2, sq. 112/38, d. 60 in	2-738	380379
h	2	5.1	1 11/16	4.3	Site 2, surf	2-153	380380
i	2 9/16	6.5	1 31/32	5.0	Site 2, tr. 1, surf	2-173	380389
j	1 31/32	5.0	1 11/16	4.3	Site 2 tr. 1, surf	2-97	380381
k	3 19/32	9.2	1 17/32	3.9	Site 2, tr. 1, surf	2-98	380382

Plate	Length Inches	Length Cm.	Width Inches	Width Cm.	Provenience	Field No.	U.S.N.M. No.
38, a	1 3/8	3.5	1/2	1.25	Site 1, sq. 84/34, d. 12-24 in	1-2083	380043
b	1 1/4	3.2	5/8	1.55	Site 1, sq. 84/30, d. 24 in	1-948	380044
c	1	2.5	1/2	1.25	Site 1, sq. 87/28, d. 12 in	1-718	380045
d	1 3/8	3.5	19/32	1.5	Site 1, sq. 84/35, d. 24-36 in	1-2472	380046
e	1 1/4	3.2	7/16	1.15	Site 1, sq. 87/38, d. 0-12 in	1-2102	380047
f	1 3/8	3.5	17/32	1.35	Site 1, sq. 85/31, d. 0-12 in	1-1469	380048
g	3/4	1.9	19/32	1.5	Site 1, sq. (?), d. (?)	1-358	380049
h	1 1/4	3.2	17/32	1.3	Site 1, sq. 82/31, d. 12-24 in	1-1447b	380050
i	1 5/8	4.1	19/32	1.5	Site 1, sq. 84/31, d. 12 in	1-1351	380051
j	1 1/4	3.2	5/8	1.55	Site 3, burial 121	3-74c	380565
k	2 3/8	6.0	19/32	1.5	Site 3, burial 16	3-40	380563
l	1 7/16	3.7	5/8	1.6	Site 3, burial 108	3-298	380564
m	1 9/16	4.0	1/2	1.25	Site 3, burial 108	3-106	380564
n	1 5/8	4.1	11/16	1.8	Site 3, burial 121	3-74d	380565
o	3.0	7.6	1/2	1.25	Site 1, sq. 89/37, d. 54 in	1-32	380090
p	1 15/16	4.9	9/16	1.3	Site 1, sq. 87/37, d. 0-12 in	1-1951	380078
q	2	5.1	11/16	1.7	Site 4, sq. 75/59, d. 16 in. (bur. 5)	4-138	380629
r	2 5/16	5.9	3/4	1.9	Site 4, sq. 75/58, d. 36 in. (bur. 9)	4-144	380630
s	2 1/16	5.25	15/16	2.4	Site 2, surf	2-155	380439
t	1 7/16	3.7	1 1/8	2.9	Site 2, tr. 2, d. (?)	2-249	380407
u	1 7/8	4.75	7/8	2.2	Site 2, sq. 107/23, d. 0-12 in	2-293	380408
v	1 7/8	4.75	27/32	2.1	Site 1, sq. 86/30, d. 24-36 in	1-1213	380112
w	2 3/4	7.0	25/32	2.0	Site 2, tr. 1, W. 104', d. 24 in	2-46	380404
x	2 27/32	7.2	7/8	2.2	Site 2, sq. 107/34, d. 4 in	2-448	380409
y	2 27/32	7.2	1	2.5	Site 1, sq. 87/38, d. 60-72 in	1-2547	380114
z	1 9/16	4.0	1 1/8	2.9	Site 1, sq. 84/30, d. 12-24 in	1-1037	380111
a'	1 3/32	2.8	23/32	1.8	Site 1, sq. 85/28, d. 12 in	1-595	380110
b'	2 1/16	5.3	1	2.5	Site 1, sq. 83/33, d. 36-48 in	1-1862	380113
c'	2 1/4	5.7	1 3/32	2.8	Site 2, tr. 1, d. 30 in	2-243	380406
39, a	1 13/32	3.6	1/2	1.3	Site 1, sq. 92/38, d. 16 in	1-529	380126
b	1 1/16	1.7	13/32	1.0	Site 1, sq. 85/30, d. 24-36 in	1-1358	380127
c	1 1/4	3.2	5/8	1.6	Site 3, burial 308 (?)	3-235	380578
d	1 5/16	3.4	9/16	1.5	Site 2, sq. 106/33, d. 2 in	2-855	380420
e	1 1/4	3.2	15/32	1.2	Site 1, sq. 80/32, d. 0-12 in	1-1579	380128
f	7/8	2.2	9/16	1.5	Site 1, sq. 78/30, d. (?)	1-843b	380129
g	1 3/16	3.0	15/32	1.2	Site 1, sq. 85/38, d. 36-48 in	1-2105	380130
h	1 9/16	4.0	3/4	1.9	Site 2, sq. 109/28, d. 44 in	2-633	380432
i	1 1/2	3.9	25/32	2.0	Site 2, sq. 109/28, d. 24 in	2-507	380431
j	1 3/4	4.5	15/16	2.4	Site 2, surf	2-154b	380428

TABLE 10.—*Size and provenience of artifacts illustrated*—Continued

Plate	Length Inches	Length Cm.	Width Inches	Width Cm.	Provenience	Field No.	U.S.N.M. No.
k	2 1/16	5.2	27/32	2.2	Site 2, surf	2–489	380430
l	1 3/4	4.5	7/8	2.2	Site 2, sq. 116/32, d. 0–12 in	2–286	380429
m	1 21/32	4.2	1 1/32	2.6	Site 1, sq. 61/37, d. (?) (bur. 25)	1–2881	380152
n	1 9/16	4.0	27/32	2.2	Site 2, sq. 111/36, d. 30 in	2–588	380433
o	1 7/16	3.7	25/32	2.0	Site 1, sq. 49/37, d. 36 in	1–2865	380151
p	2 3/8	6.1	1 9/32	3.2	Site 2, sq. 107/23, d. 14 in	2–629	380459
q	1 11/16	4.4	5/8	1.6	Site 1, sq. 85/30, d. 12 in	1–1077	380133
r	1 1/2	3.8	1 5/16	3.3	Site 1, sq. 80/39, d. 0–12 in	1–1389	280134
s	1 3/4	4.5	1 1/32	.9	Site 1, sq. 83/34, d. 48–60 in	1–2375	380136
t	1 15/16	4.9	5/8	1.6	Site 1, sq. 92/34, d. 96 in	1–1792	380135
u	1 27/32	4.7	27/32	2.2	Site 4, sq. 74/58, d. (?) (bur. 110) (?)	4–117	380638
v	1 5/16	2.4	29/32	2.3	Site 1, sq. 86/40, d. 0–12 in	1–477	380153
w	1 5/16	3.4	7/8	2.2	Site 2, tr. 1, E. 80 ft., d. 36 in	2–192a	380468
x	1 27/32	4.7	3 1/32	2.5	Site 2, tr. 1, beach, d. 40 in	2–176	380467
y	1 7/8	4.8	1 3/16	2.0	Site 2, tr. 1, dirt pile	2–719	380466
40, a	6 25/32	17.3	1 3/8	3.5	Site 1, sq. 96/38, d. 10 in	1–742	380155
b	4 1/8	10.5	1 5/16	3.3	Site 1, sq. 89/34, d. 12 in	1–201	380154
c	3 9/32	8.3	1 5/16	3.3	Site 1, sq. 87/38, d. 24–36 in	1–1438	380156
d	7 1/16	18.0	1 25/32	4.5	Site 3, burial 256	3–163	380580
e	3 7/8	9.85	1 11/32	3.4	Site 2, tr. 1, W. 115 ft., d. 30 in	2–52	380472
f	3 15/16	10.0	1 3/8	3.5	Site 2, sq. 115/42, d. 32 in (bur. 62)	2–433	380473
g	6 7/16	16.4	1 3/4	4.5	Site 2, sq. 108/26, d. 6 in	2–663	380474
h	3 13/16	9.7	1 27/32	4.7	Site 1, sq. 99/34, d. 0–12 in	1–2622	380221
i	2 5/8	6.7	1 5/8	4.1	Site 1, sq. 83/35, d. 0–12 in	1–2722	380222
41, a	3 13/16	9.7	3 1/4	8.2	Site 1, sq. 86/41, d. 12 in	1–61	380196
b	4 1/2	11.5	1 7/8	4.8	Site 1, sq. 94/40, d. 0–12 in	1–361	380197
c	4 1/8	10.5	2 3/16	5.6	Site 1, sq. 102/39, d. 9 in	1–480	380198
d	5 15/16	15.1	4 1/4	10.8	Site 4, sq. 76/59, d. 13 in (bur. 28)	4–102	380635
42, a	2 3/16	5.6	1 15/32	3.7	Site 1, sq. 86/33, d. 36–48 in	1–2139	380162
b	1 15/16	5.0	1 7/16	3.65	Site 1, sq. 87/34, d. 12–24 in	1–2573	380163
c	1 27/32	4.7	29/32	2.3	Site 1, sq. 86/34, d. 36–48 in	1–2477	380164
d	2 1/4	5.7	2 1/16	5.2	Site 1, sq. 89/30–34, d. 0–48 in	1–247	380165
e	2	5.2	1 7/8	4.3	Site 1, sq. 70/33, d. 0–12 in	1–3040	380167
f	2 1/16	5.1	1 11/16	4.3	Site 1, sq. 92/40, d. 0–12 in	1–266	380166
43, a	3 21/32	9.3	2 3/4	7.0	Site 4, sq. 77/58, d. 30 in	4–110	380610
b	3 3/32	7.85	2 27/32	7.2	Site 1, sq. 83/31, d. 12–24 in	1–1419	380209
c	3 1/4	8.25			Site 1, sq. 78/31, d. 12–24 in	1–1418	380210
d	1 29/32	4.85			Site 1, sq. 49/37, d. 0–48 in	1–2882	380211
e	2.0	5.1			Site 1, sq. 89/(?), d. 12–27 in	1–210	380212
f	5 17/32	14.1	1 27/32	4.7	Site 1, sq. 87/35, d. 60–72 in	1–2877	380253
g	2 3/32	5.35	1 11/32	3.4	Site 1, sq. 70/37, d. 0–12 in	1–2862	380252
h	4 13/16	12.2	3 13/32	8.65	Site 2, sq. 108/24, d. 36–48 in	2–388	380500
i	4 7/8	12.35	3 5/16	8.4	Site 1, sq. 86/29, d. 12–24 in	1–874	380224

Plate	Length Inches	Length Centimeter	Diameter Inches	Diameter Centimeter	Provenience	Field No.	U.S.N.M. No.
44, a	4 13/16	12.15	1 23/32	4.35	Site 2, sq. 109/24, d. 36 in	2–318	380492
b	3 21/32	9.3	1 1/2	3.8	Site, 2 surface of spit	2–23A	380490
c	4 9/16	11.6	1 3/32	3.55	Site 2, surface of spit	2–23B	380491
d	3 5/8	9.25	1 1/16	2.7	Site 2, sq. 106/29, d. 36 in	2–754	380493
e	2 3/16	5.55	7/8	2.25	Site 1, sq. 89/35 & 36, d.12–28 in	1–231	380218
f			1 3/32	2.8	Site 2, tr. 2, d.18 in	2–144	380487
g			1	2.5	Site 2, sq. 111/35, d.36 in	2–559	380486
h			1 15/16	4.9	Site 2, sq. 113/41, d.8 in	2–534	380489

Plate	Length Inches	Length Centimeters	Width Inches	Width Centimeters	Thickness Inches	Thickness Centimeters	Provenience	Field No.	U.S.N.M. No.
45, a	7 3/8	18.8	6 3/8	16.2	2 1/2	6.3	Site 1, sq. 89/39, d. 52 in	1–179	380732
b	3 15/16	10.0	3 3/4	9.5	2 7/8	7.3	Site 1, sq. 83/37, d. 0–12 in	1–2646	380234
c	4.0	10.2	4.0	10.2	3 1/4	8.3	Site 1, sq. 86/37, d. 12–24 in.	1–2073	380233

TABLE 10.—*Size and provenience of artifacts illustrated*—Continued

Plate	Maximum diameter		Height		Provenience	Field No.	U.S.N.M. No.
	Inches	Centimeters	Inches	Centimeters			
46, *a*	8 3/4	22.2	5 5/8	14.4	Site 2, tr. 1, w 31 ft.; d. 62 in	2-223	380498
b	9 3/8	24.0	7	18.0	Site 2, sq. 119/34, d. 12 in	2-211B	380497
c	10 3/8	26.6	7 1/8	18.3	Site 2, sq. 112/39, d. 14 in	2-697	380496

Plate	Length		Maximum diameter		Provenience	Field No.	U.S.N.M. No.
	Inches	Centimeters	Inches	Centimeters			
47, *a*	6 7/16	16.4	2 3/8	6.1	Site 2, sq. 112/39, d. 18 in	2-677	380517
b	6 3/16	15.7	2 1/2	6.3	Site 1, sq. 89/33, d. 15 in	1-18	380240
c	5 29/32	15.0	2 7/16	6.2	Site 1, sq. 84/35, d. 0-12 in	1-2486	380241
d	5 3/16	13.2	2 3/16	5.6	Site 1, sq. 92/33, d. 0-24 in	1-2205B	380242
e	9 3/4	24.8	3 1/2	9.0	Site 2, surf	2-124	380513
f	9	22.9	1 3/8	3.5	Site 2, tr. 1, w. 105 ft., d. 12 in	2-68	380512
g	11 3/8	29.0	3 11/16	9.4	Site 1, sq. 83/33, d. 36 in	1-1811	380243

Plate	Length		Width (or thickness)		Provenience	Field No.	U.S.N.M. No.
	Inches	Centimeters	Inches	Centimeters			
51, *a*	2 7/16	6.2	1 9/16	4.0	Site 3, burial-55	3-112	380584
b	2	5.0	1 1/2	3.7	Site 3, burial 55	3-112	380584
c	4 3/4	12.1	3 1/4	8.3	Site 3, burial 255	3-272	380585

LITERATURE CITED

BANCROFT, HUBERT HOWE

1886. The works of. 39 vols. 1886–1890. History of California, vol. 2, 1801–1824. San Francisco.

BOLTON, HERBERT E.

1931. In the south San Joaquin ahead of Garcés. Quart. Calif. Hist. Soc., vol. 10, No. 3, pp. 211–219.

COUES, ELLIOTT, EDITOR

1900. On the trail of a Spanish pioneer, the diary and itinerary of Francisco Garcés, 1775–76, 2 vols.

CULIN, STEWART

1907. Games of the North American Indians. 24th Ann. Rep. Bur. Amer. Ethnol., 1902–03, pp. 1–809.

FAGES, PEDRO

1775. A historical, political, and natural description of California. Trans. by H. I. Priestley, 1937. Univ. Calif. Press.

GAYTON, A. H.

1929. Yokuts and western Mono pottery-making. Univ. Calif. Publ. Amer. Archeol. and Ethnol., vol. 24, No. 3, pp. 239–252.

1936. Estudillo among the Yokuts: 1819. *In* Essays in anthropology in honor of Alfred Louis Kroeber, pp. 67–85. Univ. Calif. Press.

GIFFORD, EDWARD WINSLOW

1916. Composition of California shellmounds. Univ. Calif. Publ. Amer. Archeol. and Ethnol., vol. 12, No. 1, pp. 1–29.

GIFFORD, E. W., and SCHENCK, W. EGBERT
    1926. Archaeology of the southern San Joaquin Valley, California. Univ.
        Calif. Publ. Amer. Archeol. and Ethnol., vol. 23, No. 1, pp. 1–122.
HARRINGTON, JOHN P.
    1928. Exploration of the Burton Mound at Santa Barbara, California. 44th
        Ann. Rep. Bur. Amer. Ethnol., 1926–27, pp. 23–168.
HEIZER, ROBERT F.
    1937. Baked-clay objects of the lower Sacramento Valley, California.
        Amer. Antiquity, vol. 3, No. 1, pp. 34–50.
    1939. Some Sacramento Valley-Santa Barbara archeological relationships.
        The Masterkey, vol. 13, pp. 31–35.
HEIZER, R. F., and FENENGA, F.
    1939. Archeological horizons in central California. Amer. Anthrop., n. s.,
        vol. 41, No. 3, pp. 378–399.
HEIZER, R. F., and HEWES, G. W.
    1940. Animal ceremonialism in central California in the light of arche-
        ology. Amer. Anthrop., n. s., vol. 42, No. 4, pt. 1, pp. 587–603.
HEYE, GEORGE G.
    1921. Certain artifacts from San Miguel Island, California. Ind. Notes
        and Monogr., vol. 7, No. 4. Mus. Amer. Ind., Heye Foundation.
HOOTON, E. A.
    1930. Indians of Pecos Pueblo. Yale Univ. Press.
JOCHELSON, WALDEMAR
    1925. Archaeological investigations in the Aleutian Islands. Carnegie Inst.
        Washington, Publ. No. 367.
KIDDER, A. V.
    1932. Artifacts of Pecos. Yale University Press.
KRIEGER, A. D.
    No date. Report on the excavations at Howell's Point mound, Colusa
        County, California. MS.
KROEBER, A. L.
    1909. The archeology of California. Putnam Anniversary Vol.
    1925. Handbook of the Indians of California. Bur. Amer. Ethnol. Bull. 78.
    1936. Prospects in California prehistory. Amer. Antiquity, vol. 2, No. 2,
        pp. 108–116.
LATTA, F. F.
    1929. Uncle Jeff's story. Tulare Times.
LILLARD, J. B., and PURVES, W. K.
    1936. The archeology of the Deer Creek-Cosumnes area, Sacramento County,
        California. Sacramento Junior College, Dept. Anthrop., Bull. 1.
NELSON, N. C.
    1909. Shellmounds of the San Francisco Bay region. Univ. Calif. Publ.
        Amer. Archeol. and Ethnol., vol. 7, No. 4, pp. 309–356.
OLSON, RONALD L.
    1930. Chumash prehistory. Univ. Calif. Publ. Amer. Archeol. and Ethnol.
        vol. 28, No. 1, pp. 1–21.
PRIESTLEY, H. I.
    No date. Franciscan exploration of California. MS.
PUTNAM, FREDERICK W., ET ALIA
    1879. Reports upon archeological and ethnological collections from vicinity
        of Santa Barbara, California. . . . Rep. U. S. Geogr. Surv. W.
        100th Meridian, in charge First Lieut. Geo. M. Wheeler. Vol. 7.
        Archaeology.

a, View south from lake bed across sites 1 and 3 (3 on hilltop).

b, Looking north across site 1 (cleared) and Buena Vista lake bed.

c, Looking northeast toward lake bed through trench 1 at site 1.

GENERAL VIEWS OF SITE 1 AND TRENCH 1.

a, North wall of trench 1 from 89/37 to 89/42.   Light streak at left below shell layers is stratum 2C.   Site 1.

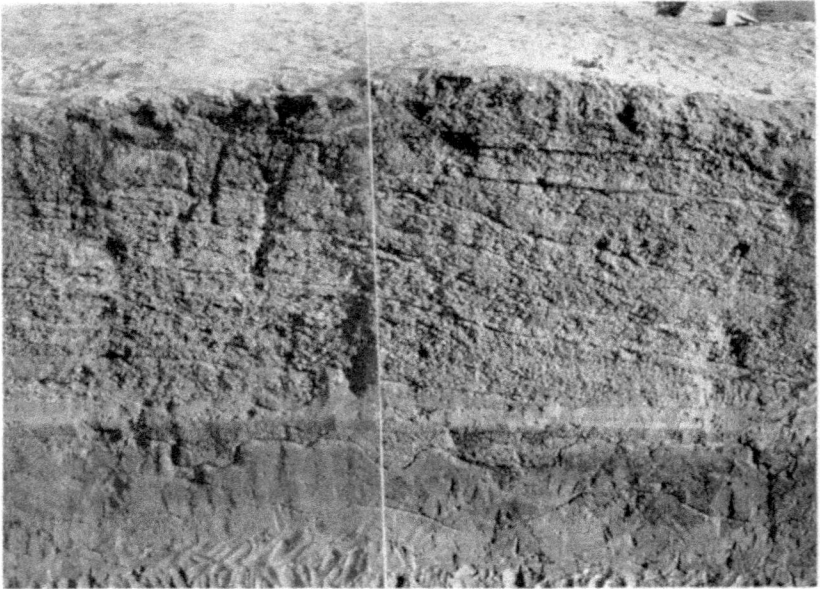

b, North wall of trench 1 in square 90/39, site 1.   Compare figure 5 for identification of layers.

STRATIFICATION IN NORTH WALL OF TRENCH 1, SITE 1.

a, North wall of trench 1, site 1, from lake bed.

b, Refuse-filled wave-cut terraces (5 and 4) in wall of trench 1, site 1.

NORTH WALL OF TRENCH 1 AND BURIED TERRACES, SITE 1.

a, Southwest end of trench 2, showing sloping layers of finely broken shell above hardpan. Site 1, squares 77/38 to 77/41.

b, Northeast end of south wall in trench 1, looking toward lake bed.   Site 1.

VIEWS IN TRENCHES 1 AND 2, SITE 1.

a, House 1 with post molds and central hearth, site 1.

c, Pestle and steatite sherds in pocket cache, site 1.

b, Clay-lined pit, site 1.   *d*, Lined basin and contents, site 1.

HOUSE 1 AND OTHER FEATURES AT SITE 1.

a, Broken steatite bowl in situ against terrace 3, site 1.

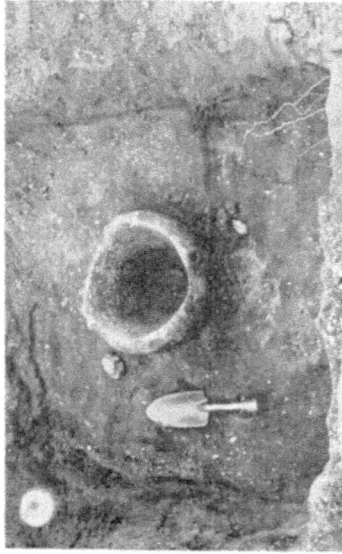

b, Stone bowl with asphaltum-plugged bottom, site 1.

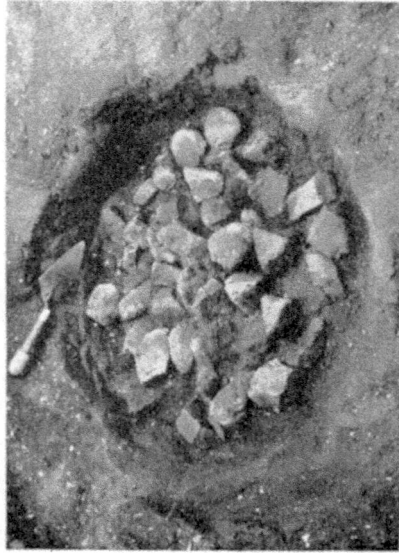

c, Rock fireplace in square 67/36, site 1.

d, Rock fireplace, site 1.

ROCK FIREPLACES AND OTHER FEATURES AT SITE 1.

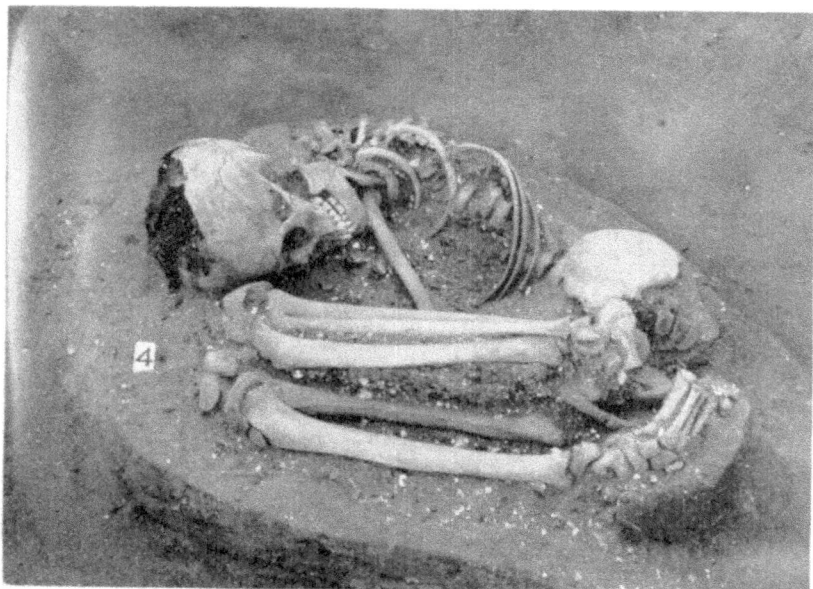

a, Flexed burial at 69-inch depth, site 1.

b, Flexed double burial at 36-inch depth, site 1.

FLEXED BURIALS AT SITE 1.

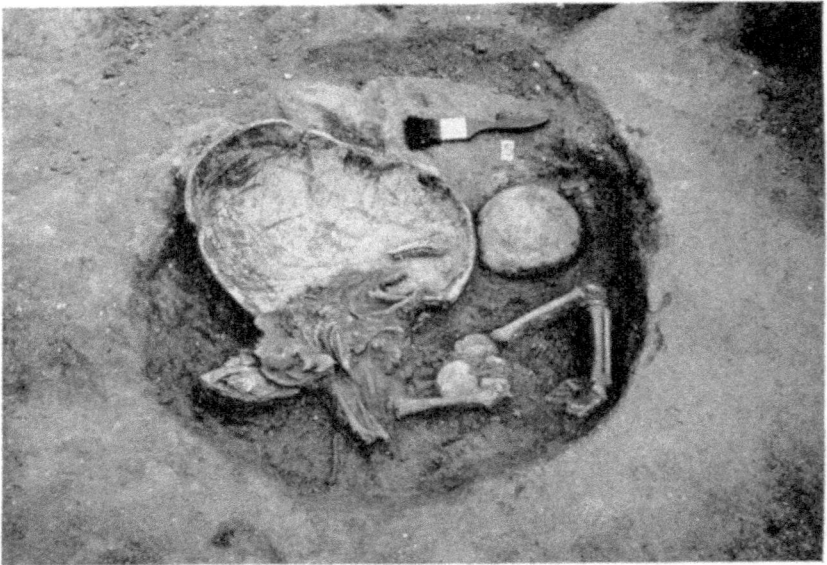

a, Child burial No. 5 with steatite bowls in situ, site 1.

b, Animal "burial" at site 2.

CHILD BURIAL, SITE 1, AND ANIMAL BURIAL, SITE 2.

a, General view of site 2 (cleared), sandspit, and lake bed before excavation; looking south-east from tip of Buena Vista Hills.

b, Sites 2 (at foot of hill), 4, and 5, looking west from lake bed.

c, Recent beach and wave-cut terraces at site 2.

GENERAL VIEWS OF SITE 2 AND SURROUNDINGS

a, Trench 1 and part of camp site excavations at site 2, looking southeast.

b, Cooking pits, post molds, and other features at 20-inch level on camp site, site 2; looking southeast across sandspit and lake bed.

TRENCH 1 AND CAMP SITE AT 20-INCH LEVEL, SITE 2

a, West end of north wall in trench 1, site 2.

b, South wall of trench 1, site 2, from square 107/33 to east end. Compare figure 10 for explanation of stratification.

STRATIFICATION IN TRENCH 1, SITE 2.

a, House 4 and burial 71 at 9-inch level, site 2.   Sandspit in left background.

b House 1 at 12-inch level, site 2.

HOUSES 1 AND 4 ON CAMP SITE, SITE 2.

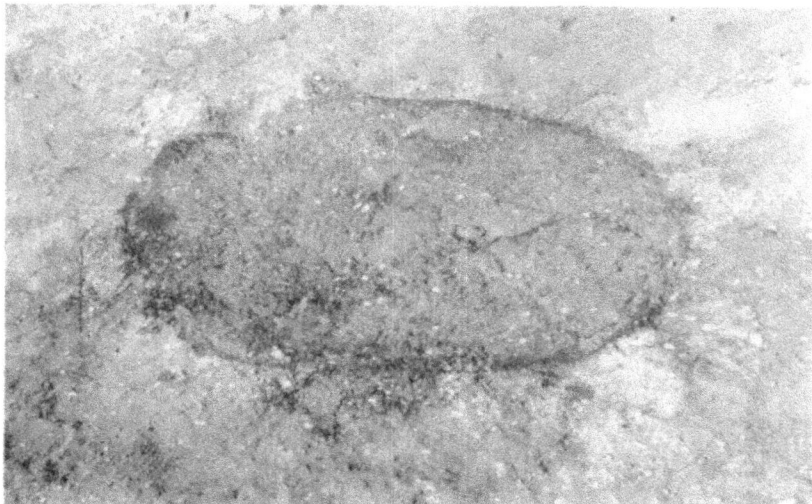

a, Unopened grave of burial 108 in roasting pit at 36-inch level, site 2.

b, Clay-lined basin in square 109/33 at 15-inch level, site 2.

UNOPENED GRAVE AND CLAY-LINED BASIN AT SITE 2.

a, Rock fireplace in square 105/34 at 24-inch level, site 2.

b, Pitch-covered twined basket, site 4.

c, Flexed child burial, site 2.

d, Flexed child burial, site 1.

CHILD BURIALS, ROCK FIREPLACE, AND PITCH-COVERED BASKET. SITES 1, 2, AND 4.

a

b

EXTENDED BURIALS FROM DEEP LEVELS AT SITE 2.

a, Flexed pit burial at site 2.

b, Flexed double burial in roasting pit at site 2.

FLEXED PIT BURIALS FROM UPPER LEVELS AT SITE 2.

a, Grave post with burial 251, site 3.

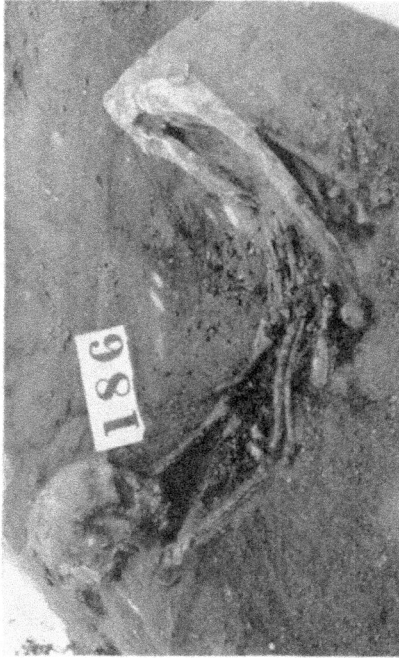

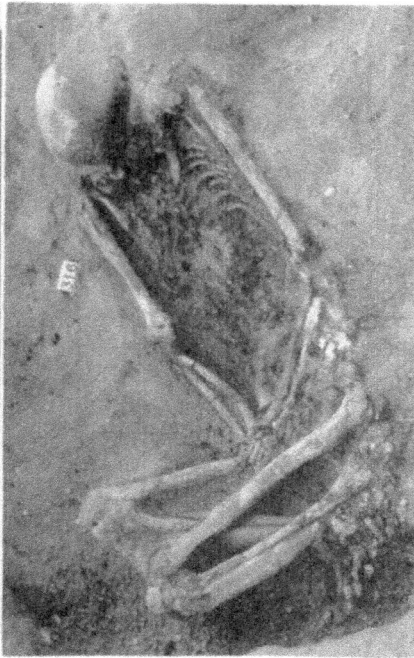

b, *c*, Semiflexed burials at site 3.

GRAVE POST AND SEMIFLEXED BURIALS AT SITE 3.

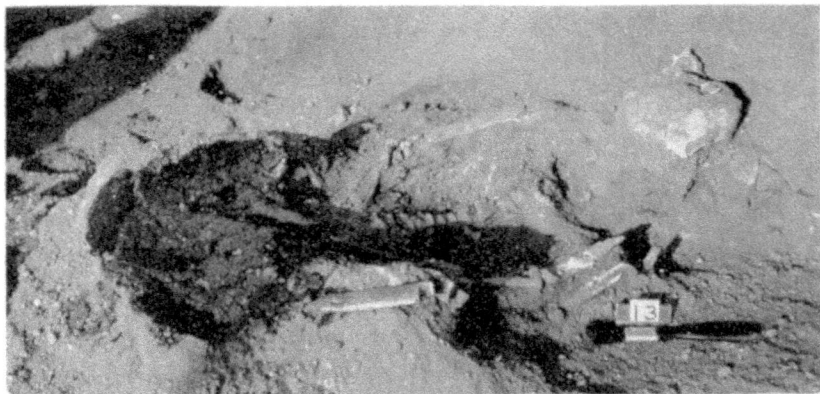

a

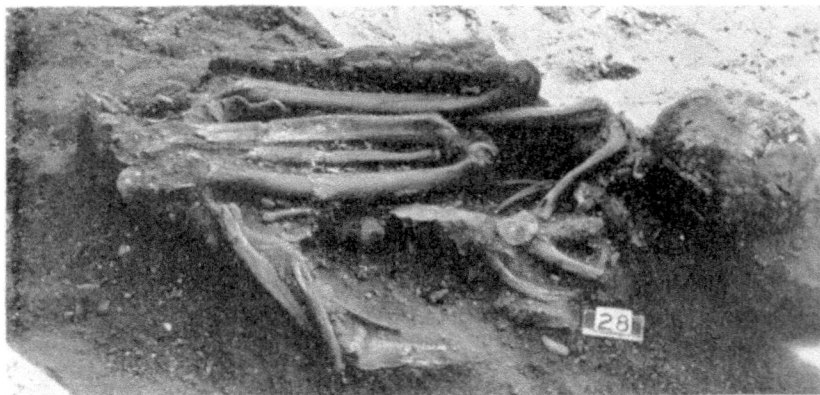

b

c

Note textiles about feet of No. 13.

FLEXED (NO. 28) AND SEMIFLEXED BURIALS AT SITE 4.

OBJECTS OF ASPHALTUM AND BAKED CLAY, SITES 1 AND 5.

POTSHERDS, BAKED CLAY, AND SANDSTONE (f) OBJECTS, SITE 1.

FIBER AND ASPHALTUM BRUSH (SITE 1) AND BONE ORNAMENT (SITE 3)

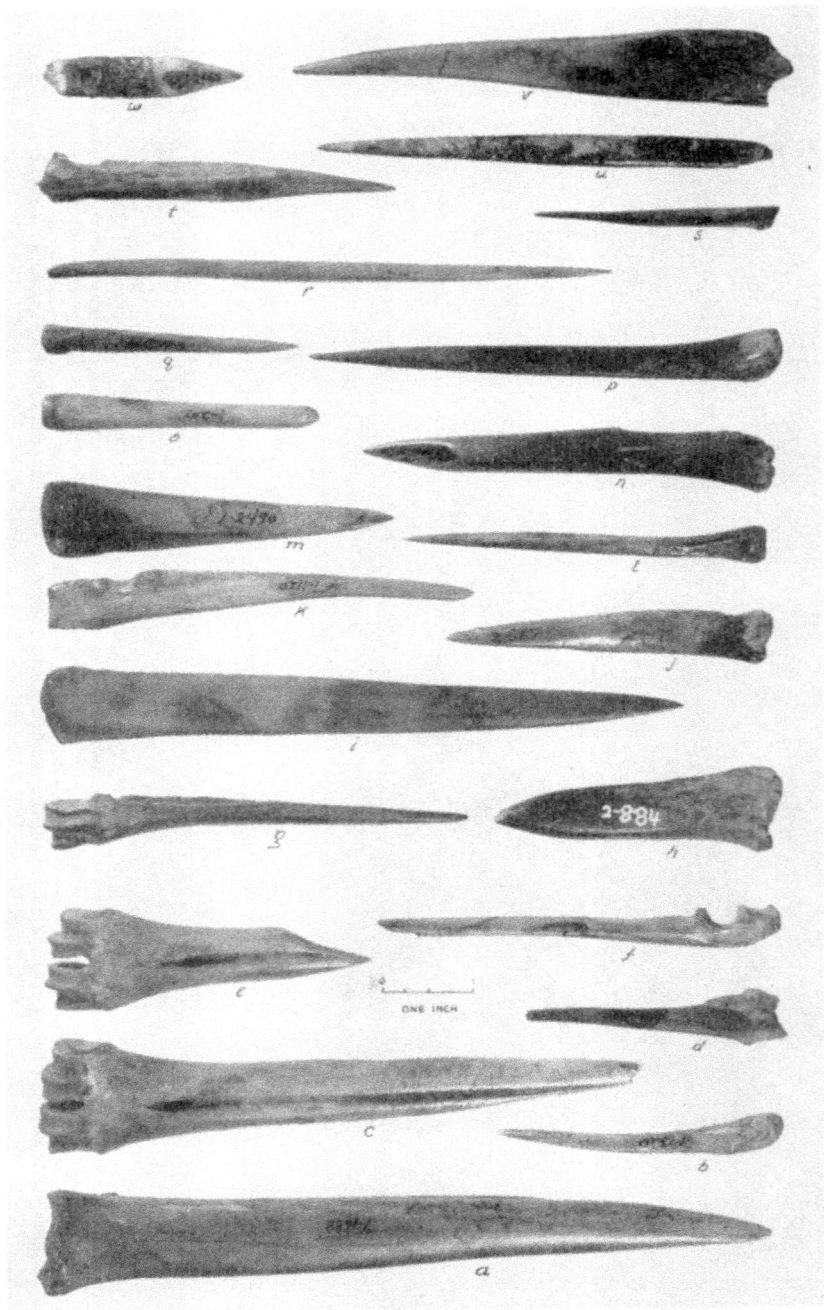

BONE AWLS FROM SITES 1 AND 2.

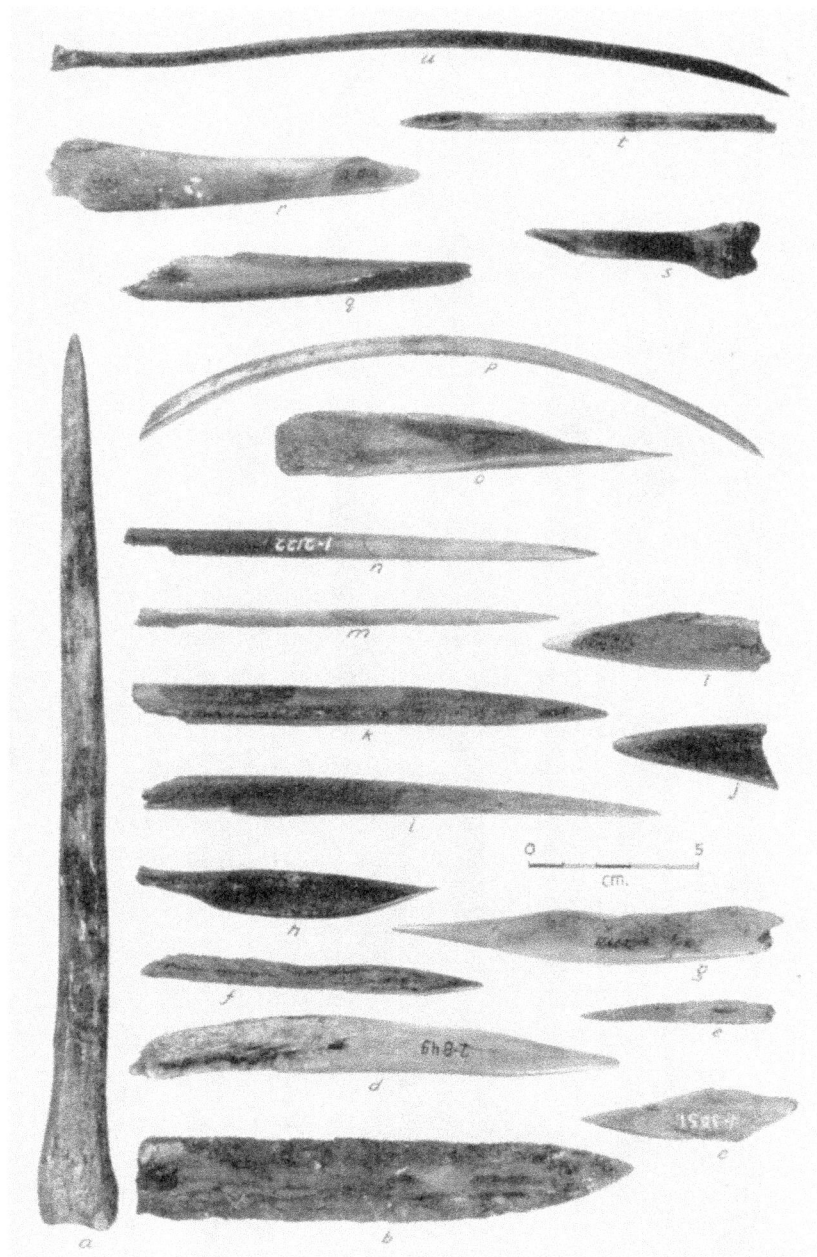

BONE AWLS FROM SITES 1 AND 2.

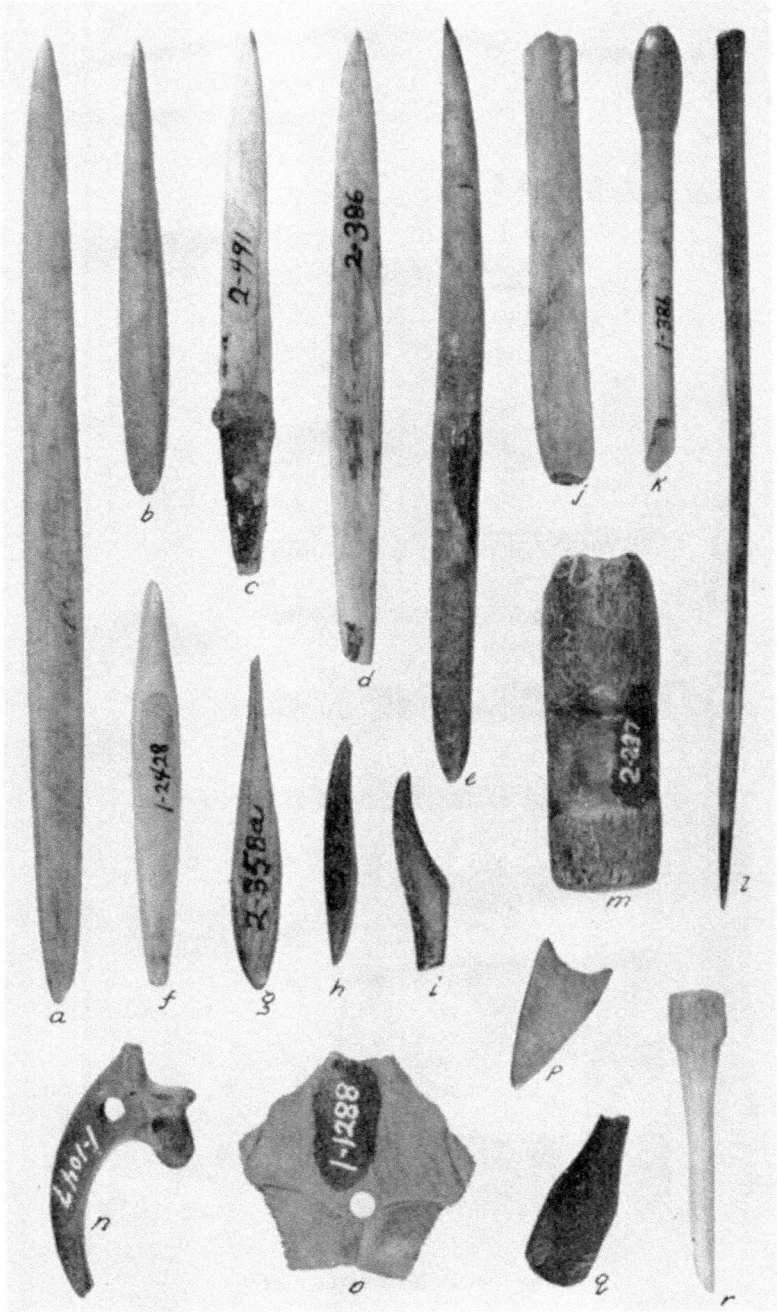

MISCELLANEOUS BONE OBJECTS FROM SITES 1 AND 2.

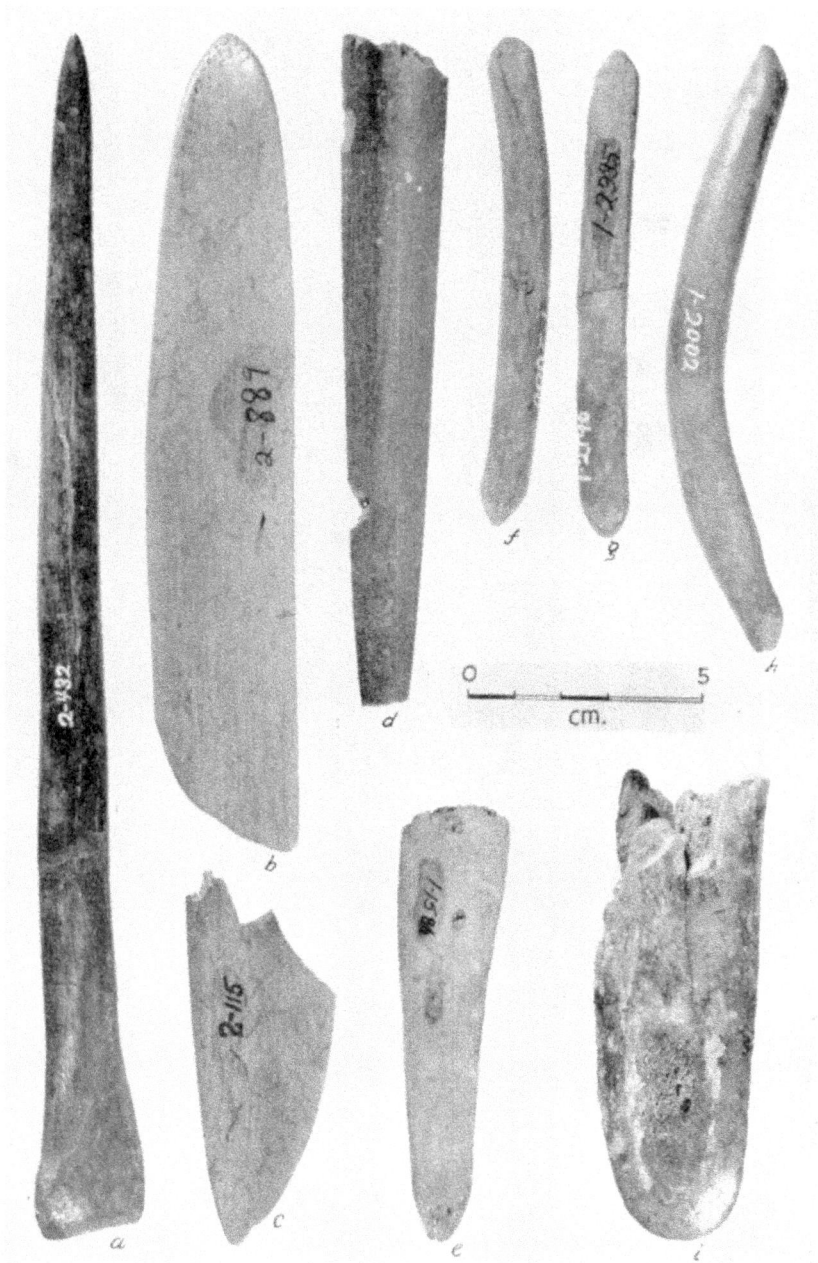

BONE AND HORN OBJECTS FROM SITES 1 AND 2.

BONE WHISTLES, BEADS, AND TUBES FROM SITE 1.

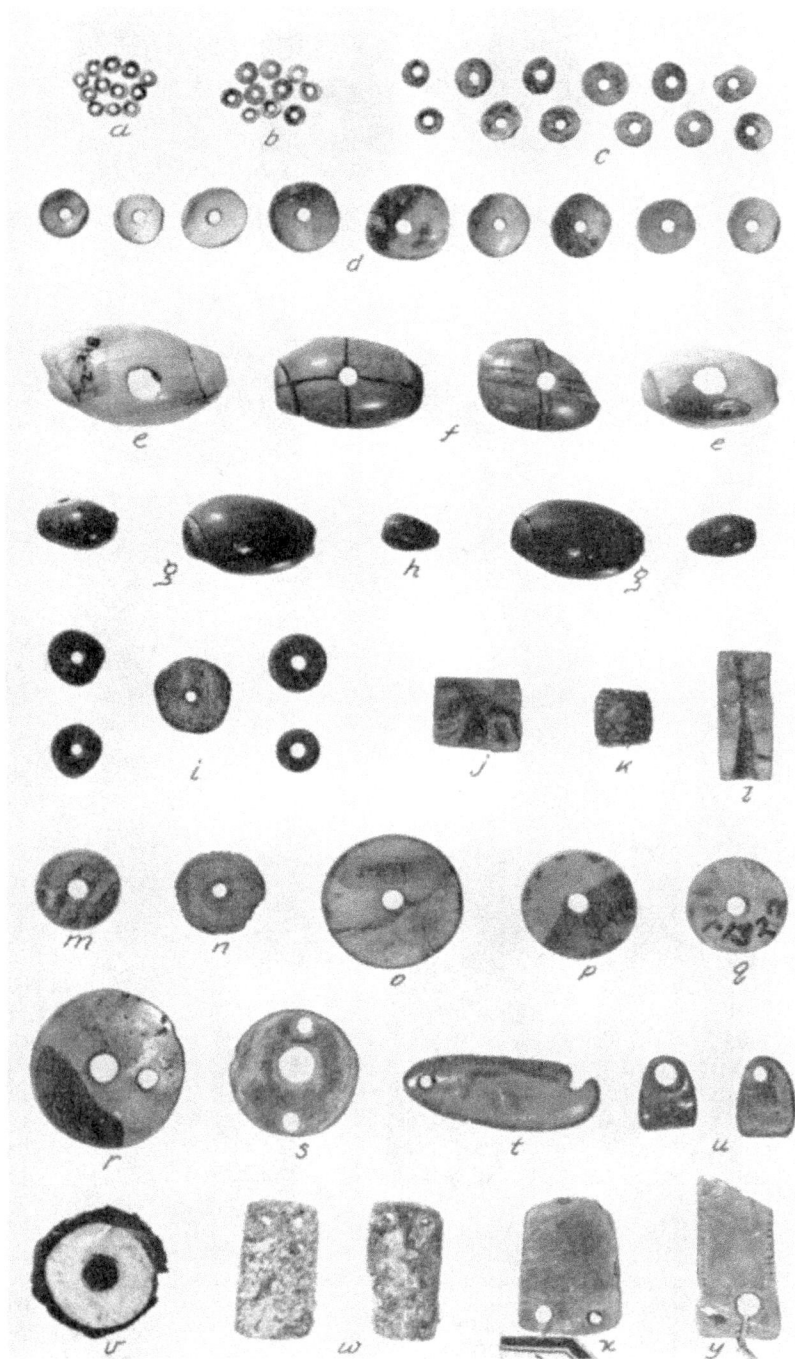

SHELL BEADS AND ORNAMENTS FROM SITES 1, 2, AND 3.

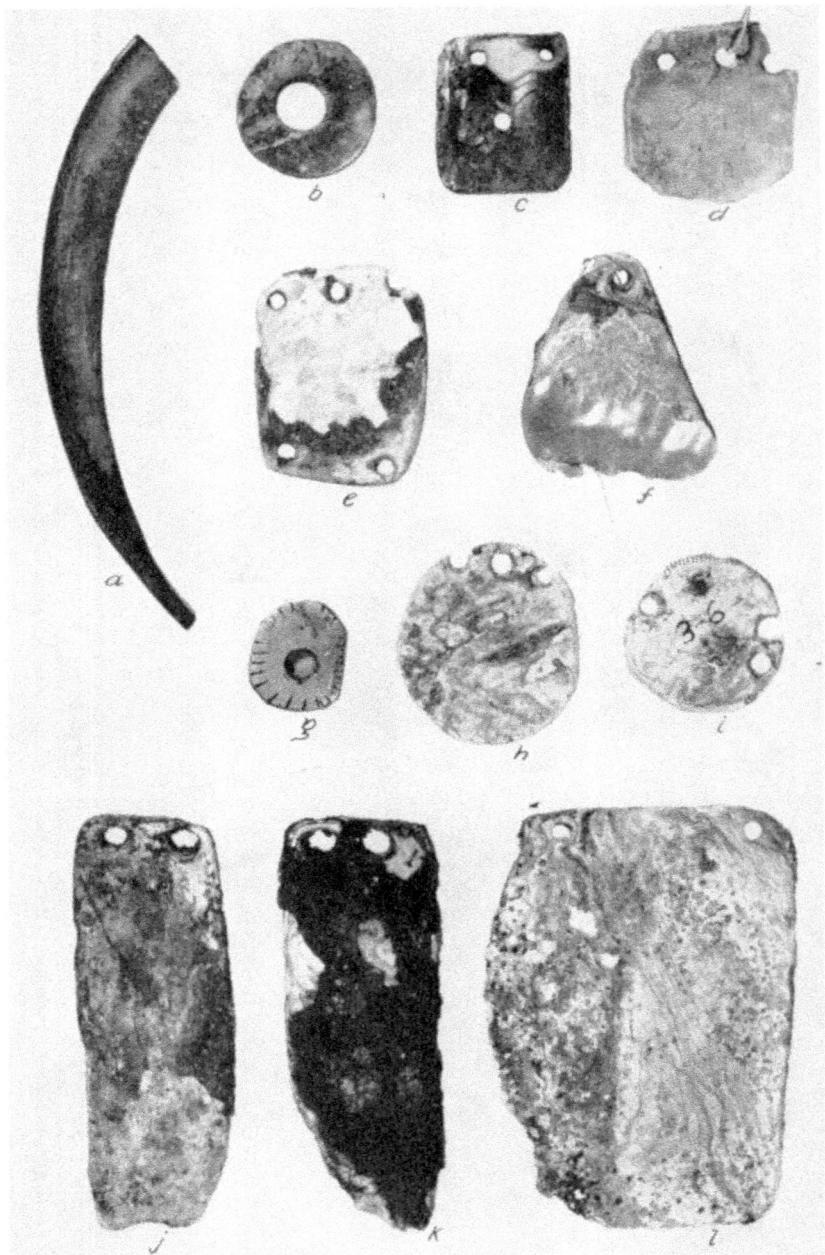

SHELL PENDANTS FROM SITES 1, 2, AND 3.

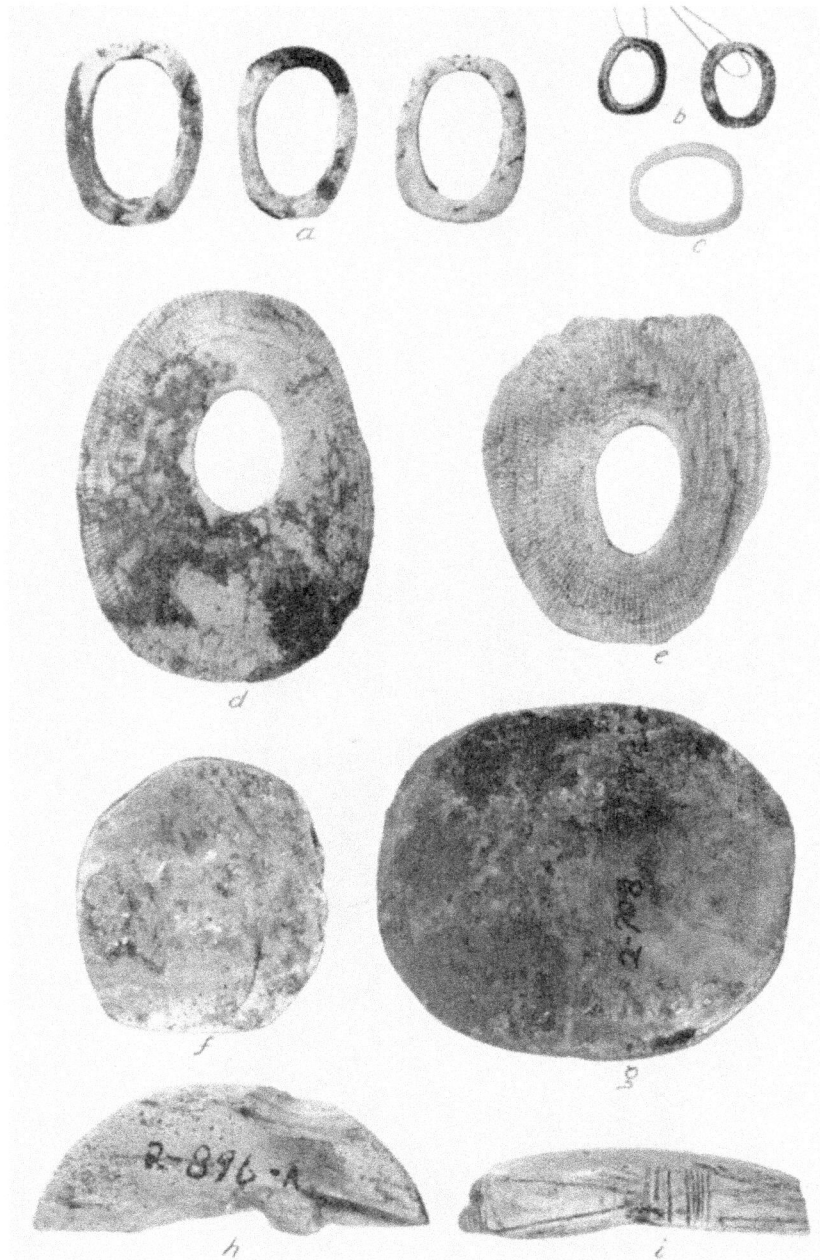

ORNAMENTS OF ABALONE, CLAM, AND LIMPET SHELL FROM SITE 2.

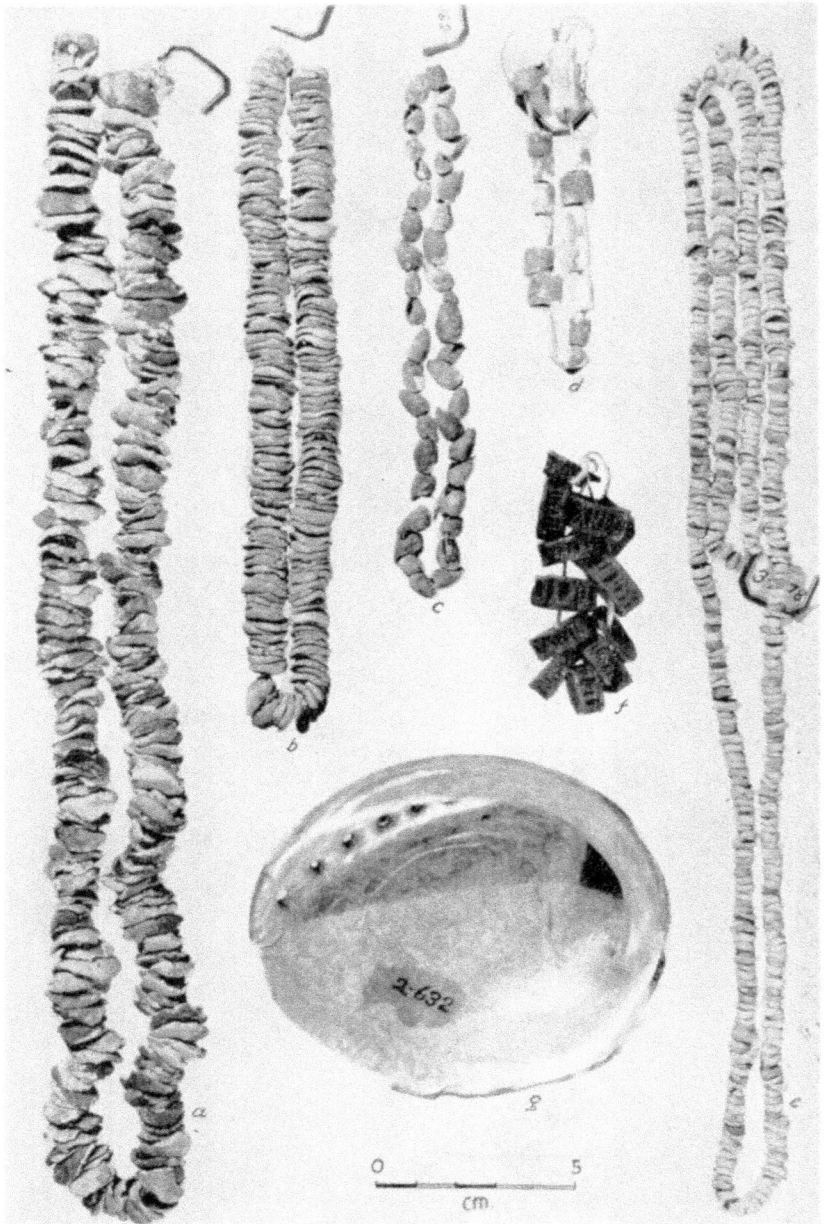

OBJECTS OF SHELL AND PIERCED FISH VERTEBRAE FROM SITES 2, 3, AND 4.

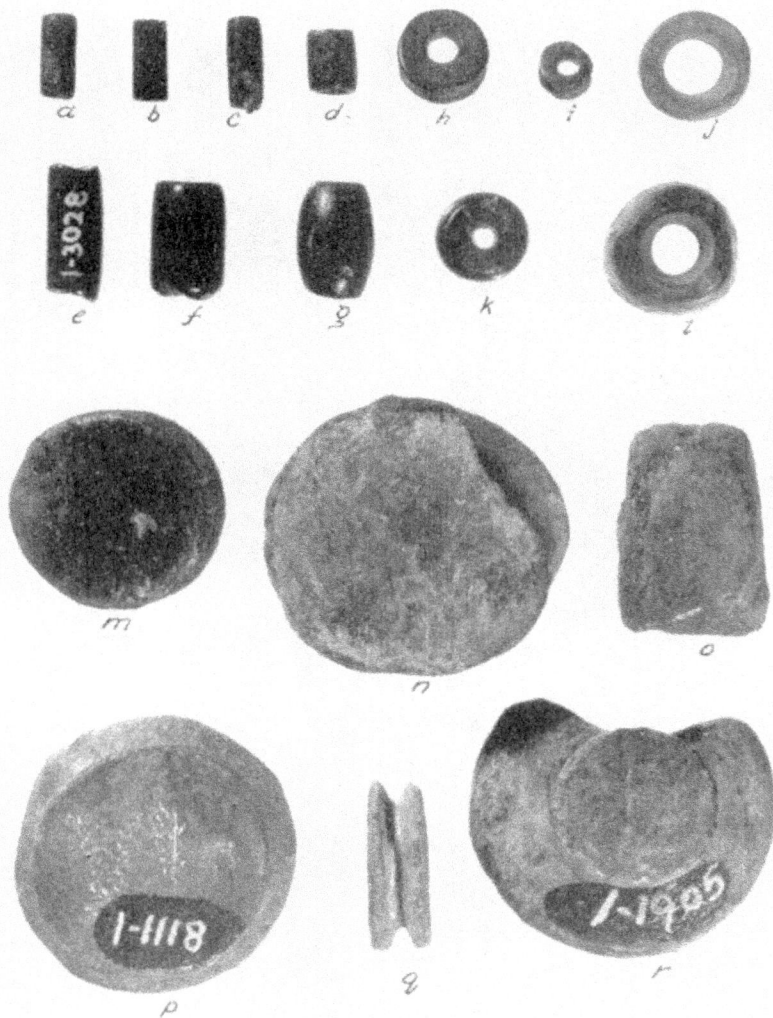

SERPENTINE BEADS AND STEATITE LABRETS FROM SITES 1 AND 3.

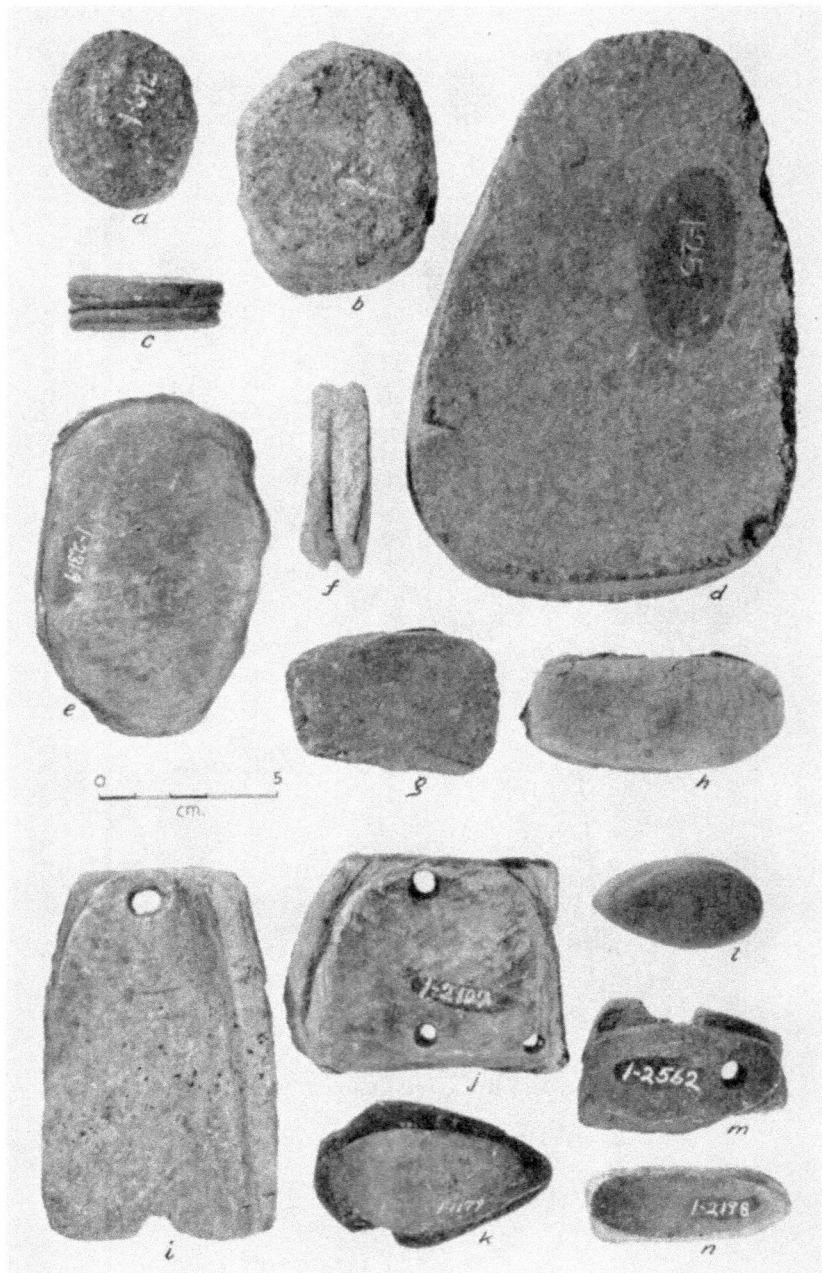

GROOVE-EDGED STEATITE OBJECTS FROM SITE 1.

MISCELLANEOUS STEATITE OBJECTS FROM SITE 1.

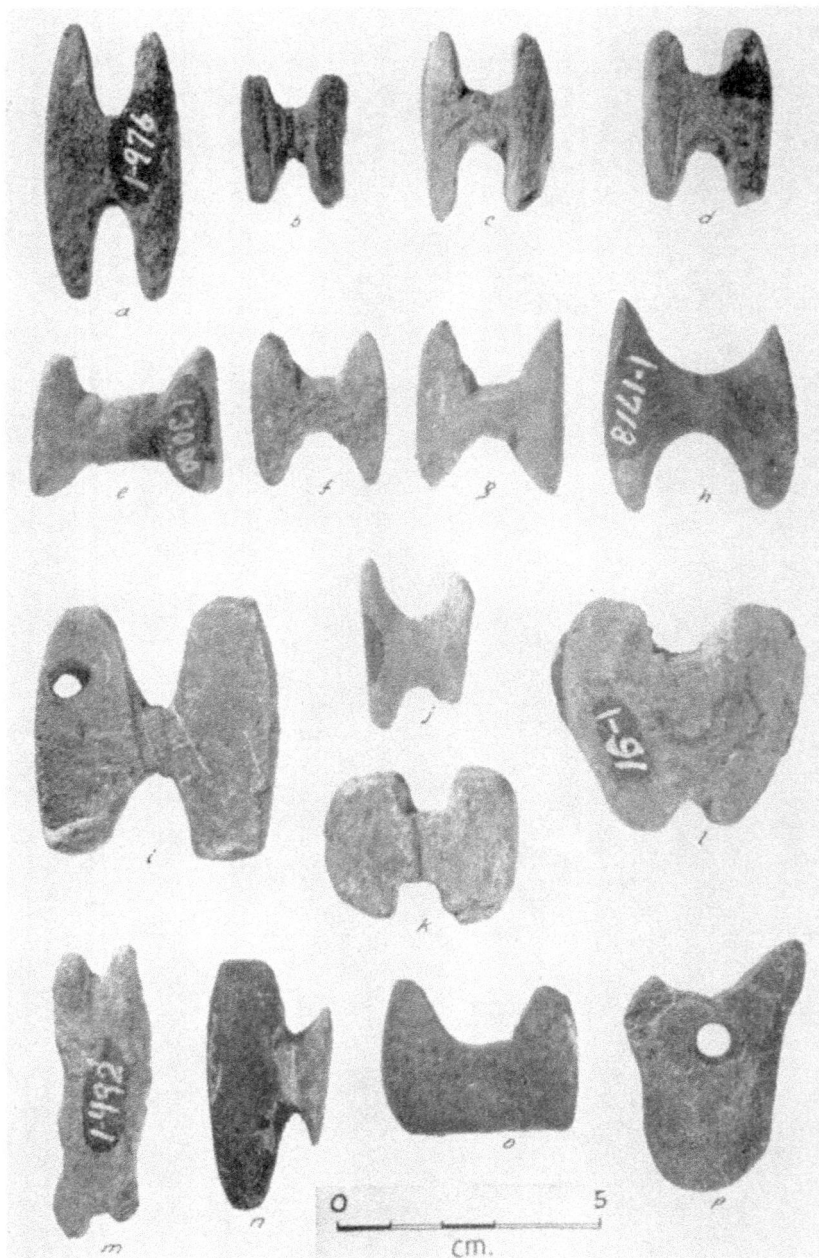

REEL-SHAPED STEATITE OBJECTS FROM SITE 1.

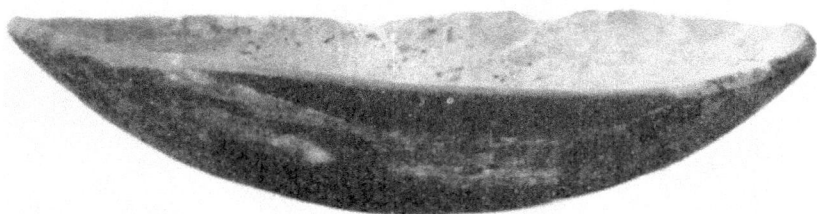

STEATITE BOWLS FROM SITE 1.

STEATITE BOWLS FROM SITE 1.

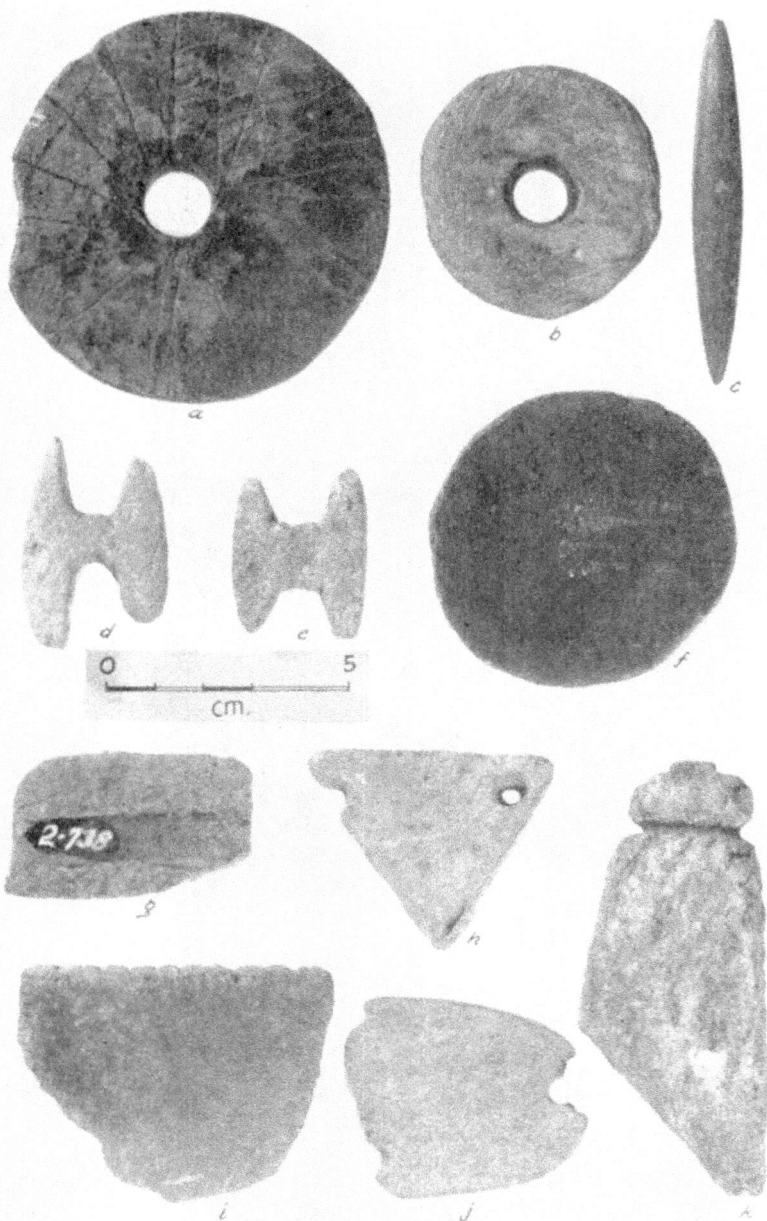

MISCELLANEOUS STEATITE OBJECTS FROM SITE 2.

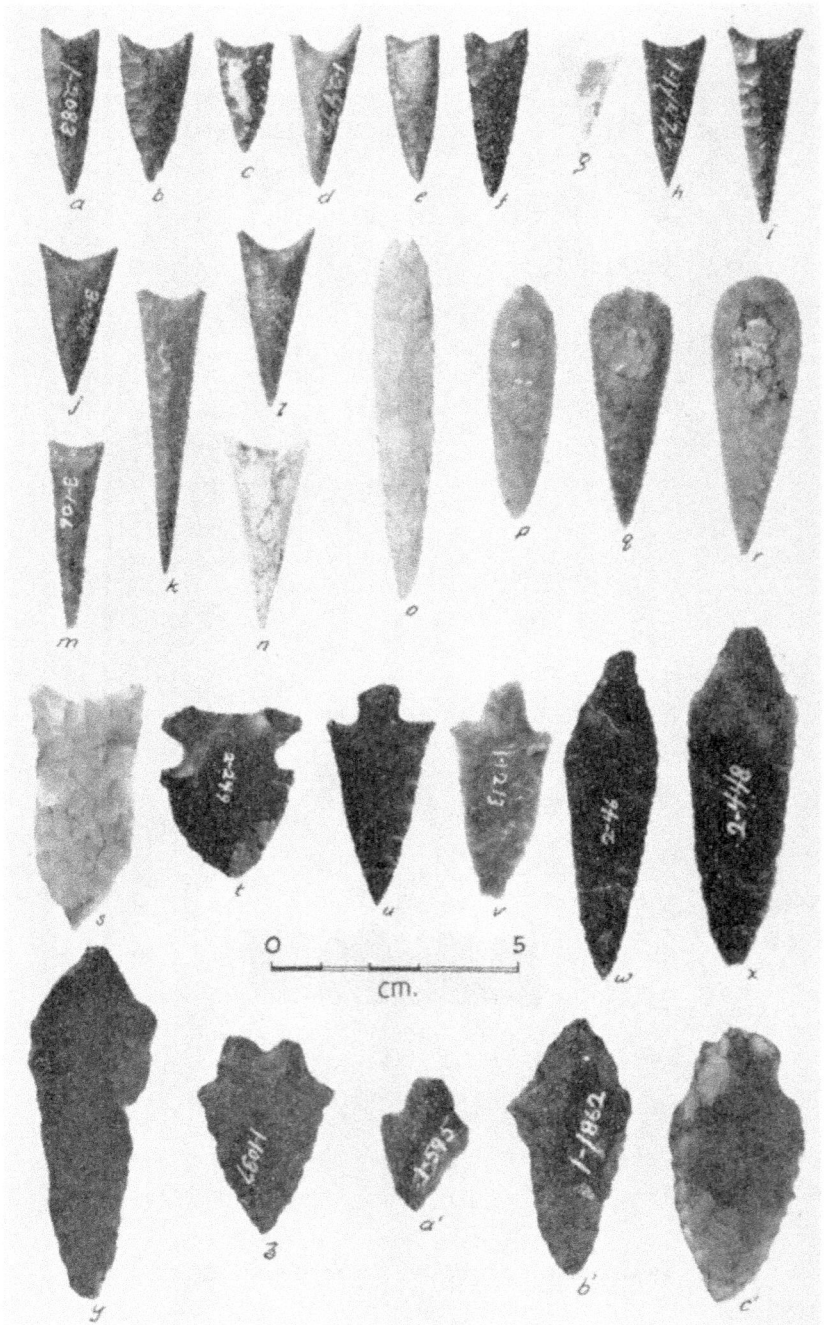

PROJECTILE POINTS FROM SITES 1, 2, 3, AND 4.

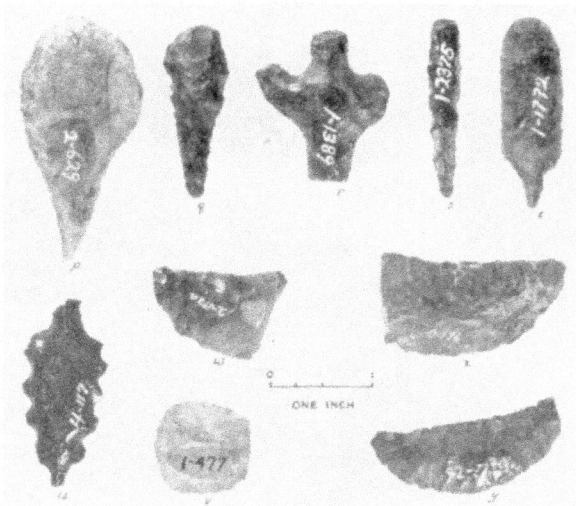

OBSIDIAN AND CHIPPED FLINT FROM SITES 1, 2, 3, AND 4.

CHIPPED BLADES AND GROUND-STONE KNIVES FROM SITES 1, 2, AND 3.

SAWS AND HAND AX FROM SITES 1 AND 4.

SCRAPER KNIVES WITH ASPHALTUM FOR HAFTING FROM SITE 1.

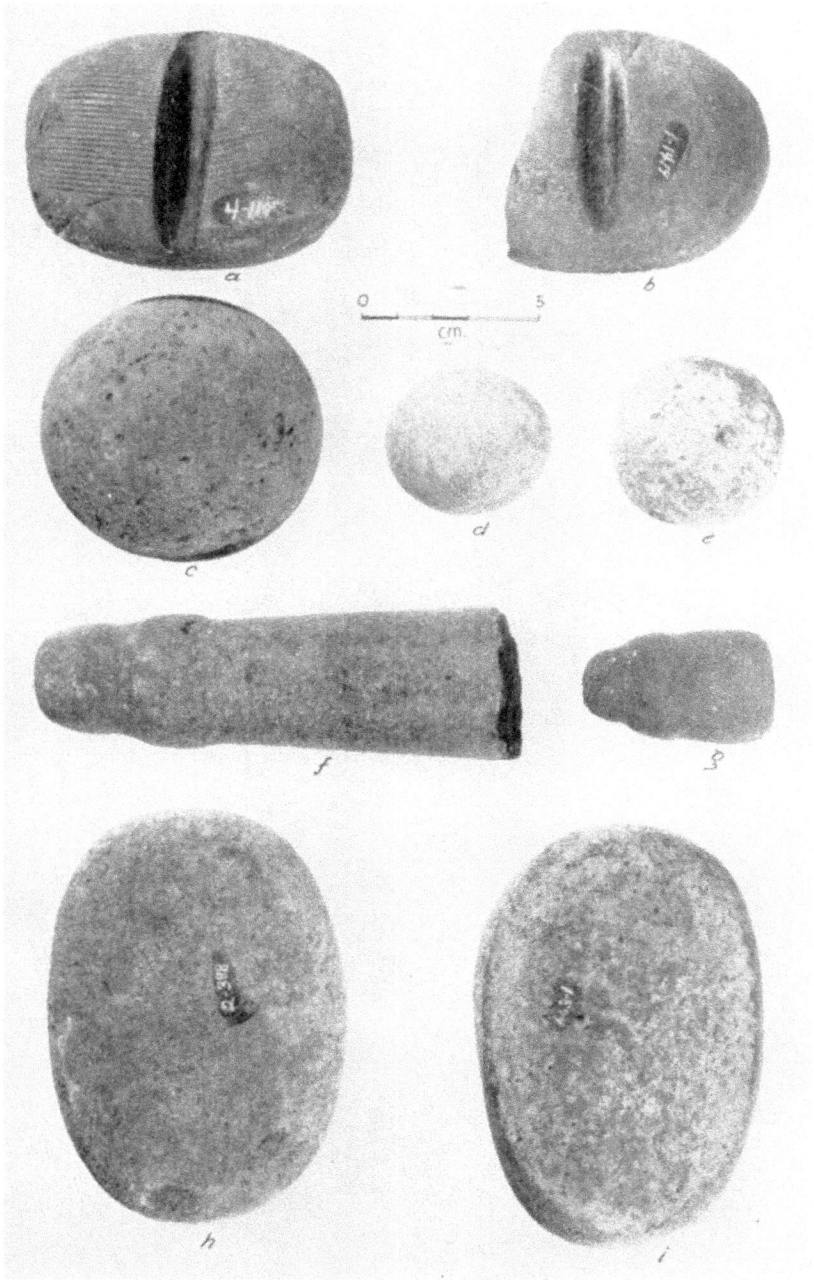

GROUND-STONE OBJECTS FROM SITES 1, 2, AND 4.

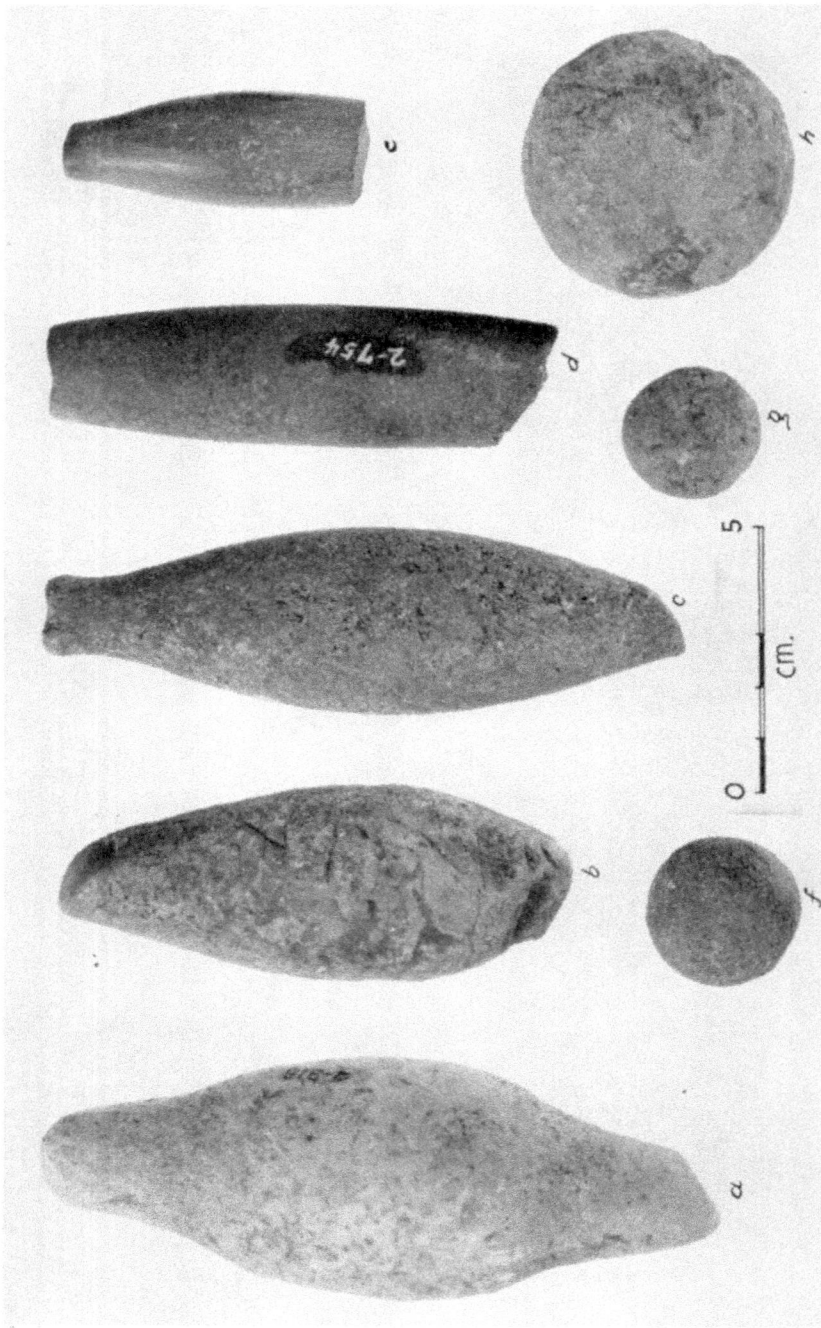

GROUND-STONE OBJECTS FROM SITES 1 AND 2.

HOPPER MORTAR STONES FROM SITE 1.

PORTABLE STONE MORTARS FROM SITE 2.

Diameter of *b*, 9⅜ inches.

PESTLES FROM SITES 1 AND 2.

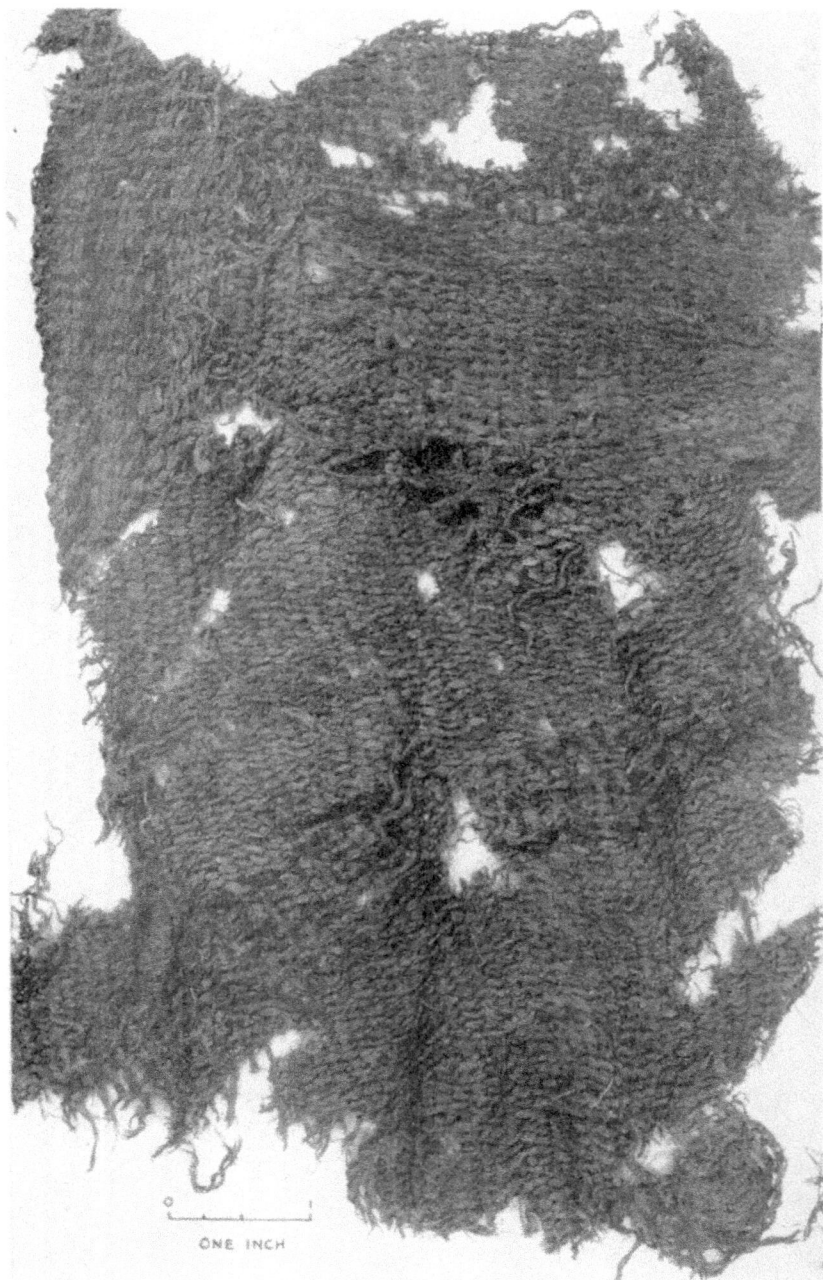

ONE INCH

PLAIN TWINED SOFT TEXTILE WITH BLACK DESIGN FROM SITE 3.

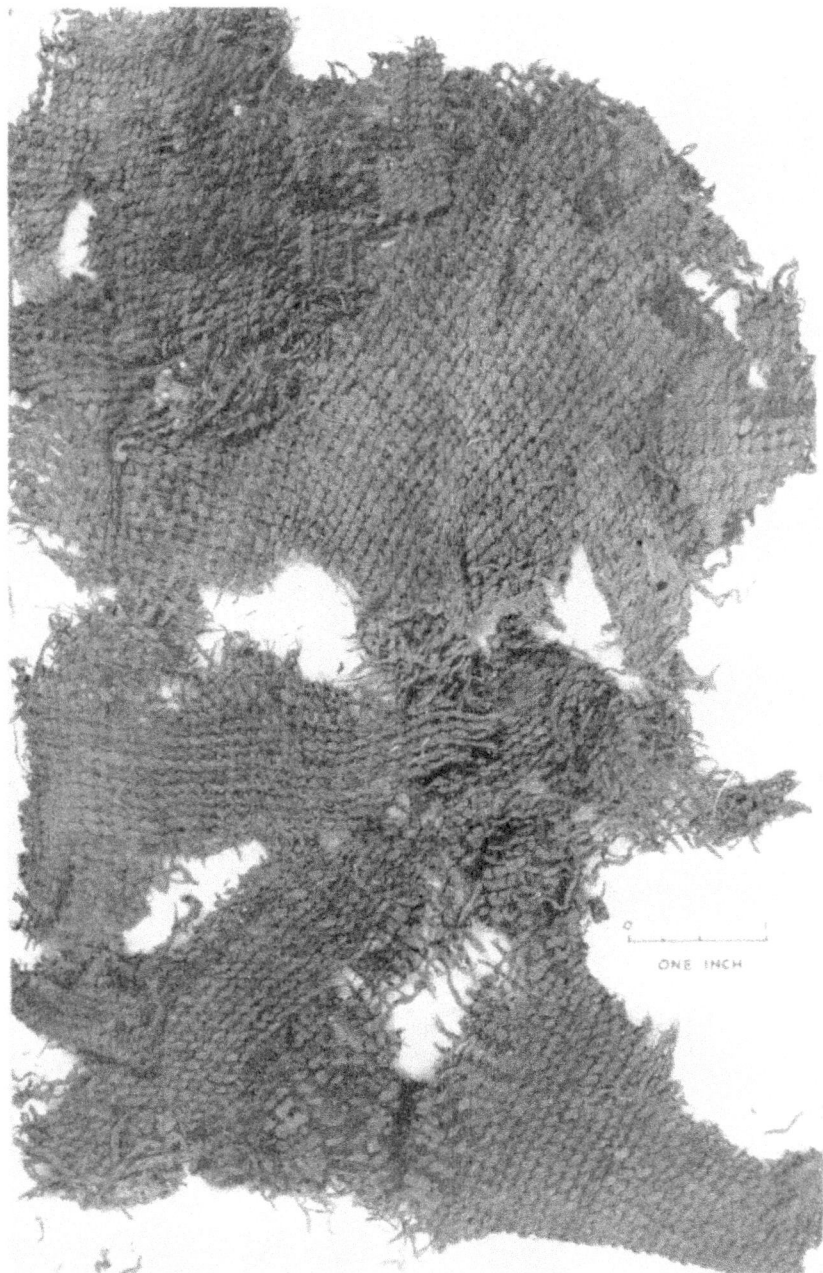

ONE INCH

SOFT TEXTILE WITH DESIGN IN WRAPPED TWINING AND BLACK FROM SITE 3.

SOFT WRAPPED TWINED TEXTILE, COILED AND TWINED BASKETRY, FROM SITE 3.

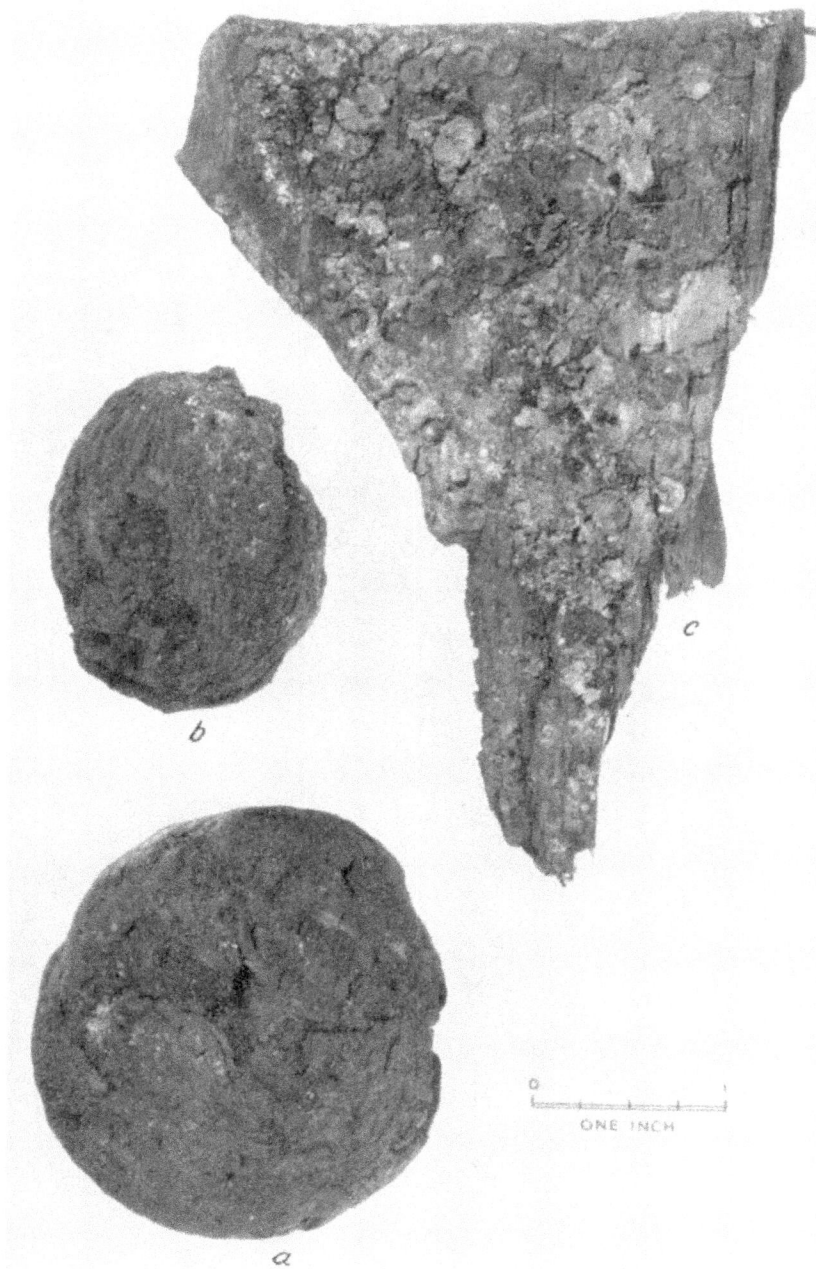

WOODEN BURLS AND SHELL-INLAID SLAB FROM SITE 3.

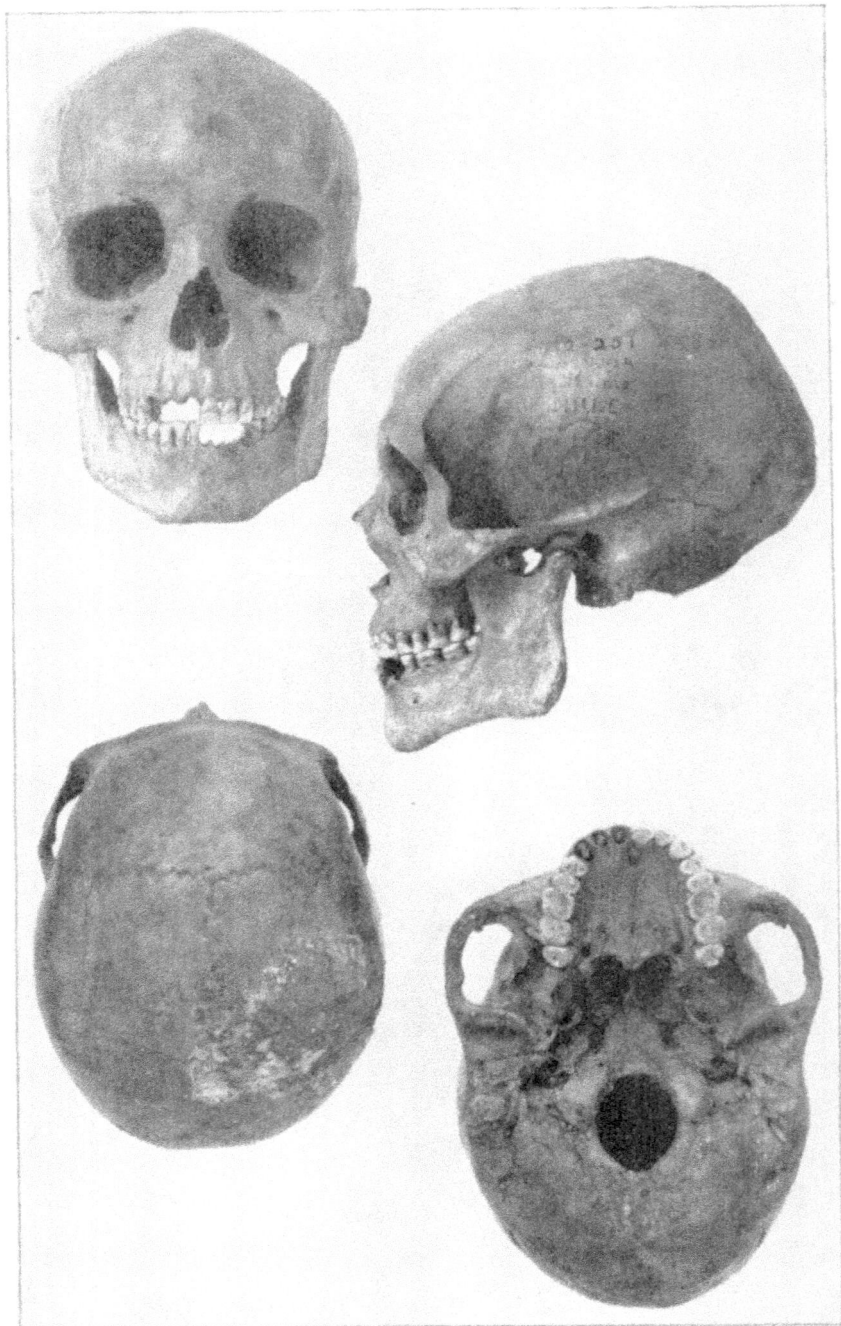

FOUR VIEWS OF MALE SKULL U. S. N. M. NO. 372251 (BURIAL 1, SITE 1), ORIENTED IN THE EYE-EAR PLANE.

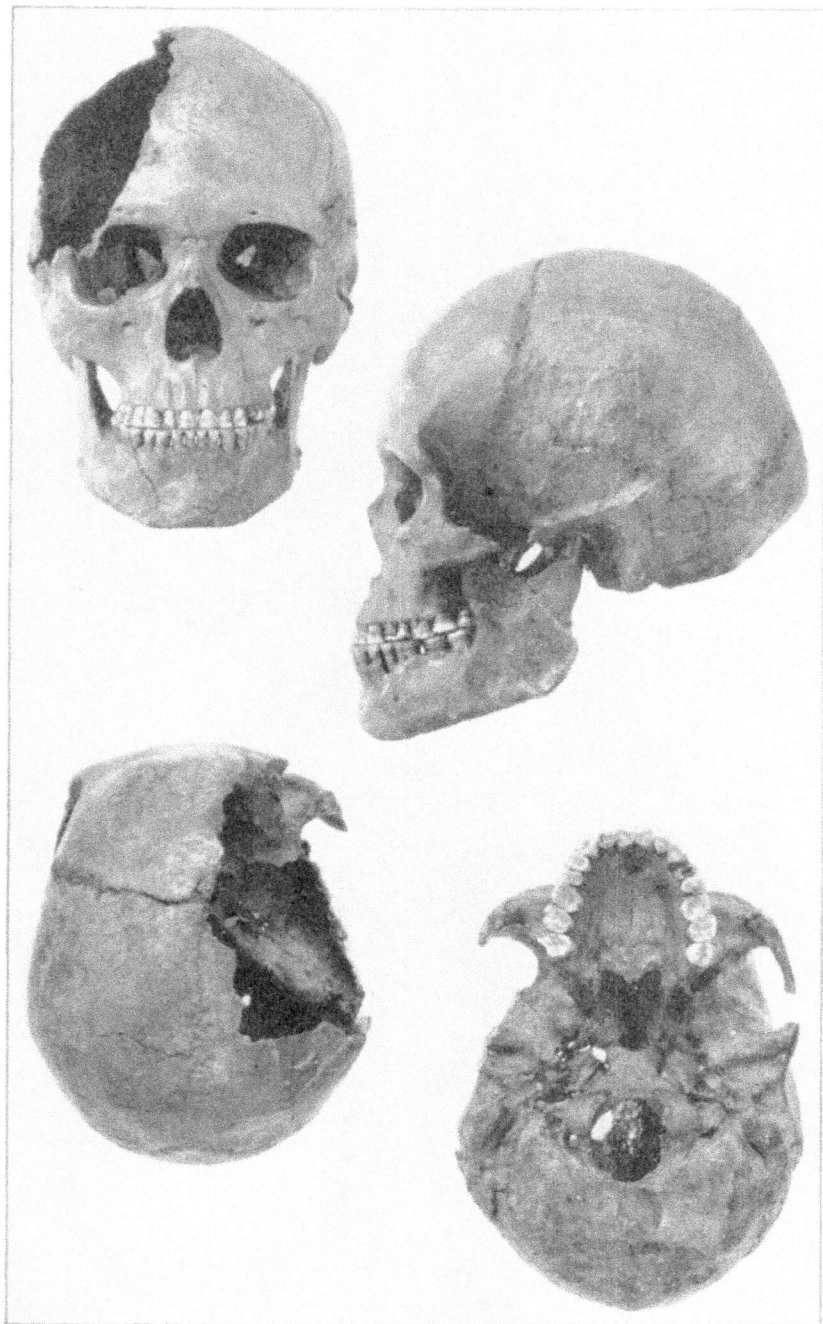

FOUR VIEWS OF MALE SKULL U. S. N. M. NO. 372252 (BURIAL 2, SITE 1), ORIENTED IN THE EYE-EAR PLANE.

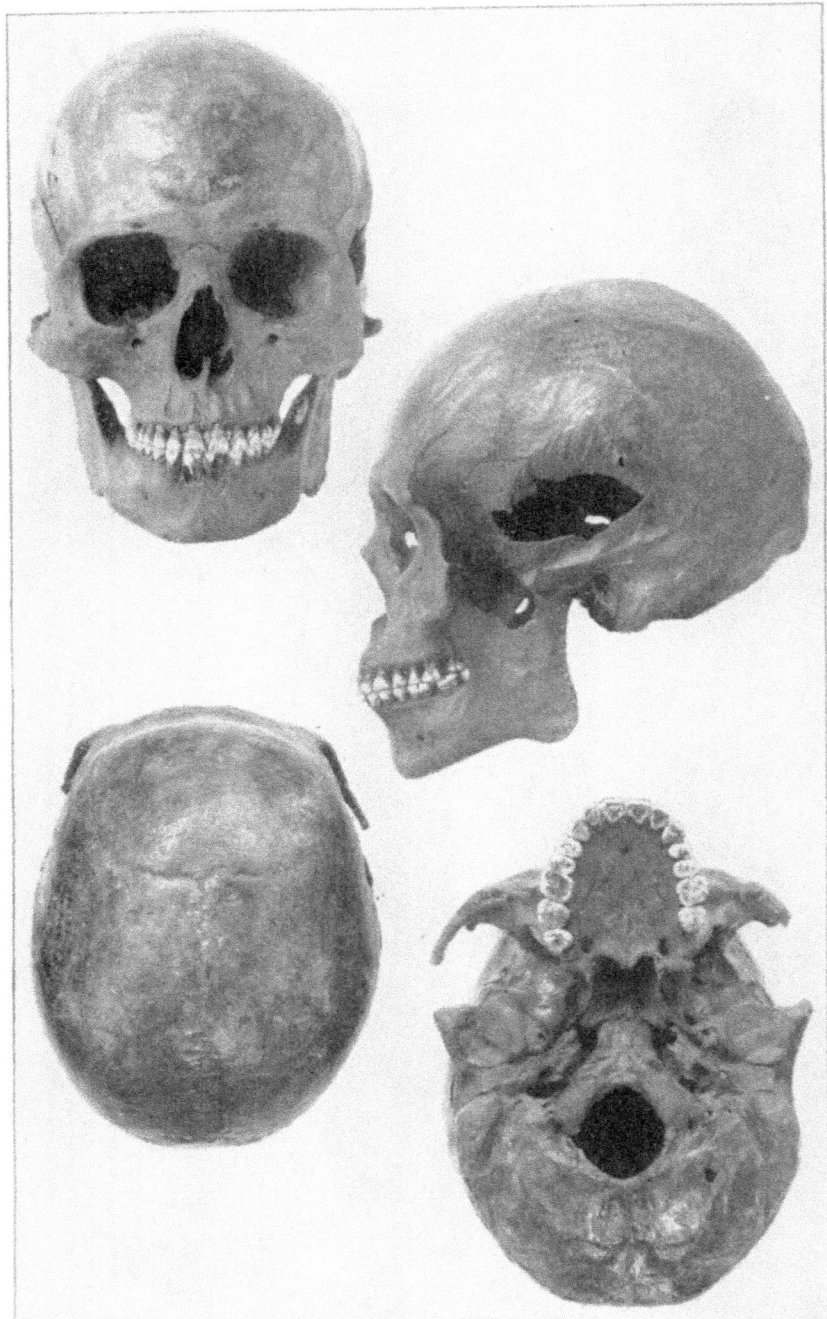

FOUR VIEWS OF MALE SKULL U. S. N. M. NO. 372272 (BURIAL 14, SITE 2), ORIENTED IN THE EYE-EAR PLANE.

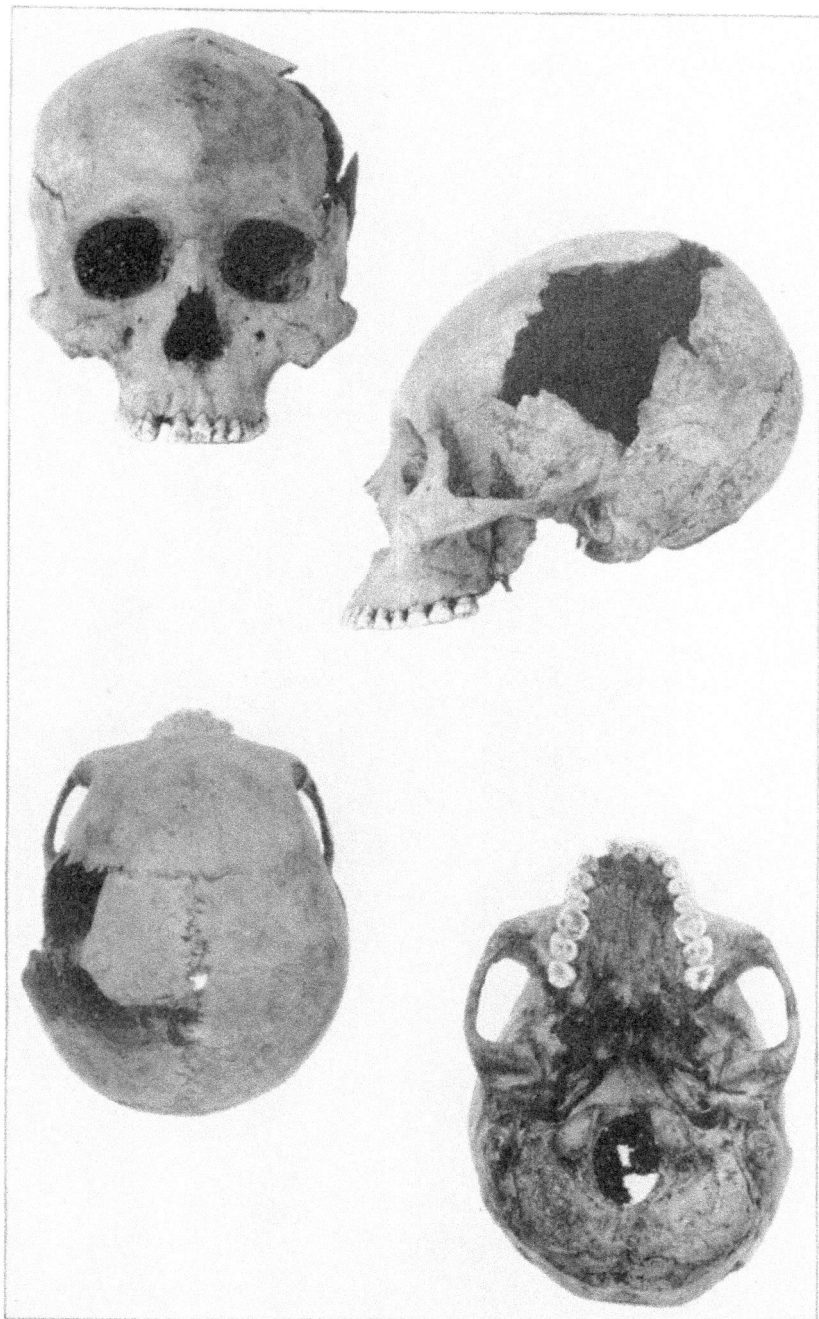

FOUR VIEWS OF MALE SKULL U. S. N. M. NO. 372284 (BURIAL 46, SITE 2), ORIENTED IN THE EYE-EAR PLANE.

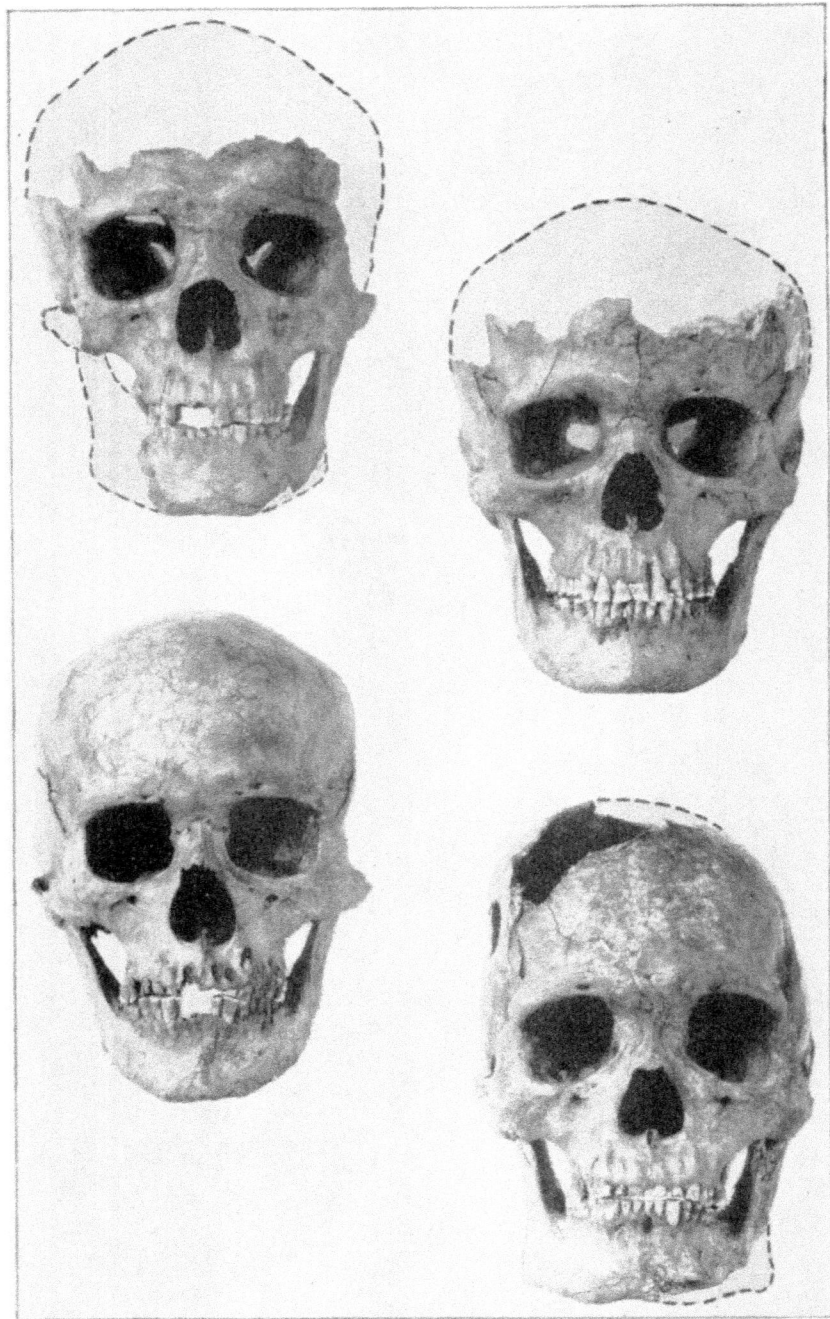

FRONT VIEWS OF FOUR SKULLS FROM SITE 2, ORIENTED IN THE EYE-EAR PLANE.

Upper left (U. S. N. M. No. 372297), female (burial 86); upper right (U. S. N. M. No. 372286), female (burial 50); lower left (U. S. N. M. No. 372270), male (burial 2); lower right (U. S. N. M. No. 372298), male (burial 89).

PATHOLOGICAL CHANGES IN LONG BONES.

Left, periostitis (syphilis ?) of left tibia (U. S. N. M. No. 372297, burial 86, site 2); right osteomyelitis (?) of left femur (U. S. N. M. No. 372257, site 1).

ROGERS, D. B.
1929. Prehistoric man of the Santa Barbara coast. Santa Barbara.
SCHENCK, W. EGBERT
1926. The Emeryville Shellmound: Final report. Univ. Calif. Publ. Amer. Archeol. and Ethnol., vol. 23, No. 3, pp. 147–282.
SCHENCK, W. EGBERT, and DAWSON, ELMER J.
1929. Archaeology of the northern San Joaquin Valley. Univ. Calif. Publ. Amer. Archeol. and Ethnol., vol. 25, No. 4, pp. 289–413.
SETZLER, F. M., and STRONG, W. D.
1936. Archaeology and relief. Amer. Antiquity, vol. 1, No. 4, pp. 301–309.
STIRLING, M. W.
1935. Smithsonian archeological projects conducted under the Federal Emergency Relief Administration, 1933–34. Ann. Rep. Smithsonian Inst. 1934, pp. 371–400.
STRONG, WILLIAM DUNCAN
1935. An introduction to Nebraska archeology. Smithsonian Misc. Coll., vol. 93, No. 10.
1935a. Archeological explorations in the country of the eastern Chumash. Explorations and Field-work Smithsonian Inst. 1934, pp. 69–72.
WALKER, EDWIN F.
1935. A Yokuts cemetery at Elk Hills. The Masterkey, vol. 9, No. 5, pp. 145–150.
WALKER, WINSLOW M.
1935. Excavating ancient Yokuts shellmounds in California. Explorations and Field-work Smithsonian Inst. 1934, pp. 73–76.
WHEELER SURVEY. *See* PUTNAM, F. W., ET ALIA
WILSON, THOMAS
1899. Arrowpoints, spearheads, and knives of prehistoric times. Ann. Rep U. S. Nat. Mus. 1897, pp. 811–988.
ZALVIDEA, P. JOSE MARIA DE
1806. Diary of an inland expedition by P. Jose Maria de Zalvidea, from July 19 to August 14, 1806. Trans. from MS. by H. I. Priestley, from Arch. Sta. Barbara Esp. y Com. Tom 4 Ind. diary.

SKELETAL REMAINS FROM THE BUENA VISTA SITES, CALIFORNIA

BY T. D. STEWART

Division of Physical Anthropology, United States National Museum

---

In view of the identification at Buena Vista Lake of two main periods of occupation, together representing apparently a considerable time interval, it is indeed unfortunate that most of the numerous burials encountered were poorly preserved. No skeletal remains of any significance were recovered from the lower level. Of those recovered from the upper level many are subadults, and especially infants. Since there is little justification culturally for distinguishing between individuals, full descriptions of the separate specimens will not be given.

METHODS

The measurements on this small collection have been taken in accordance with Hrdlička's technique (1939). The measurements on the skull thus are comparable with most of those available for California collections, notably those of Gifford (1926) and Hrdlička (1927). I would call attention, however, to the fact that Hrdlička's measurement of orbital breadth is taken from lacrimale and not dacryon, and hence results in a smaller mean than Gifford's. This difference in definition was detected by von Bonin and Morant (1938, pp. 99–100). In the present case I have followed Hrdlička's practice.

Personal error.—It happens that Hrdlička also has measured the skulls of the present collection, as a routine procedure. For this reason it is possible to evaluate the differences in our techniques. Gifford (1926) has given similar figures for Kroeber and Loud as compared with Hrdlička. Furthermore, since Hrdlička has measured Otis' series of 1880, it is possible also to include the differences between their methods for the few comparable measurements. The reason for considering Otis is that Gifford included the former's (1876) measurements in the computation of his averages.

Table 1, in which the results of Kroeber, Loud, Otis, and myself are compared with those of Hrdlička (as mean differences), rather assumes that this standard has remained constant over a period of about 30 years. Although it is unreasonable to expect this of a full anthropometric technique, and especially in the case of one with such a mounting experience, nevertheless, it is the only check on personal error in this case, and, I might add, much more of a check than is usually available. This comparison shows that Hrdlička fairly consistently obtains slightly higher averages than Kroeber, Loud, and myself. The nose measurements are the only exception. In general I come closest to Hrdlička's results; my worst showing is in menton-nasion height, in which I am conservative to the extent of 3.1 mm. in correcting for tooth wear. In California crania dental attrition is usually extreme (Leigh, 1928) and the correction therefor is a subjective matter.

As regards the three measurements by Otis that are comparable by definition, length is the only one showing an unusual difference. Otis states (1876, 1880) that his length is "the greatest longitudinal diameter, measured from the glabella to the most prominent part of the occiput." Obviously, however, he measured from ophryon instead of glabella.

Error due to sexing.—Hrdlička and I agree in our sexing of the crania from Buena Vista. I have utilized the pelvis for this purpose whenever it was available. There is no close check on the sexing given by Gifford (1926), but in this connection von Bonin and Morant (1938) comment as follows:

It is certainly curious that Gifford's Santa Cruz series should be distinguished by the smaller size of its type, not only from both Hrdlička's but also from Gifford's Santa Rosa series. The hypothesis that differences in sexing are responsible for these relationships seems to be a plausible one . . . [Pp. 101–102.]

A comparison of Otis' (1880) and Hrdlička's (1927) records for the Santa Baraba County series shows that they agreed on the sexing of 63 out of 90 skulls; they differed on 27 (15: Hrdlička male, Otis female; 12: Hrdlička female, Otis male). According as they sexed this series these two observers obtained the following averages for the two measurements in which the technique is comparable:

Observer	Male		Female	
	Diameter lateral	Bizygomatic maximum	Diameter lateral	Bizgyomatic maximum
	mm.	*mm.*	*mm.*	*mm.*
Hrdlička_____	(44) 138. 5	(26) 135. 7	(35) 133. 9	(20) 126. 6
Otis_____	(42) 138. 1	(27) 134. 2	(37) 135. 4	(19) 129. 8
Difference_____	−0. 4	−1. 5	+1. 5	+3. 2

Discounting the small difference due to technique, as shown in table 1, it will be seen that Otis tends to get averages for females that are too high, and the reverse for males. Upon reviewing this material I have concluded that Hrdlička's sexing is probably correct, hence these average differences may be said to be due to an error of sexing.

TABLE 1.—*Personal errors: Average differences (mm.) between the results of four observers and those of Hrdlička based on three different series of California crania*

Measurement	No.	Stewart	No.	Kroeber [1]	No.	Loud [1]	No.	Otis [2]
Diameter antero-posterior maximum	9	−0.1	19	−1.1	20	+1.1	80	−4.4
Diameter lateral maximum	9	−.6	18	−.7	20	−.7	79	+.3
Basion-bregma height	6	−.2	13	−.9	14	−.9	26	[2] +3.7
Menton-nasion height	8	−3.1						
Alveolar point-nasion height	14	−.4	9	−1.0	10	−1.9		
Diameter bizygomatic maximum	11	−.4	8	−.6	9	−.2	46	+.6
Basion-nasion	8	−.1	10	+.5	11	−.3		
Basion-subnasal point	8	−.8						
Basion-alveolar point	8	−.1	7	−.5	7	−.5		
Orbital height, mean	14	−.5						
Orbital breadth, mean	14	−.2						
Nasal height	14	−.03	15	+.8	15	+.6		
Nasal breadth	14	+.07	15	+.5	15	+.2		
External alveolar length	15	−.5						
External alveolar breadth, maximum	14	−.4						

[1] Gifford (1926), p. 349.   [2] Differs by definition.
[2] Otis (1880) vs. Hrdlička (1927); Santa Barbara County series.

It is noteworthy that in general a like trend may be demonstrated with Gifford's (1926) averages for his Santa Barbara series in comparison with a similar combination of Hrdlička's (1927) series; that is, Gifford's averages for the females are slightly higher than Hrdlička's, and those for the males are lower. While this result may be determined partly by the inclusion of Otis' measurements, it, nevertheless, tends to confirm the opinion of von Bonin and Morant quoted above.

The significance of the errors due to technique and sexing will become more apparent when we compare the present material with other California series. The present collection now will be described.

MATERIAL

Remains from site 1.—Of the 19 specimens from this site only 4 are adult. The subadults have the following age distribution:

Age period:	No.	Determinants
Fetus	2	Maximum length of femur: 43–49 mm.; humerus: 40–45 mm.
Newborn	9	Maximum length of femur: 70–79 mm.; humerus: 60–67 mm.
Near 2 years	1	2d temporary molars erupting.
Near 6 years	2	1st permanent molars erupting.
12–15 years	1	2d permanent molars erupted; major epiphyses ununited.
Total	15	

The oldest of these subadults is brachycranic (cranial index 82.4), high headed (mean height index 86.7) and leptorrhinic (nasal index 43.4).

Of the adults only two (372251–2) have skulls. (All specimen numbers refer to the catalog of the United States National Museum.) These are shown in plates 52 and 53, and the measurements are given in table 2. The skeleton of 372251 yields some long bone measurements which are given in tables 3 and 4.   The spine of this skeleton contains the modal number of segments (7C, 12T, 5L).   Neither humerus has a septal aperture.   The left femur has no third trochanter.

The two remaining adults are represented by single bones: 372256, a very small female, by a lower jaw; 372257, by a pathological femur (pl. 57).   The nature of the pathology represented in this femur [1] is uncertain.   On account of the absence of the rest of the skeleton it is unknown as to what parts were involved and whether or not the condition was bilaterally symmetrical.   The presence of sinuses is, not typical of syphilis and suggests osteomyelitis.

Remains from site 2.—The age range of the 44 specimens recovered from this site is as follows:

Age period:	No.	Determinants
Newborn_____	2	Maximum length of femur 78 mm. ; humerus 66 mm.
Under 1 year_____	1	Temporary incisors erupting ; maximum length of humerus 82 mm.
Under 6 years_____	4	1st permanent molar erupting.
Near 8 years_____	3	1st permanent molar erupted ; permanent incisors erupting.
12–15 years_____	4	2nd permanent molar erupted ; major epiphyses un- united.
15–20 years_____	2	Estimate based upon teeth alone.
Adult_____	28	Basilar suture closed, etc.
Total_____.	44	

The measurements of the adult skulls and long bones are given in tables 2, 3, and 4.   In addition, the following indices are derived from the incomplete skull of the oldest subadult (372288): Cranial index 75.3, mean height index 88.6, mean orbital index 97.0, nasal index 47.7.   Typical skulls are shown in plates 54–56.

In only three cases are complete spines present: 372292 has an extra thoracic vertebra, which probably bore very rudimentary ribs, but otherwise the modal number of segments (7C, 5L) ; 372298 and 372334 have the modal number of segments throughout.   The fifth lumbar vertebra of 372298 has a separate neural arch divided at the spine (*Spina bifida*).

It is noteworthy that of the 19 distal ends of humeri recovered (9 right, 10 left) only two (10.5 percent) show septal apertures (1 right, medium; 1 left, slight).

Third trochanter of the femur is not a feature of this collection; in the few cases where present it is of slight development.

There was found only one case of major pathology in this group: the tibiae of 372297,[2] an adult female, show symmetrical marked osteitis probably due to syphilis (pl. 57).

---

[1] Found in the wall of trench 1, square 88/36, at a depth of 6 feet 10 inches.
[2] Found in a pit from the 16-inch level in square 104/33.

Remains from site 3.—Parts of only seven individuals were recovered at this site. Of these only two are elderly; all the rest are young adults. The skulls of 372308–9 are measurable (see table 2); 372309 also yields a few long bone measurements (see tables 3 and 4). The right humerus of 372309 shows a medium-sized septal aperture (left ?). The femora of this specimen do not have third trochanters.

Remains from site 4.—Only two specimens, both adults, are noted as coming from this site; neither is measurable.

Remains of questionable origin.—The site identification was not preserved on three specimens. Two of these are adults; the third is an adolescent of approximately 15 years (nearly complete union of proximal ulnar epiphysis). The skull of one of the adults (372331), imperfectly reconstructed, has a cranial index near 84.

Summary of material.—A total of 75 specimens were recovered at the 4 Buena Vista sites. Site 2 yielded the largest number. All age periods are represented, but adults predominate only 43 to 32. In the adult group measurements have been obtained on 20 skulls and parts of 14 skeletons. Fortunately, males predominate in the measurable specimens. It is chiefly through the skulls that relationships can be traced, so in the comparisons that follow attention will be directed primarily to these.

TABLE 2.—*Measurements (cm.) and indices of individual skulls*

MALE

Collector's No.	U.S.N.M. No.	Age [1]	Diameter antero-posterior maximum	Diameter lateral maximum	Basion-bregma height	Cranial index	Mean height index	Cranial module
Site 1:								
1	372251	M	18.6	14.2	13.4	*76.3*	*81.7*	15.40
2	372252	M	18.2	14.2?	13.6	78.0	*84.0*	15.33
Site 2:								
2	372270	O	18.7	13.9	14.8?	*74.3*	*90.8*	15.80
10	372334	O	(18.2)	14.2	14.0	(*73.0*)	(*86.4*)	(15.47)
14	372272	M	18.8	14.4?	13.9	*76.6*	*83.7*	15.70
20	372275	O	18.7	14.2?	14.0?	*75.9*	*85.1*	15.63
41	372282	Y						
46	372284	Y	17.1	14.2?	13.1	[2] *83.0*	*83.7*	14.80
67	372292	M						
68	372293	O	18.5	14.8	14.2	80.0	*85.3*	15.83
83	372296	M						
89	372298	O	(19.0)	(14.0)		(*73.7*)		
Site 3:								
61	372308	O	17.8	14.6	(13.0)	*82.0*	(*80.2*)	(15.13)

FEMALE

Collector's No.	U.S.N.M. No.	Age [1]	Diameter antero-posterior maximum	Diameter lateral maximum	Basion-bregma height	Cranial index	Mean height index	Cranial module
Site 2:								
30	372277	O	18.0	14.0	13.8	*77.8*	*86.2*	15.27
38	372281	O?						
50	372286	M	16.4	14.4?		[2] *87.8*		
75	372294	O?	17.1	13.0	13.5	*76.0*	*89.7*	14.53
86	372297	O?						
?	372300	M	17.6	14.2		*80.7*		
Site 3:								
63	372309	Y			(13.0)			

[1] Y=young; M=middle aged; O=old.
[2] Probably some occipital flattening.

Table 2.—*Measurements (cm.) and indices of individual skulls*—Continued

MALE

Collec- tor's No.	Menton- nasion height	Alveolar point- nasion height	Diam- eter bizy- gomatic maxi- mum	Facial index, total	Facial index- upper	Basion- nasion	Basion- sub- nasal point	Basion- alveolar point	Facial angle	Alveolar angle
Site 1:										
1	12.4	7.5	14.4	86.1	52.1	10.1	8.4	9.5	71°	53°
2	⁸ 12.0	7.2	14.0?	85.7	51.4	10.0	9.1	10.5	66	46
Site 2:										
2	⁸ 12.2	7.2	14.3?	85.3	50.3					
10										
14	12.2	7.6	14.8?	88.4	51.4	10.7	9.2	10.6	70	48
20						10.0				
41										
46		7.7	13.7		56.2	9.6	8.8	10.6	61	44
67	⁸ 12.3	7.3	14.0	87.8	52.1	10.0	8.8	10.4	66	46
68										
83	⁸ 12.5	7.5								
89	⁸ 12.3	7.1	14.5?	84.8	49.0					
Site 3:										
61		7.4	14.0?		52.8	(10.2)				

FEMALE

Site 2:										
30										
38	⁸ 10.9	6.6								
50	⁸ 11.5	6.8	13.7	83.9	49.6	9.7	8.5	9.9	68	48
75		6.3?	13.3		47.4	10.1	8.8	10.2?	71	44
86	⁸ 11.8	7.3	13.8?	85.5	52.9					
7	⁸ 11.9	7.2	13.9	85.6	51.8					
Site 3:										
63	⁸ 11.0	6.4	12.8?	85.9	50.0	9.⁶	8.5	9.7	70	48

MALE

Collec- tor's No.	Orbital height, mean	Orbital breadth, mean	Orbital index	Nasal height	Nasal breadth	Nasal index	External alveolar length	External alveolar breadth, maxi- mum	External alveolar index
Site 1:									
1	3.72	4.0	93.0	5.4	2.4	44.4	5.4	6.5	120.4
2	3.12	3.85	81.0	5.1	2.4	47.0	5.6	6.2	110.7
Site 2:									
2	3.28	3.72	88.2	5.2	2.8	53.8	5.8	6.7?	115.5
10									
14	3.6	3.9	92.3	5.4	2.4	44.4	5.7	6.1	107.0
20									
41				(5.2)	2.4	(46.2)	6.1	6.6	108.2
46	3.3	3.68	89.7	5.0	2.3	46.0	6.0	5.9	98.3
67	3.38	3.75	90.1	4.9	2.6	53.1	5.6	6.6	117.8
68							5.4	6.2	114.8
83	3.4 L.	4.05 L.	84.0 L	5.2	2.7	51.9	5.7	6.7	117.5
89	3.45	3.85	89.6	5.1	2.7	52.9	5.8	6.5	112.1
Site 3:									
61	3.3 L.	3.8 L.	86.8 L	4.9	2.3	46.9	5.6	6.4	114.3

FEMALE

Site 2:									
30									
38	3.4 R.	3.7 R.	91.9 R	4.6	2.3	50.0	5.4	5.9	109.2
50	3.2	3.75	85.3	4.6	2.5	54.3	5.4	6.6	122.2
75	3.2	3.8	84.2	4.5	2.4	53.3	5.5	5.8	105.4
86	3.35	3.65	91.8	5.0	2.6	52.0	5.7	6.4	112.3
7	3.6	3.75	96.0	5.2	2.6	50.0	5.6		
Site 3:									
63	3.2	3.6	88.9	4.6	2.6	56.5	5.3	6.1	115.5

⁸ Corrected for tooth wear.

TABLE 3.—*Measurements (cm.) of individual bones of upper extremity*

MALE

Collector's No.	U.S.N.M. No.	Maximum length of humerus		Maximum length of radius		Maximum length of ulna		Maximum length of clavicle	
		R.	L.	R.	L.	R.	L.	R.	L.
Site 1:									
1	372251	33.0	33.0		24.1		26.3		15.5
Site 2:									
2	372270	31.0		24.1	23.2		25.2		
10	372334	32.8	32.8		25.2				
16	372273		32.7				28.1	14.2	15.0
20	372275				26.3		28.5		15.5
44	372283			25.3	24.9				
62	372290	31.1							
67	372292	30.5	30.8	22.7	22.8	24.8	25.0	14.2	14.7
89	372298								15.5

FEMALE

Site 2:									
50	372286		33.8	24.4					
86	372297	28.6							
Site 3:									
63	372309	31.1							

TABLE 4.—*Measurements (cm.) of individual bones of lower extremity*

MALE

Collector's No.	U.S.N.M. No.	Maximum length of femur		Bicondylar length of femur		Length of tibia in position		Maximum length of fibula	
		R.	L.	R.	L.	R.	L.	R.	L.
Site 1:									
1	372251		44.0		43.2		36.9		
Site 2:									
2	372270					36.7	36.6	35.5	35.1
16	372273		47.5		47.0	39.3		37.0	37.2
20	372275					37.5	37.8	36.1	
44	372283					37.3	37.1		
51	372335								34.6
67	372292			40.9		33.6		32.3	32.8
68	372337	42.5	42.3	42.4	42.2	35.8	35.9		
89	372298								35.4

FEMALE

Site 2:									
1	372269				44.7				
86	372297	40.0		39.6					
Site 3:									
63	372309	42.7		42.1		34.4	34.4	33.5	

COMPARISONS

In order to evaluate fully the measurements on the Buena Vista series it is desirable first to review the data on California skeletal material that are available for comparison. This material for the most part is limited to skulls.

GENERAL, HISTORICAL

Although the first Otis catalogue, containing a few measurements on 182 California skulls, appeared in 1876, it gave no summary or interpretation. Thus Carr's paper in the Wheeler report of 1879 is the first attempt to differentiate the California physical types. The 315 specimens upon which Carr's report chiefly is based consisted of Otis' 182 combined with 133 from the Peabody Museum; all were from the Santa Barbara Islands. Carr used Otis' measurements of length, breadth, height, and capacity as reported in the catalogue of 1876, in combination with his own for the Peabody series, and supplemented with a few facial measurements of the latter series. As we have seen, Otis measured maximum skull length from ophryon instead of glabella. By comparing Carr's individual measurements as given in the twelfth annual Peabody report (1880) with Hooton's figures for the same material (Gifford, 1926) it seems that Carr measured skull length from glabella (and probably in the midline of the occiput) and, like Otis, took the maximum height from basion.

With these considerations in mind, it is significant that Carr already recognized the essential features of the island physical type:

... the typical or average skull of this collection is small and low and of medium length as compared with its breadth; ... it has a retreating forehead, a prominent occiput, and is slightly scaphocephalic or roof-shaped along the sagittal suture. Its chief development is in the occipital region; so much so, indeed, that a plane perpendicular to the horizon drawn through the auricular openings would divide the skull into two unequal parts, of which the posterior portion would be much the larger. The face is small and narrow, even as compared with the Peruvians. It is more prognathic than the white man, though it by no means reaches the extreme in that respect. The nasal opening is of medium size, while the orbit is large. The malar bones are broad and slope back from the median line of the face, differing widely in this respect as also in the prominence of the nasal bones from the Greenland Eskimo, whose face is flat. [Carr, 1879, p. 286.]

Moreover, he distinguished, on the basis of cranial index, between the northern islands (San Miguel, Santa Cruz) and the southern islands (San Nicholas, San Clemente and Santa Catalina):

... if we ... subdivide these skulls according to the islands from which they were obtained, we shall find other factors entering into the calculation that cannot be explained save on the hypothesis that different races occupied these two groups of islands at the time represented by this collection. Take, for instance, San Miguel of the northern group and Santa Catalina of the southern—extreme cases, it is true, but all the better for my purpose. In the collection from the former of these islands there are sixteen brachycephalous and seventeen orthocephalous crania—not a single dolichocephalous specimen among them; while in the latter there are thirty-one dolichocephali and eight orthocephali, but no brachycephali. Eliminating the orthocephali as common to both, and we have in one case sixteen short skulls against thirty-one that are long in the other. This condition of affairs is not reconcilable with the theory of a difference in cranial forms among people of the same race. [P. 289.]

In addition Carr called attention to the fact that the physical type of the Santa Barbara mainland is similar to that of the adjacent (northern) islands. It is noteworthy, however, that he did not emphasize the regional differences in head height clearly recognizable in his tables.

The second Otis catalogue, listing at least 483 specimens from California, appeared in 1880. Following this, Virchow (1889) gave a detailed report on 28 specimens from Santa Catalina and Santa Cruz Islands. It is interesting to note that Virchow combines the specimens from these two localities and makes no mention of the earlier studies in America. Also, Virchow carried out his measurements in relation to the Frankfort plane, giving, for instance, horizontal length and vertical height.

Boas gave a brief indication of the significance of this new material in 1895. Listing the cranial indices of 677 specimens, without regard to sex, he distinguished five regions: 1, Southern islands; 2, northern islands; 3, Santa Barbara mainland; 4, San Francisco Bay; and 5, Round Valley. In another table the length-height indices of the northern and southern islands are distinguished. Apparently the measurements of Carr, Otis, and possibly Virchow are used here without question. Boas interprets these data as follows:

In northern California we meet immediately an exceedingly long-headed small population which represents a most northerly extension of a Sonoran type, which was also found definitely in the most southerly islands of southern California. The tribes of southern California, which belonged to many linguistic groups, are closely affiliated in their type with the Yuma tribes and the dark, short-headed Navaho. In going from the south to the north on the southern California islands, there is a gradual diminishing of Sonoran type. [Boas, 1895, p. 402, translation.]

It should be noted that the skulls of the Indians of the California Islands are very small. They are about 6% smaller than those of the Indians of the plains. This indicates that the population was probably of small stature so that in the relation of head form and stature they must have been like the tribes of Cape Mendocino. [Boas, 1895, p. 404, translation.]

In 1896 Allen gave full measurement on 12 skulls from the "Santa Barbara Islands" and 5 from the mainland, all from the collections of the Academy of Natural Sciences of Philadelphia. In 1904 Matiegka supplied detailed information regarding 15 skulls and 4 skeletons from Santa Rosa, another of the northern islands. In 1905 Pocock reported briefly on 4 specimens from the San Francisco region. None of these reports adds materially to the picture as already known. However, from this time on a somewhat different anthropometric technique comes into use, so these more recent figures are not always entirely comparable with the earlier ones.

In 1906 begins the period of reexamination when Hrdlička reports the results of remeasuring 27 skulls of the Otis series from the San Francisco Bay region. To this group he adds 20 new specimens from the same region, making a total of 47. The conclusion reached from this study is that:

The skulls are those of one single physical type of people. . . .
As to its relations, the California mainland physical type is practically identical with that of the Santa Barbara mainland, and with that of at least a large part of the adjoining archipelago. Beyond the boundries of the state no indication of this type has yet been found in the immediate north or in the northwest. Along the eastern border of California are the Pa-Utes. Of the physical type of these people but little is as yet known, but the few crania that have been described or are in our collections are very close indeed to the Californians. . . .
In the immediate south are the Mission Indians, who represent perhaps a comparatively recent immigration into that country and are of the physical type of the Mohave. Ancient crania from the California Peninsula are also of a different type. Arizona and Sonora show no population, recent or ancient, allied physically to the Californians. In Mexico, however, are several great Indian peoples who in many features approach the Californians to such a degree that an original identity must be held as probable. One of these is the Otomi, of the States of Hidalgo and Mexico. A large group of peoples in the States of Puebla, Michoacan, and farther south, even including the Aztecs, and finally the Tarahumare, in Chihuahua, are all physically related to the Otomi as well as to the Californians. [Hrdlička, 1906, p. 64.]

Nearly 20 years elapse before further studies on the California physical type appear. Then in 3 succeeding years—1925, 1926, 1927 —come important studies by Oetteking, Gifford, and Hrdlička, respectively. Oetteking had only five more or less complete skulls from Santa Barbara, which he described in minute detail. Thus this constitutes perhaps the best characterization of an already well established type.

Gifford (1926) reported, in addition to data on the living, measurements on about 515 (by my count) adult skulls from all parts of the state, none of which had been recorded heretofore. Also, he gave most of Carr's Peabody series as remeasured by Hooton. From these data, together with Otis' 1876 and Hrdlička's 1906 figures—altogether nearly 900 skulls—Gifford identified seven cranial types. Of these seven types only two—San Francisco, Santa Barbara (northern islands and coast)—are represented by fairly large samples; the samples of two others—San Joaquin, Santa Catalina (southern islands and coast)—are probably not statistically adequate; and three—Yuki, Buena Vista, Great Basin—are inadequately represented.

Hrdlička (1927) reported in the Catalogue of Crania his measuements on all of the California crania in the United States National Museum—a total of 397 specimens. The majority of this collection consists of the Otis series already referred to. Hrdlička concludes that:

The material from California shows considerable uniformity. The type is characterized as follows: The cephalic index ranges from dolicho- to meso-cephalic; the height of the vault is medium to submedium; in size the skull is rather small; the face is of medium dimensions; the orbits range about medium; the nasal index is submedium to medium. . . . In general the Californians here represented are plainly of one type, with here and there secondary variations. This type appears to be practically identical with that of the Shoshoneans. [Hrdlička, 1927, p. 127.]

In all of the foregoing studies no attempt was made to distinguish between the regional skull types by statistical means. Recently (1938) von Bonin and Morant have attempted to do this on the basis of Gifford's and Hrdlička's (1927) data. Limiting their consideration to males and using mostly the same subdivisions recog-nized heretofore, but otherwise combining smaller groups to obtain adequate samples, von Bonin and Morant arrive at six series, among which they make comparisons by the coefficient of racial likeness. Although in this case the number of characters available for establishing the coefficient is far below the ideal, and the coefficient itself is probably open to criticism, this means of comparison gives a convenient measure of resemblance. The results show the closest relationships (lowest coefficients) among the six groups to be the following:

Santa Barbara County vs. Northern islands_____ 5. 56
Santa Barbara County vs. San Francisco Bay_____ 7. 85
Northern California vs. Central California_____ 7. 89
Northern California vs. Santa Barbara County_____ 11. 47
Northern California vs. San Francisco Bay_____ 12. 35

The least relationships (highest coefficients) among these groups are indicated thus:

Southern islands vs. Central California_____ 94. 03
Southern islands vs. Northern California_____ 92. 08
Southern islands vs. Santa Barbara County_____ 70. 10
Southern islands vs. Northern islands_____ 56. 53
Southern islands vs. San Francisco Bay_____ 52. 39

The remainder show intermediate relationship:

San Francisco Bay vs. Central California_____ 18. 43
Northern islands vs. Northern California_____ 21. 30
Northern islands vs. San Francisco Bay_____ 25. 00
Santa Barbara County vs. Central California_____ 31. 37
Northern islands vs. Central California_____ 37. 15

Von Bonin and Morant (1938) comment on these results as follows:

There appears to be a fairly close association between the relationships of the types and their geographical positions in the case of five of the series, but the remaining one—from Santa Catalina, San Clemente and San Nicolas Islands—is widely removed from the others. A comparison of the means shows at once that the last type has high coefficients with all the others chiefly on account of

its greater calvarial length and lower cephalic and height-length indices. Even
if it be excluded, the Californian types show greater diversity than is generally
found for adjoining populations inhabiting a small region. In particular the
neighbouring Costanoan and Yokut groups are far less similar than might have
been expected. [P. 102.]

The results of this mathematical exercise thus advance us very
little beyond Carr's conclusions of 60 years ago. If there is any
advance, in fact, it is due to the inclusion of data from new areas—
chiefly San Joaquin Valley. Comparisons are still being made on a
geographical basis instead of culturally and chronologically. Personal error, error due to sexing, and differences in technique are still
being loaded on the scales on the side of racial diversity.

To illustrate these points further I will merely call attention to
the following points: 1, Rogers (1929) and Heizer (1939) have found
earlier dolichocranic populations in the northern islands and in the
Sacramento-San Joaquin Delta, respectively. A simple geographical
classification of materials does not take these facts into consideration.
2, As von Bonin and Morant have pointed out, the differences between Gifford's and Hrdlička's series from Santa Cruz Island (see
von Bonin and Morant, 1938, table 1, p. 98) can only mean error
due to sexing. In this case the difference between the average cranial
capacities amounts to 113 cc. Such differences probably have a considerable effect upon the Coefficient of Racial Likeness. 3, Examination of von Bonin and Morant's table 1 shows that California
geographical groups differ chiefly in skull shape (cranial index),
relative skull height and absolute size. In general, a low longheaded
group (Shoshonean) can be distinguished from a high, medium
roundheaded group. Degrees of roundheadedness are probably influenced by deformity, a factor not recorded in Gifford's data.
Throughout the State face proportions, including eyes and nose, do
not vary notably. Whether or not size reflects more than environ-
mental factors is uncertain; if not, the Coefficient of Racial Likeness
gives it too much weight.

BUENA VISTA, SKULL

With these general considerations in mind we may turn to the
present collection. As we have seen, Gifford (1926) identified a
Buena Vista cranial type. Since, however, he based this type upon
only six males selected from the collections of two sites, there is no
statistical justification for separating it from that of the San Joaquin
Valley in general. The averages for this so-called Buena Vista type
suggest that they are derived merely from large males. The example
illustrated shows only contour differences such as are probably not
constant for the group as a whole.

Culturally and chronologically, the present collection from Buena Vista points partly to the Delta and partly to the Santa Barbara coast. It so happens that the national collections contain skeletal remains from the upper and intermediate horizons of mounds near Stockton in the lower San Joaquin Valley. These have been measured by Dr. Hrdlička, and are available to me through his kindness. I am thus able to present my measurements on the Buena Vista crania in comparison with his for the Santa Barbara coast (1927) and the lower San Joaquin Valley series (table 5). In this comparison errors due to technique are at a minimum (see table 1 for my personal error in relation to Hrdlička).

There can be no question that these Buena Vista and San Joaquin groups are identical; and on the other hand, that they are distinct from the coastal group. As compared with Gifford's San Joaquin averages those of Hrdlička from the same area show chiefly a longer head, relatively. This is due probably to the inclusion of deformed skulls in Gifford's series. In general the skulls of the San Joaquin and Santa Barbara coast peoples differ mainly in size and height.

TABLE 5.—*Craniometric comparisons*

Measurements (cm.) and indices	Sex	Santa Barbara (Hrdlička)	San Joaquin (Hrdlička)	Buena Vista (Stewart)
Diameter antero-posterio maximum	M	17.9 (48)	18.3 (26)	18.3 (8)
	F	17.1 (37)	17.4 (33)	17.3 (4)
Diameter lateral maximum	M	13.8 (45)	14.3 (26)	14.3 (9)
	F	13.4 (38)	13.8 (33)	13.9 (4)
Basion-bregma height	M	13.2 (45)	14.0 (25)	13.9 (8)
	F	12.4 (38)	13.4 (33)	13.6 (2)
Cranial index	M	77.2 (44)	78.2 (26)	78.3 (8)
	F	78.5 (36)	79.7 (33)	80.6 (4)
Mean height index	M	82.9 (41)	85.6 (25)	84.9 (7)
	F	81.5 (34)	86.2 (33)	88.0 (2)
Cranial module	M	15.0 (41)	15.5 (25)	15.5 (7)
	F	14.3 (34)	14.9 (33)	14.9 (2)
Alveolar point-nasion height	M	7.0 (47)	7.4 (25)	7.4 (9)
	F	6.5 (35)	6.7 (28)	6.8 (6)
Diameter bizygomatic maximum	M	13.5 (28)	14.1 (28)	14.2 (8)
	F	12.6 (25)	13.0 (35)	13.5 (5)
Facial index, upper	M	51.3 (25)	52.5 (23)	51.9 (8)
	F	51.3 (23)	51.4 (28)	50.3 (5)
Orbital height, mean	M	3.45(45)	3.51(29)	3.39(9)
	F	3.31(34)	3.40(35)	3.32(6)
Orbital breadth, mean	M	3.83(44)	3.92(29)	3.84(9)
	F	3.69(33)	3.79(35)	3.71(6)
Orbital index, mean	M	89.6 (44)	89.5 (29)	88.3 (9)
	F	89.5 (33)	89.7 (35)	89.7 (6)
Nasal height	M	4.9 (49)	5.1 (28)	5.1 (9)
	F	4.6 (37)	4.7 (31)	4.8 (6)
Nasal breadth	M	2.4 (51)	2.5 (28)	2.5 (9)
	F	2.3 (39)	2.4 (32)	2.5 (6)
Nasal index	M	48.4 (48)	49.1 (28)	48.9 (9)
	F	51.0 (37)	52.1 (31)	52.7 (6)

It will be recalled that Hrdlička (1927) has asserted that the California type is practically identical with the Shoshonean. The latter type he has said (1927, p. 101) "is not far from the Algonkin, but differs from this by a perceptibly lower vault." These remarks were made before the San Joaquin material became available. Logically, therefore, the San Joaquin skull type, with its high vault, is metrically indistinguishable from the Algonkin. In this connection it will be recalled that von Bonin and Morant found a coefficient racial likeness of 12.93 between the Central Californians and the "Western Algonkins."

TABLE 6.—*Average lengths of long bones in four California series*

MALE

Site	Femur, bicondylar length	Femur, maximum length	Tibia, maximum length	Humerus, maximum length	Radius, maximum length
Buena Vista	43.1 (5)	44.1 (4)	36.8 (11)	32.0 (9)	24.3 (9)
San Joaquin	44.8 (13)	----------	37.6 (16)	32.6 (12)	25.5 (11)
Santa Rosa	44.5 (6)	44.9 (6)	37.4 (6)	32.5 (6)	25.6 (6)
Southern islands	----------	43.0 (14)	35.5 (16)	30.5 (12)	----------

FEMALE

Site	Femur, bicondylar length	Femur, maximum length	Tibia, maximum length	Humerus, maximum length	Radius, maximum length
Buena Vista	42.1 (3)	41.4 (2)	34.4 (2)	31.2 (3)	24.4 (1)
San Joaquin	40.5 (17)	----------	34.2 (17)	29.0 (13)	22.2 (17)
Santa Rosa	39.8 (2)	40.4 (2)	33.8 (2)	28.6 (2)	21.7 (2)
Southern islands	----------	40.3 (16)	33.2 (19)	28.4 (13)	----------

In all of the foregoing, the material from the four sites at Buena Vista has been considered as a unit. Because the metrical ranges for the various California series show so much overlapping, it is impossible to place individual skulls from Buena Vista either with the Santa Barbara or San Joaquin groups. However, attention may be called to the fact that of the three skulls from the culturally related sites 1 and 3 (table 2) two are quite lowheaded and hence more nearly like the Santa Barbara group.

The morphological details of the Buena Vista skulls are best seen in photographs of the better preserved specimens (pls. 52–56).

BUENA VISTA, SKELETON

As for the skeleton, there are few measurements available from California with which to compare the Buena Vista series. Matiegka (1905) gives figures for four skeletons from Santa Rosa; Gifford (1926) reports Hooton's measurements of 27 skeletons from the southern islands (Santa Catalina, San Clemente). In addition, Dr. Hrdlička has permitted me to use his unpublished measurements of 18 skeletons from the lower San Joaquin Valley. Because the numbers are so inadequate, table 6 can be said only to suggest a lower stature in the southern islands than elsewhere. Also, it would appear that the Buena Vista series is clearly affiliated with the higher statured San Joaquin group.

Only one morphological feature of the skeleton will be mentioned, namely septal apertures of the humerus. There are 22 distal ends of humeri in the Buena Vista collection. Of these three show apertures (13.6 percent).

Comparative figures for California are lacking (Hrdlička, 1932), but an examination of 40 humeri from the San Joaquin Valley in the national collections shows 17 (42.5 percent) with apertures. Since both series are inadequate and include the two sexes and sides unequally, they are not entirely comparable.

Attention has been called to the fact that one skeleton from site 2 (372297, pl. 57) showed pathological changes attributable to syphilis. If this diagnosis is correct, we are face to face with the old controversy as to whether syphilis is a pre- or post-Columbian disease in North America. It is a matter of record that this disease was among those that decimated the coastal peoples during the eighteenth and nineteenth centuries. On the other hand, there is an interval of about 200 years between the first European contacts on the Pacific coast and the suggested date of abandonment of the Buena Vista sites. If, then, syphilis was introduced to the coast of California by the early navigators, which is not impossible (see Cook, 1937), then the pathological specimen from site 2 must be later than 1542.

The skeletons in the national collections from the lower San Joaquin, which Professor Lillard considers (1936, and a personal communication) "precontact," include a number with pathological lesions resembling syphilis. Unfortunately, there are no records of pathology for the skeletons from the oldest levels in this region. At the present state of knowledge, however, and judging by conditions elsewhere in North America, the burden of proof rests with those who claim that syphilis was present in pre-Columbian times.

CONCLUSIONS

Briefly stated, the following points have been brought out in the present study:

1. The available measurements on California crania are not equally reliable as regards technique and sexing. The reexamination of several series furnishes an estimate of personal error that aids in the evaluation of the data.

2. Most cranial studies in the California area are based on geographical distributions and largely ignore cultural and temporal relationships.

3. The skeletal remains from the Buena Vista sites are clearly related to those of the protohistoric levels from the lower San Joaquin Valley, and not to those from the Santa Barbara coast.

4. The presence of pathological lesions attributable to syphilis on some of the long bones from Buena Vista raises the question of

whether or not this disease was present in California during prehistoric times. It is maintained that the burden of proof rests with those who claim antiquity for the disease in America.[1]

LITERATURE CITED

ALLEN, HARRISON

1896. Crania from the mounds of the St. John's River, Florida; a study made in connection with crania from other parts of North America. Journ. Acad. Nat. Sci. Philadelphia, vol. 10, pt. 4, pp. 367–448.

BOAS, FRANZ

1895. Zur Anthropologie der nordamerikanischen Indianer. Zeitschr. f. Ethnol., vol. 27, pp. 366–411.

CARR, LUCIEN

1879. Observations on the crania from the Santa Barbara Islands, California. In Rep. U. S. Geogr. Surv. W. 100th Meridian (Wheeler), vol. 7 (Archaeology), pp. 277–292.

1880. Measurements of crania from California. 12th Ann. Rep., Peabody Mus. Amer. Archaeol. and Ethnol., pp. 497–505.

COOK, S. F.

1937. The extent and significance of disease among the Indians of Baja California, 1697–1773. Ibero-Americana, vol. 12.

GIFFORD, E. F.

1926. California anthropometry. Univ. Calif. Publ. Amer. Archeol. and Ethnol., vol. 22, No. 2, pp. 217–390.

HEIZER, ROBERT F.

1939. Some Sacramento Valley-Santa Barbara archeological relationships. The Masterkey, vol. 13, No. 1, pp. 31–35.

HRDLIČKA, A.

1906. Contribution to the physical anthropology of California, based on collections in the department of anthropology of the University of California and in the U. S. National Museum. Univ. Calif. Publ. Amer. Archeol. and Ethnol., vol. 4, No. 2, pp. 49–64.

1927. Catalogue of human crania in the United States National Museum collections. The Algonkin and related Iroquois; Siouan, Caddoan, Salish and Sahaptin, Shoshonean, and Californian Indians. Proc. U. S. Nat. Mus., vol. 69, art. 5.

1932. The humerus: Septal apertures. Anthropologie, Prague, vol. 10, pp. 31–96.

1939. Practical anthropometry. Philadelphia.

LEIGH, R. W.

1928. Dental pathology of aboriginal California. Univ. Calif. Publ. Amer. Archeol. and Ethnol., vol. 23, No. 10, pp. 399–440.

LILLARD, J. B., and PURVES, W. K.

1936. The archeology of the Deer Creek-Cosumnes area, Sacramento County, California. Sacramento Junior College, Dept. Anthrop., Bull. 1.

MATIEGKA, H.

1905. Ueber Schädel und Skelette von Santa Rosa (Santa Barbara-Archipel bei Californien). Sitzungsber. d. königl. Böhmischen Ges. d. Wissenschaften, Math.-Naturw. Cl. 1904, art. 2. Prague.

---

[1] This argument has been amplified in the author's contribution to the Swanton Volume (Stewart, 1940), which was written after this report was prepared.

OETTEKING, BRUNO
1925. Skeletal remains from Santa Barbara, California. I. Craniology. Ind. Notes and Monogr., No. 39, Mus. Amer. Ind., Heye Foundation.

OTIS GEORGE
1876. Check list of preparations and objects in the Section of Human Anatomy of the United States Army Medical Museum for use during the International Exhibition of 1876 in connection with the representation of the Medical Department U. S. Army, No. 8. Washington.
1880. List of the specimens in the Anatomical Section of the United States Army Medical Museum. Washington.

POCOCK, W. I.
1905. Crania from shell-bearing sand-hills near San Francisco, now in the Cambridge Museum. Man, vol. 5, No. 81, pp. 148–152.

ROGERS, D. B.
1929. Prehistoric man of the Santa Barbara coast. Santa Barbara.

STEWART, T. D.
1940. Some historical implications of physical anthropology in North America. In Essays in historical anthropology in North America. Published in honor of John R. Swanton. Smithsonian Misc. Coll., vol. 100, pp. 15–50.

VIRCHOW, R.
1889. Beiträge zur Craniologie der Insulaner von der Westküste Nordamerikas. Verhandl. Ber. Ges. f. Anthrop., Ethnol. u. Urgesch., pp. 382–403.

VON BONIN, GEBHARDT, and MORANT, G. M.
1938. Indian races in the United States. A survey of previously published cranial measurements. Biometrika, vol. 30, pp. 94–129.

INDEX

Abel, Stanley, acknowledgment to, 3
Aleutian Islands, knife fragments mentioned, 69
Allen, Harrison, work referred to, 180
Archeology, 17–133
  linked with ethnography of Yokuts, 151–153
Arrowpoints, 61–65, 111
  See also Projectile points
Arrowshaft buffers (?), 131
Arrow-shaped object, 45
Arrow straighteners, 53–54, 96, 128–129
Artifacts, Buena Vista compared with other cultures, 147–149
  comparative age, 26
  European make, 48
  found in burials, 87
  location in horizon, 20
  manner of grouping, 37
  number of entries in field catalog, 37
  size and provenience of artifacts illustrated, 162–169
  summary of vertical distribution, 157–161
  See also Cultures, summary; *individual names*
Ash pits, 32
  See also Firepits; Fireplaces; Pits
Asphaltum, Buena Vista source of supply, 37–38
  present in graves, 36, 87, 109, 125
  reference to, 32, 122, 126, 127
  used for inlay, 51, 52–53, 121
  used on artifacts, 44, 65, 67, 70, 89. 90, 92, 94, 100, 102, 103, 115, 130
  work in, 37–40, 88–89
Associated Oil Company, acknowledgment to, 2
Awls, bone, 40–42, 89–90
  sharpener (?), 101
Ax, hand, description, 130
Balls, 38, 68, 100
Barbat, W. F., acknowledgment to, 3
Bars, steatite, 54, 96
Basins, clay-lined. *See* Clay-lined basins
Basketry, 109, 116, 120
  and textiles, 126–127
  basket hopper mentioned, 70
  coiled, 39, 103
  in graves, 125
  waterproofing baskets, 39, 89

Beads, 30
  bone, 36, 91, 110, 112
  clay, 45, 93
  glass, 48–49
  in graves, 36, 110, 125
  opaque, 48–49
  serpentine, 53, 54–55, 113–114
  shell, 36, 49, 50, 51, 52, 89, 94, 95, 105, 110, 113, 125, 128, 132
  spire-lopped, 52
  steatite, 54–55, 110, 125
  See also Disks; Shell
Biperforate objects, steatite, 55
Bipointed objects, 42, 90–91, 96
Birds, bone used for artifacts, 40, 42, 45, 92
  distribution of remains, identified at U. S. National Museum, 11
  species, San Joaquin Valley, known to aboriginal man, 9
Bitumen, 132
Blades, 61, 62, 98, 99, 146
  See also Knives
Board of County Supervisors, Taft, acknowledgment to, 3
Boas, Franz, quoted, 180
Bolton, Herbert E., quoted, 12, 13
Bone and horn, work in, 40–45, 89–92, 112
  in graves, 87
Bowls, 102
  in graves, 36, 110
  sandstone, 110
  steatite, 30, 35, 36, 59, 126
  See also Potsherds; Vessels
Brush, 38
Buenavista, location of village, 16–17, 151
Buena Vista Basin, description, 3–6
  linked with coastal areas to the south, 65
  rainfall, 8
  travel routes, 7–8
Buena Vista Lake, description, 4–6, 121
  vegetation, 8–9
Burial grounds, description, 105–106, 122
  native and prehistoric, 19
Burial practices, 36–37, 86, 105, 106, 107, 125–126

245824—41

189

○

www.ingramcontent.com/pod-product-compliance
Lightning Source LLC
Chambersburg PA
CBHW031151270326
41931CB00006B/229